Jonathan Alexander
Karen Yescavage
Editors

Bisexuality and Transgenderism: InterSEXions of the Others

Bisexuality and Transgenderism: InterSEXions of the Others has been co-published simultaneously as *Journal of Bisexuality*, Volume 3, Numbers 3/4 2003.

Pre-publication
REVIEWS,
COMMENTARIES,
EVALUATIONS . . .

" A VALUABLE RESOURCE for readers of all sexual orientations. . . . Rich, challenging, honest, and progressive. I recommend this book to anyone interested in learning more about diversity in gender identity and human sexuality."

Walter Bockting, PhD
Coordinator of Transgender
Health Services, Program in Sexuality
University of Minnesota Medical School
Author of *Transgender and HIV: Risks, Prevention, and Care*

Harrington Park Press

Bisexuality and Transgenderism: InterSEXions of the Others

Bisexuality and Transgenderism: InterSEXions of the Others has been co-published simultaneously as *Journal of Bisexuality*, Volume 3, Numbers 3/4 2003.

The *Journal of Bisexuality* Monographic "Separates"

Below is a list of "separates," which in serials librarianship means a special issue simultaneously published as a special journal issue or double-issue *and* as a "separate" hardbound monograph. (This is a format which we also call a "DocuSerial.")

"Separates" are published because specialized libraries or professionals may wish to purchase a specific thematic issue by itself in a format which can be separately cataloged and shelved, as opposed to purchasing the journal on an on-going basis. Faculty members may also more easily consider a "separate" for classroom adoption.

"Separates" are carefully classified separately with the major book jobbers so that the journal tie-in can be noted on new book order slips to avoid duplicate purchasing.

You may wish to visit Haworth's website at . . .

http://www.HaworthPress.com

. . . to search our online catalog for complete tables of contents of these separates and related publications.

You may also call 1-800-HAWORTH (outside US/Canada: 607-722-5857), or Fax: 1-800-895-0582 (outside US/Canada: 607-771-0012), or e-mail at:

docdelivery@haworthpress.com

Bisexuality and Transgenderism: InterSEXions of the Others, edited by Jonathan Alexander, PhD, and Karen Yescavage, PhD (Vol. 3, Nos. 3/4, 2003). *The first book devoted to exploring the common ground–and the important differences–between bisexuality and transgenderism.*

Women and Bisexuality: A Global Perspective, edited by Serena Anderlini-D'Onofrio, PhD (Vol. 3, No. 1, 2003). *"Nimbly straddles disciplinary and geographical boundaries. . . . The collection's diversity of subject matter and theoretical perspectives offers a useful model for the continued development of interdisciplinary sexuality studies." (Maria Pramaggiore, PhD, Associate Professor of Film Studies, North Carolina State University)*

Bisexual Women in the Twenty-First Century, edited by Dawn Atkins, PhD (cand.) (Vol. 2, Nos. 2/3, 2002). *An eclectic collection of articles that typifies an ongoing feminist process of theory grounded in life experience.*

Bisexual Men in Culture and Society, edited by Brett Beemyn, PhD, and Erich Steinman, PhD (cand.) (Vol. 2, No. 1, 2002). *Incisive examinations of the cultural meanings of bisexuality, including the overlooked bisexual themes in James Baldwin's classic novels* Another Country *and* Giovanni's Room, *the conflicts within sexual-identity politics between gay men and bisexual men, and the recurring figure of the predatory, immoral bisexual man in novels, films, and women's magazines.*

Bisexuality in the Lives of Men: Facts and Fictions, edited by Brett Beemyn, PhD, and Erich Steinman, PhD (cand.) (Vol. 1, Nos. 2/3, 2001). *"At last, a source book which explains bisexual male desires, practices, and identities in a language all of us can understand! This is informative reading for a general audience, and will be especially valuable for discussions in gender studies, sexuality studies, and men's studies courses." (William L. Leap, PhD, Professor, Department of Anthropology, American University, Washington, DC)*

Bisexuality and Transgenderism: InterSEXions of the Others

Jonathan Alexander, PhD
Karen Yescavage, PhD
Editors

Bisexuality and Transgenderism: InterSEXions of the Others has been co-published simultaneously as *Journal of Bisexuality*, Volume 3, Numbers 3/4 2003.

Harrington Park Press®
An Imprint of The Haworth Press, Inc.

New York • London • Victoria (AU)
www.HaworthPress.com

Published by

Harrington Park Press®, 10 Alice Street, Binghamton, NY 13904-1580 USA

Harrington Park Press is an imprint of The Haworth Press, Inc., 10 Alice Street, Binghamton, NY 13904-1580 USA

Bisexuality and Transgenderism: InterSEXions of the Others has been co-published simultaneously as *Journal of Bisexuality*, Volume 3, Numbers 3/4 2003.

The development, preparation, and publication of this work has been undertaken with great care. However, the publisher, employees, editors, and agents of The Haworth Press and all imprints of The Haworth Press, Inc., including The Haworth Medical Press® and Pharmaceutical Products Press®, are not responsible for any errors contained herein or for consequences that may ensue from use of materials or information contained in this work. Opinions expressed by the author(s) are not necessarily those of The Haworth Press, Inc. With regard to case studies, identities and circumstances of individuals discussed herein have been changed to protect confidentiality. Any resemblance to actual persons, living or dead, is entirely coincidental.

Cover design by Brooke R. Stiles

Library of Congress Cataloging-in-Publication Data

Alexander, Jonathan.
    Bisexuality and transgenderism : interSEXions of the others / Jonathan Alexander, Karen Yescavage.
    p. cm.
    Includes bibliographical references and index.
    ISBN 1-56023-286-2 (hard cover : alk. paper) – ISBN 1-56023-287-0 (soft cover : alk. paper)
    1. Bisexuality. 2. Transsexualism. I. Yescavage, Karen. II. Journal of bisexuality. III. Title.
HQ74.A43 2004
306.76'5–dc22
                                        2004000568

Indexing, Abstracting & Website/Internet Coverage

This section provides you with a list of major indexing & abstracting services. That is to say, each service began covering this periodical during the year noted in the right column. Most Websites which are listed below have indicated that they will either post, disseminate, compile, archive, cite or alert their own Website users with research-based content from this work. (This list is as current as the copyright date of this publication.)

Abstracting, Website/Indexing Coverage . . . . Year When Coverage Began

- *Abstracts in Anthropology* **2000**
- *Book Review Index* **2000**
- *CNPIEC Reference Guide: Chinese National Directory*
   of Foreign Periodicals **2000**
- *e-psyche, LLC <http://www.e-psyche.net>* **2001**
- *Family Index Database <http://www.familyscholar.com>* **2003**
- *Gay & Lesbian Abstracts <http://www.nisc.com>* **2000**
- *HOMODOK/"Relevant" Bibliographic Database,*
   Documentation Centre for Gay & Lesbian Studies,
   University of Amsterdam (selective printed abstracts in
   "Homologie" and bibliographic computer databases covering
   cultural, historical, social and political aspects)
   <http://www.ihlia.nl/> **2000**
- *IBZ International Bibliography of Periodical Literature*
   <http://www.saur.de> **2002**
- *Index to Periodical Articles Related to Law* **2000**
- *Journal of Social Work Practice "Abstracts Section"*
   <http://www.carfax.co.uk/jsw-ad.htm> **2000**

(continued)

Special Bibliographic Notes related to special journal issues
(separates) and indexing/abstracting:

- indexing/abstracting services in this list will also cover material in any "separate" that is co-published simultaneously with Haworth's special thematic journal issue or DocuSerial. Indexing/abstracting usually covers material at the article/chapter level.
- monographic co-editions are intended for either non-subscribers or libraries which intend to purchase a second copy for their circulating collections.
- monographic co-editions are reported to all jobbers/wholesalers/approval plans. The source journal is listed as the "series" to assist the prevention of duplicate purchasing in the same manner utilized for books-in-series.
- to facilitate user/access services all indexing/abstracting services are encouraged to utilize the co-indexing entry note indicated at the bottom of the first page of each article/chapter/contribution.
- this is intended to assist a library user of any reference tool (whether print, electronic, online, or CD-ROM) to locate the monographic version if the library has purchased this version but not a subscription to the source journal.
- individual articles/chapters in any Haworth publication are also available through the Haworth Document Delivery Service (HDDS).

Bisexuality and Transgenderism: InterSEXions of the Others

CONTENTS

ABOUT THE EDITORS

Karen Yescavage, PhD, is Associate Professor of psychology and women's studies at Colorado State University-Pueblo. Her research interests are in sexuality studies generally and queer studies particularly. She has published on topics such as bisexual representation in film, transphobia, and the "introduction" of sexual orientation in the classroom.

Jonathan Alexander, PhD, is Associate Professor of English at the University of Cincinnati, where he teaches writing and sexuality studies. His primary areas of scholarly and pedagogical interest are in writing studies, the use of technology in the teaching of writing, and sexuality studies. Jonathan also works as a diversity trainer and a sexual health educator. He writes poetry and science fiction in his spare time. To find out more about Jonathan, visit his Website at <http://oz.uc.edu/~alexanj/>.

Karen and Jonathan's next project will be on the future of sex, addressing a multitude of issues such as sex in space, bio-ethics of alternative modes of reproduction, the future of sex education, and the global impact of STDs.

About the Contributors

Jennifer L. Ailles is a doctoral candidate in English, specializing in Renaissance literature, gender theory, and cultural and performance studies, at the University of Rochester. Her dissertation focuses on the embodiment of disease in early modern English drama, particularly textual moments that merge political and mythological rhetoric(s) with highly racialized and gendered discourses of medicine, midwifery, witchcraft, and infection. She has taught courses on Shakespearean adaptation, women warriors, and representations of witches in film and literature. She is also the former Project Manager of the "Canadian Adaptations of Shakespeare" Project at the University of Guelph.

Thaniel Chase was born in Flint, Michigan, where people worked in factories. It was hard to believe in other options. He escaped in literature, art, and theater. He took all the drugs he could get. He tried a variety of sexual identities. He stopped using drugs and alcohol. When he realized he was FTM, things made more sense. He lives in Denver with his partner and many animals. He wrestles with the usual: seeking meaningful work, being middle-aged without becoming his father, learning to love someone else without losing what he values about himself. He is relatively happy.

David Clowers was born nine months after the attack on Pearl Harbor and grew up in YMCA camps and Waukesha, Wisconsin. After high school, he attended Kalamazoo College, the University of Michigan for a BA and MA in English and the University of Chicago for a JD. Along the way, he taught English Literature for three years at Drake University. Since Law School, he has practiced law in Milwaukee and Sturgeon Bay, Wisconsin, maintaining a general practice with an emphasis on disability cases. After failed attempts at short stories and novels, for the past four years, he has written poetry. He has been married twice.

Charlotte Cooper is a freelance writer living in the East End of London, England. Her debut novel, *Cherry* (Millivres 2002), is a dirty romp through the seedy underbelly of modern dyke life that was seized by Canada Customs for obscenity. Read all about it on <www.CharlotteCooper.net>.

Coralee Drechsler originally from British Columbia, Canada, completed her undergraduate degree in Sociology at Okanagan University College. After working for two years, she began her master's degree in sociology at the University of Saskatchewan, where she was also a Graduate Teaching Fellow. Her master's degree was conferred in 2002 and, since then, she has worked as a part-time research associate with the Community Health and Epidemiology Department at the U of S, in addition to doing contract research work, most notably with Health Canada. She is currently living in Hamilton, Ontario, with her partner of seven years, where she hopes to begin a PhD program.

kari edwards is the winner of New Langton Art's Bay Area Award in literature (2002) and author of *Iduna* (O Books, 2003), *a day in the life of p.* (Subpress Collective, 2002), and *A Diary Of Lies–Belladonna #27* (Belladonna Books, 2002). Her work can also be found in: *Aufgabe, Van Gogh's Ear, 88: A Journal of Contemporary American Poetry, Narratively, Bathhouse, Avoid Strange Men, Bird Dog Magazine, RealPoetik, Blazevox 2k3, Raised in a Barn* and *The International Journal of Sexuality and Gender Studies.*

Sharyn Graham is a lecturer in the School of Social Science at Auckland University of Technology in New Zealand. Her recently submitted PhD dissertation, entitled "Hunters, Wedding Mothers, and Androgynous Priests: conceptualizing Gender Among Bugis in South Sulawesi, Indonesia," was undertaken at the University of Western Australia. Sharyn's academic interests center around notions of gender and sexuality, particularly in Indonesia.

Jamison Green is an internationally respected writer, educator, and advocate for transgender civil rights, health, and social safety. He serves on the boards of two nonprofit groups, Gender Education & Advocacy and the Transgender Law & Policy Institute, led FTM International from 1991 to 1999, and has been one of the driving forces behind San Francisco's and worldwide progress in the area of transgender and transsexual issues for over a decade. His articles appear in anthologies, journals, magazines, and on PlanetOut.com. His book, *Becoming a Visible Man*, will be published by Vanderbilt University Press in 2004.

Matthew Kailey is a Denver, Colorado, author, speaker, and workshop facilitator focusing on gender and sexuality. He is a regular presenter at various colleges and universities in Colorado and Wyoming, including the University of Wyoming, the University of Colorado, the University of Denver, Metro State University, and AIMS Community College. In addition, he speaks at businesses and corporations regarding on-the-job gender transition, facilitates workshops at a variety of conferences, and trains health providers and HIV/AIDS organizations on transgender issues. He is a columnist for *The Gender Identity Center of Colorado Journal* and a journalist with *Out Front Colorado.*

Deborah L. Kerr is a research assistant in the Department of Radiology, Department of Psychology, Washington University, St. Louis, MO.

Barbara A. Lehmann is Assistant Professor in the Department of Social Work, Augsburg College, Minneapolis, MN.

Mark McLelland is a researcher in the Center for Critical and Cultural Studies at the University of Queensland, Australia. He is the author of *Male Homosexuality in Modern Japan*, and the co-editor of *Japanese Cybercultures.* He is currently completing a new book, *Kono Sekai-Queer Japan from 1945 to the Age of the Internet*, and a new edited collection: *Genders, Transgenders and Sexualities in Modern Japan.*

Robin M. Mathy is associated with the Kellogg College and Evidence-Based Health Care, University of Oxford, Oxford, England; Wolfson College and International Relations, University of Cambridge, Cambridge, England; and the Division of Child & Adolescent Psychiatry, Department of Psychiatry, University of Minnesota Medical School, Minneapolis, MN.

Michaela D. E. Meyer is a PhD candidate in the School of Communication Studies at Ohio University. She earned her Master's of Science in journalism from Ohio University in 2001, and her Bachelor of Philosophy from Miami University, Oxford, in 1999. Her primary areas of interest are rhetoric, interpersonal communication and sexuality. The author is grateful to professors Elizabeth Graham and Lena Myers for their support of this project. She also thanks the editors of this volume for their insightful commentary and their commitment to mentoring a young scholar.

Milla Rosenberg is an independent scholar, activist, photographer, and journalist. S/he has a forthcoming essay on integration in *Race in Post-Integration America*, and she has photographed for *CMJ: New Music Monthly* and *URB* magazine. Milla is currently a contributing reporter for *Gay People's Chronicle*, a statewide newspaper serving lesbian, gay, bisexual, and transgender people in Ohio.

Laura Anne Seabrook is a pagan, goth, writer, cartoonist, and artist, who also reads tarot. Western Australian by birth, she currently resides in the Hunter Valley in New South Wales with her pets. She has worked in the public service, has a bachelor of visual arts degree, and has interests in science fiction, folk and fringe culture. She has a regular comic feature in a local publication, *Out Now*, and has had her prose and poetry published elsewhere.

Cristina Lucia Stasia is a second-year doctoral student and university fellow in the English department at Syracuse University. She earned her BA Honors in English/women's studies from the University of Alberta and completed her MA in English at Syracuse University. Her thesis interrogated the relationship between third-wave feminist theories and popular representations of girl power. She works in film and gender/sexuality theories. As a teaching fellow in the Writing Program, she teaches her students how to critically think and write using popular culture. She writes regularly for *Good Girl*.

Ann Tweedy's poetry has been published in *Clackamas Literary Review*, *The Yalobusha Review*, *Berkeley Poetry Review*, *The Drag King Anthology*, and elsewhere. "Holding Out for Spring" was selected by Jane Hirshfield as first runner-up in the GSU Review's Third Annual Writing Contest. Originally from Southeastern Massachusetts, Ann currently lives in Northern Washington, where she works as a lawyer for an Indian tribe.

Jillian Todd Weiss is a lawyer and transgender scholar. She is an instructor in the Department of Sociology and Anthropology at Northeastern University, as well as the Department of Political Science, and a PhD candidate in the Law, Policy & Society Program at Northeastern. She is interested in how the intersection of law, gender and sexuality affects law and organizational policy. Her dissertation is a study of the primary influences on the adoption of transgender human resources policy by U.S. employers. You may learn more about this and her other writings at her Website, <http://hometown.aol.com>.

Introductions

Bisexuality and Transgenderism: InterSEXions of the Others

Jonathan Alexander
Karen Yescavage

http://www.haworthpress.com/web/JB
Digital Object Identifier: 10.1300/J159v03n03_01

[Haworth co-indexing entry note]: "Bisexuality and Transgenderism: InterSEXions of the Others." Alexander, Jonathan, and Karen Yescavage. Co-published simultaneously in *Journal of Bisexuality* (Harrington Park Press, an imprint of The Haworth Press, Inc.) Vol. 3, No. 3/4, 2003, pp. 1-23; and: *Bisexuality and Transgenderism: InterSEXions of the Others* (ed: Jonathan Alexander, and Karen Yescavage) Harrington Park Press, an imprint of The Haworth Press, Inc., 2003, pp. 1-23. Single or multiple copies of this article are available for a fee from The Haworth Document Delivery Service [1-800-HAWORTH, 9:00 a.m. - 5:00 p.m. (EST). E-mail address: docdelivery@haworthpress.com].

SUMMARY. This introduction to the collection *Bisexuality and Transgenderism: InterSEXions of the Others* provides an overview of how considering bisexuality and transgenderism (each broadly defined) can inform and challenge larger cultural understandings of sexuality and gender. The authors provide an overview of extant literature on the subject, propose some of their own productive "intersections" between bisexuality and transgenderism, and introduce the pieces contained in the collection. *[Article copies available for a fee from The Haworth Document Delivery Service: 1-800-HAWORTH. E-mail address: <docdelivery@haworthpress.com> Website: <http://www.HaworthPress.com> © 2003 by The Haworth Press, Inc. All rights reserved.]*

KEYWORDS. Bisexuality, transgender, transsexuality, LGBT, queer, sexuality, gender

In a recent review, historian John D'Emilio (1999) reminds us of what has become a commonplace in thinking about the LGBT/queer community: "Within all of these identities are some who are as mainstream as can be, and some who march to their own drummer" (p. 49). We differ in terms of identity: some of us feel that we were born with our genders or our desires fixed and unchanging; others do not. We differ in terms of political praxis: some feel we should assimilate into the mainstream culture; others celebrate the creation of separate "queer" space. We're variously gay, post-gay, queer, bi-queer, butch, femme, top, bottom, feminist, masculinist, intersexual, genderfuckers, trans, pre-op, post-op, confused, certain, ambivalent, and generally awed by the diversity of our ranks. We are obviously not all the same (nor have we ever been), and we do not all configure our desire in the same way.

For many queers, the inclusion in particular of bisexuals and the transgendered has been a cause for celebration–or concern. Many welcome the expansion of the LGBT umbrella to cover bisexuals and the transgendered, who are often welcomed as queer brothers, sisters, and genderfuckers. Others, however, question whether bisexuals and the transgendered really "belong" in the lesbian and gay community, if they share common ground and common cause with lesbians and gays. The strangeness of the situation is certainly not lost on either bisexuals or the transgendered. As Clare Hemmings (personal communication, May 5th, 2003) put it in an e-mail to Jonathan, ". . . the phrase GLBT may trip off the tongue of every self-aware sexual activist these days, but we know that this is commonly the last moment where B or T difference is really engaged with. One might say that a common bi and trans skeptical humor in relation to a gay and lesbian political fantasy of unity results–I like to think so anyway."

That skepticism signals important work that needs to be done in thinking about what bisexuality and transgenderism bring to the LGBT community–and to the traditionally gendered, heteronormative society at large.

This collection explores what bisexuality and transgenderism, viewed in tandem, can teach us about gender and sexuality. Far from being "strange bedfellows," bi- and trans-lives potentially offer theoretical, cultural, social, and political challenges–and complications–to our collective and individual understandings of desire. What are these challenges and complications? How can they be used–personally and politically? How might BT lives complicate one another? What could be the "common ground" among BT experiences, and where do divergences "queery" the assumptions each makes about desire, identity, and sexual politics? While some might think of B's and T's as mere "additions" tacked on to LG, we think that bisexuality and transgender have much to say to–and about–each other. They also have much to say to the larger culture about the nature, construction, and politicization of sex, sexuality, and gender in our culture.

A note about definitions: To keep the discussion (both in this introduction and throughout the collection) lively and varied, we have chosen to keep our definitions of bisexuality and transgenderism fairly open and fluid. As such, bi (or B) refers to a variety of bi-erotic practices and intimate relationships and trans (or T) encompasses a range of gender play and performance, from genderfucking to cross-dressing and transsexuality. Limiting definitions–at this point, we feel–might have foreclosed on considering some of the more challenging, and enlightening, identities, practices, and experiences currently represented by B and T.

Also, note that we are not confusing bisexuality and transgenderism, and our intention isn't to lump them together in the same category–though an individual may certainly identify as both bi and trans. Rather, our metaphor highlights the intersection of two groups, perhaps with different ultimate aims and goals, but crossing paths periodically and inhabiting common ground. Tracing those paths, examining that ground–this is our aim.

LOOKING BACK . . .

In the last few years, some writers, including scholars, activists, and "lay" members of the LGBT/queer community, have begun considering what bisexuality and transgender have to tell us about sexuality and gender in general. In this section, we highlight some of the dominant trends and issues that this literature discusses.

To start, many queer writers see that bisexuals and transgenderists have much in common–at least on the surface. For instance, in *Trans Liberation*, trans activist Leslie Feinberg (1998) characterizes the broader queer movement as optimally inclusive of multiple gender identities and desires:

> We are a movement of masculine females and feminine males, cross-dressers, transsexual men and women, intersexuals born on the anatomical sweep between female and male, gender-blenders, many other sex and gender-variant people, and our significant others. All told, we expand understanding of how many ways there are to be a human being. (p. 5)

For Feinberg, acknowledging the "many ways there are to be a [gendered] human being" is also acknowledging the many ways our desires take shape and find expression; to exist in the interstices of gender, to "gender-blend," is also to appreciate the "sweep" of erotic attachment and potential desires–from vanilla straight to kinky bi (or vice versa).

Along similar lines, Kate Bornstein has explored in her work, from *Gender Outlaw* to *My Gender Workbook*, the number of ways in which our sociocultural conceptions of gender constrain our sense of self and our ability to play with and experience a variety of desires. As a transgender activist, Bornstein encourages us to break out of our often restrictive understanding of gender and explore what it means to "play" with gender, to cross gender boundaries, to resist conformity to static notions of stereotypical gender. We should not *have* to be manly men and femme women–not if that doesn't feel "right" for us. Moreover, for Bornstein (1998), gender conformity and restriction is directly tied to our experience of desire:

> The probability is that your relationship is based on, or has nestled itself into something based more on the relationship between two identities than on the relationship between two people. That's what we're taught: man/man, woman/woman, woman/man, top/bottom, butch/femme, man/woman/man, etc. We're never taught person/person. That's what the bisexual movement has been trying to teach us. (p. 203)

Breaking out of rigid gender identities might allow us to experience desires for individuals as opposed to identity categories (which we're "supposed" to desire, given our gender and sexual orientation identities). In this way, Bornstein links transgender and bisexual viewpoints to forward a provocative agenda for liberation from the constraints of gender.

Of course, transgenderism encompasses a variety of different identities and ways of being in the world. Besides gender-bending trans activists Feinberg and Bornstein, other transgenderists, particularly some transsexual activists and writers, have also discussed intersections between transsexuality and bisexuality. The complexity of the intersections they highlight reflect the difficulties that members of both communities have found in negotiating common ground–politically, socially, and personally. Writing from her experience as a transsexual in her "Essay for the Inclusion of Transsexuals," which appeared in the groundbreaking collection *Bisexual Politics*, Kory Martin-Damon (1995) maintains that transsexuals should be welcomed into the bisexual community and movement, and that bi's and tran's have much common ground for celebrating both community and a shared vision of the world. Her realization of this was not easy, however, and, in her essay, Martin-Damon poignantly narrates her struggle to identify both as a transsexual and as bisexual. Initially, she tells us, she experienced great confusion about her gender identity, both in terms of what gender she was "supposed" to identify with and what gender she was "supposed" to desire; such confusion limited her sense of possible identifications, potential pleasures, and preferred relationships. Part of her struggle involved various attempts to find acceptance among bi and trans communities, all the while negotiating her multiple desires, for both men and women, and her varying *identification* with men and women.

Ultimately, Martin-Damon was able to locate a stable sense of self as both bisexual *and* transsexual–understanding both as identities that resist the limitations of living life as only gay or straight, male or female:

> If asked, I say I am bisexual. If I were to say I am gay or straight, it would in some sense be a lie, even if I choose to identify either way for the rest of my life. Similarly, I am both genders and neither. As one FTM said . . . , "I never knew what it was like to be a woman, even though I gave birth to six children. But I also don't know what it's like to be a man." (pp. 247-248)

For Martin-Damon, the personal is also clearly the political, and she argues forcefully for the inclusion of transsexuals within the larger bisexual community, particularly since she envisions both as boundary-crossing identities/communities:

> The bisexual community should be a place where lines are erased. Bisexuality dismisses, disproves, and defies dichotomies. It connotes a loss of rigidity and absolutes. It is an inclusive term. Heterosexuality and homosexuality (even if reality is not always practiced) are exclusive and

unilateral, referring only to the attraction to one gender. Transsexuals, despite the gender of our choice, have been two genders. Many of us will always have the genitals we were born with, whether by choice or because of aesthetics or finances. Setting aside our individual sexual orientation, where do we as transsexuals belong? Where does a male-identified person with female genitals belong? (p. 247)

The common ground between bisexuality and transsexuality might have more to teach us–about sexuality, gender, and each other–than the perceived differences between them. Or, as Martin-Damon puts it, "The inclusion of transgendered people can only empower any movement (such as the bisexual movement) that seeks to bring about changes in social mores and gender norms. No other group of people has broken so many gender rules and barriers, or redefined so many gender roles" (p. 249).

Many of these sentiments are echoed in a special issue of the (now defunct) bisexual community magazine, *Anything That Moves*, entitled "Forging a Bi-Trans Alliance." In "The Joker Is Wild: Changing Sex + Other Crimes of Passion," Max Wolf Valerio (2003) suggests that

Transsexuality and bisexuality both occupy heretical thresholds of human experience. We confound, illuminate and explore border regions. We challenge because we appear to break inviolable laws. Laws that feel "natural." And quite possibly, since we are not the norm or even average, it is likely that one function we have is to subvert those norms or laws; to break down the sleepy and unimaginative law of averages.

Transsexuals and bisexuals can both celebrate the capacity of human beings to experience and claim revelation. The bisexual breaks the rule that you must choose between man and woman; the transsexual violates the rule that you must be recognizably and distinctly either a man or a woman your entire life from birth to death. The idea that people carry within them the capacity and the desire to radically alter their biological sex and social gender–or the ability to love and lust after both men and women, or one sex then the other–is experienced by many as heresy. The willful claiming of a unique and perplexing revelation. (http://www.anythingthatmoves.com/ish17/jokers-wild.html)

For Valerio, the intersection between trans and bi lives, identities, and communities is that both offer radical border crossings, question what is socially constructed as "natural," and offer alternatives for experiencing and expressing desire.

As such, alliances between the bi and trans communities seem not just appropriate but commensensical. And, in "Bisexuality and Transgenderism," Kevin Lano (2003) notes that the bi community has often welcomed members of the trans community: "From the earliest years of the bi community, significant numbers of TV/TS and transgender people have always been involved in it. The bi community served as a kind of refuge for people who felt excluded from the established lesbian and gay communities" (http://www.anythingthatmoves. com/ish17/report-from-uk.html).

We know, though, that such alliances are not always easily established. For instance, in an earlier article, Yescavage (1999) explored her struggle to be a genuine ally to those in the trans community. Specifically, she explores the cognitive dissonance she experienced as a bisexual, feminist activist who had difficulty understanding, and hence truly respecting, transwomen. While the journey was not pleasant–confronting one's own prejudices never is–it was both intrapsychically enlightening as well as politically liberating for her.

While much of the popular writing about transgenderism and bisexuality reveals a fairly well-intentioned inclusivity and sense of common ground, other writers, particularly sexuality studies scholars, have noted that the commonalities are fraught with unexamined assumptions. In particular, the notion that both bisexuality and transgenderism share "boundary crossing"–of sex and gender–as a common aim is an assumption that runs roughshod over some of the particularities of *living* as bisexual and as transgendered. For instance, Jay Prosser (1998) has written eloquently in *Second Skins: The Body Narratives of Transsexuality* that

> . . . transsexual and transgendered narratives alike produce not the revelation of the fictionality of gender categories but the sobering realization of their ongoing foundational power . . . (p. 11)

While the writers we've discussed might advocate that we play with gender and our desires, exploring their fluidity and opening up to the possibility of multiple-gender, bi-erotic desire, Prosser reminds us that gender categories are very significant for many people–transsexual, transgendered, and even bisexual. Prosser's concern is that notions from queer theory, such as Judith Butler's concept of gender "performativity," make gender seem like something that one "puts on" in the morning, like a set of clothes. Bornstein's work, for instance, has been criticized for seemingly reducing gender to a question of shopping. But even Butler (1993) has made pains, like Prosser, to note that gender identities and "performances" should not be construed so simply:

[Gender performativity] consists in a reiteration of norms which precede, constrain, and exceed the performer and in that sense cannot be taken as the fabrication of the performer's "will" or "choice" . . . The reduction of performativity to performance would be a mistake. (p. 234)

Indeed, many transsexuals undertake surgical reassignment surgery primarily *because* they value living *as a particular gendered being*. Likewise, many bisexuals enjoy relationships with men *as men* and with women *as women*.

So, do transgender and bisexuality intersect along the lines of exploring and exploding gender/sexuality identities and boundaries, or do they help to reify normative categories of gender and sexual orientation? A part of Clare Hemmings' (2002) *Bisexual Spaces: A Geography of Sexuality and Gender* analyzes just this conundrum in thinking about the intersections between bisexuality and transgender. Hemmings notes how ". . . there are a number of similarities in the ways that bisexuality and transsexuality are given and give meaning within queer and feminist studies currently . . ." (p. 99). On one hand, "both transsexuals and bisexuals are seen as traitors, as not feminist or queer enough to be considered viable political subjects in their own right" (p. 100). Bisexuals, for instance, strike many as embracing heterosexual privilege, and transsexuals are viewed as reifying norms of gender as they seek to become "real men" or "real women." We can see some of these tensions playing out in the *Anything That Moves* issue on bi/trans intersections. In "Talking about the iSsues no onE's eXpressing: Telling it like it is in the world of bi-trans romance," Heather Franek (2003) maintains that

Many MTFs I have met have grown up with very male ideas about what makes a woman a woman, and adopt these ideals when they make their transitions. I have seen MTFs argue that biceps are not pretty, that any woman who does not like being whistled at on the street is just "uncomfortable with her sexuality," and that other transwomen are "boy-girls" or "she-males" because they don't bother to shave their legs or armpits. Does one have to get rid of one's arm hair and stop exercising in order to be feminine?

By the same token, I've seen FTMs argue that their abusive behavior towards others was an effect of testosterone injections which "cannot be controlled," even though millions of genetic men and adolescent boys manage to control their tempers every day. P.K. [the author's partner] gets extreme disapproval in her MTF community for not being "woman enough" to satisfy the MTF Guardians of True Womanhood; for not passing well enough, for not making her voice high enough, for letting it

show that she grew up as a man. (http://www.anythingthatmoves.com/ish17/
issues-no-ones-expressing.html)

On the other hand, Hemmings (2002) is quick to acknowledge that "[t]rans-sexuality and bisexuality are also positioned at the cutting edge of debates about gender, sexuality, and political meaning" (p. 100). For instance, Marjorie Garber's (1995) famous *Vice Versa: Bisexuality and the Eroticism of Every-day Life* consistently figures bisexuality as being able to teach us "something fundamental . . . about the nature of human eroticism" (p. 15); on a more personal level, she notes that it is, for some who experience it, "a matter of personal realization and personal freedom" (p. 34).

The end result for Hemmings (2002) is that we understand bisexuality and transgenderism as *either* transgressive *or* normative:

> Just as bisexuality can be contained with queer discourse through its con-signment to the middle ground of behavior or potential, transsexuality has commonly appeared in queer contexts as all that is subversive of gender norms when figured as transgenderism, as gendered surface rather than depth. And just as bisexuality is understood as normative when config-ured as identity, transsexuality becomes problematic when insisted upon as real, a property of the self, because of a perceived reinscription of dominant (i.e., heterosexist) gender and/or sexual discourse. (p. 117)

Other scholars are coming to similar understandings. In her new historical survey and analysis, *How Sex Changed: A History of Transsexuality in the United States*, Joanne Meyerowitz (2002) argues that transsexuality in partic-ular is a simultaneous reification of gender norms and expectations *and* a mo-bilization of gender:

> Transsexuals, some argue, reinscribe the conservative stereotypes of male and female and masculine and feminine. They take the signifiers of sex and the prescriptions of gender too seriously. They are "utterly invested" in the boundaries between female and male. Or they represent individual autonomy run amok in the late modern age. [. . .] . . . some theories iden-tify transsexuals as emblems of liberatory potential. (pp. 11-12)

Hemmings (2002) suggests the same about bisexuality: "Bisexuality is . . . posited as a consistent and self-evident challenge to lesbian, gay, and straight oppositions, the fluidity and transgressive nature of the former contrasted with the static and conservative nature of the latter" (5). At the same time, she argues, "It is entirely myopic to imagine that bisexuality has no role in the maintenance of dominant structures of sexuality" (p. 6). As she put it in an e-mail interview, "[i]f desiring across sexes is always a critique of desiring a particular sex, we also get to claim ourselves to be transgressive without having to examine our behaviors more carefully. It must be clear to most of us [by] now that being bisexual doesn't 'explode binaries' in itself, that we can be actively bisexual and not challenge much of anything in fact."

Hemmings and Meyerowitz bring us to a crossroads, as it were, in thinking about bisexuality and transgenderism—where both identities seem to be either "transgressive" of sex/gender norms or representative of normative practices themselves. But do these crossroads offer us only a conundrum, an either/or choice, another binary opposition? Or do they intersect in other more provocative, more complex ways?

WHAT WE HOPED THIS COLLECTION WOULD ACCOMPLISH . . .

Our sense is that there is more to the story of bisexuality and transgender intersections than this binary suggests. In our "Call for Papers" for this collection, we sought to push beyond simplistic thinking about B and T lives. Our challenge, we were to discover, was not in avoiding the binary, but in how to stay open to theses that were as wide ranging as the bi and trans communities themselves. The fact that both groups seem to subvert the binary constructions of gender (male/female) and sexuality (gay/straight) was our starting point; but that was only a *starting* point.

As our contributors reflected upon their lives and developed relevant arguments about bi/trans intersections, we too formulated a set of intersections that we feel provides support for the transgressive capabilities of the others to *both* challenge systems *as well as* continue to keep us rooted within the fundamental framework of gendered living. Further, upon listening to each other and reflecting on our many discussions, as well as discussing these issues with others in various bi and trans communities, several other intersections emerged. None of these are necessarily mutually exclusive, but rather interconnected, just like the lives of bisexuals and the transgendered. Furthermore, we do not assert that the list is exhaustive or that *all* bisexuals or *all* transgendered individuals will identify with each of them. Rather, these are points of mutually enlightening discussion, many of which took time to unfold—or, we should say, they became apparent as *we* unfolded.

Mutability Intersection

Anyone who is exposed to bisexuality and transgenderism quickly observes that bi and trans individuals challenge the notion that one *has to choose* to be (with) one gender. Bs and Ts have been called many names, suggesting that one's identity *should be* fixed (as well as single-sexed). Fortunately, both groups generally take pride in the freedom to choose, *or not* to choose. We believe that the contribution of bisexuals and the transgendered to the lesbian and gay communities is to highlight the importance of this *freedom*.

The Others Intersection

Many straights are unaware of the fairly common experience that many Ts and Bs have of being the marginalized others in the LGBT community. Many of our contributors report how Ts and Bs have been asked to march, so to speak, at the *end* of the Pride parade, *if they were asked–or allowed–at all*. We hope that by highlighting the experience of "othering" within the LGBT community, we can learn from the experience of exclusivity and begin tearing down these unnecessary barriers. Why might bi/trans individuals be treated as "other"? The next intersection offers an explanation.

Projected Fears Intersection

Some gays and lesbians believe bisexuals are *too afraid to commit* to a life as a full-fledged homosexual. Interestingly, some transgender folks are similarly accused. In both the lesbian and gay communities, one could argue that it is projected self-contempt that explains some of the biphobia. Some gays and lesbians may fear the ability to love/lust after the "othering" gender because of the temptation to reject their "queer" desires. This hostility toward bisexuals seems to imply an underlying envy of the capacity to have "normal," i.e., hetero, relationships, or it may be an envy of the "heterosexual privilege" that some bisexuals might enjoy. More fundamentally, perhaps, bisexuality seems to query the "origin" of desire and sexual orientation as innate; put another way, when gays rhetorically question, "Who would *choose* to be queer?", bisexuality by its very nature implies, "Some do." Whether this is true or not,[1] the fact is that we all choose whether or not we will *express* our desires–and how openly (or not) we will do so. In that respect, we are all the same. Regardless of whether we were born with or choose our desires, *all of us should be free to express them* (assuming, of course, that they are expressed with others fully capable of consenting).

Transgenderists are often accused of a similar fence-sitting, unwilling to commit to a gender identity, and some transsexuals have been characterized as suffering from unacknowledged "internalized homophobia," which prompts them to undergo transition from one gender to another in order to avoid living as gay or lesbian. Based on our experience and research, it seems completely irrational to us to think that someone would transition genders rather than be gay or lesbian, given the extreme amount of hatred and difficulty associated with transitioning. Easier to understand is the possibility that there is, in the lesbian and gay communities, an insecurity with one's own gender identification that causes this kind of discomfort. Given the pervasive stereotype that gay men are effeminate and lesbians are manly, some psychological baggage about one's gender identity is likely to exist. For example, a gay male student recently drove this point home saying, "I've had to struggle to accept transmen, because I didn't want them 'showing me up'!" For him, his manhood was threatened because a (former) woman was "showing him up," i.e., acting more like a (stereotypical) man than he was. His struggle is likely exacerbated because he is also Latino, coming from a culture where machismo is held in high regard and gender roles are (or can be) traditionally prescribed.

Those of us who are also aware of the theory of inversion (see Katz, 1995)–which claims that men and women who express desires for the same gender have (heterosexual) brains that have been inverted or reversed–may find transsexuality in particular or transgenderism in general tweaking certain insecurities. This theory has (re)gained recent attention as researchers report that gay men and lesbians demonstrate some cognitive abilities that are more similar to women and men, respectively ("Gays and lesbians have 'gender-bender' brains" http://breaking.examiner.ie/2003/03/25/story93076.html). What if the inversion theory has merit and gays and lesbians, as well as bisexuals, are actually a type of transsexual, i.e., they are more like transsexuals than vice versa? Ah, sweet irony . . . or unbridled fear? Would that put homosexuality back on the DSM as a disorder since gender identity disorder (transsexuality) is (still) one?

Of course, we are hardly suggesting that *all* gays and lesbians have such projected fears or communal insecurities about B and T folk. But some might, fearing an instability or impermanence to their identities, which leads us to our next intersection.

Impermanence Intersection

We have found that some people identify with bisexuality for a brief period of time as they traverse the landscape from straight to gay (or–though much less frequently–from gay to straight). This tends to cause a good bit of outrage by those who seemingly want permanent residents in a lesbian and gay community and not necessarily a lesbian, gay and bisexual "neighborhood." Similarly, some trans individuals seek to leave behind their past gendered self as well as their trans identities following completion of their change. Again, some trans activists see this as detrimental to the movement and characterize such individuals as traitors, leaving behind the "freaks" as soon as they can be perceived convincingly as "normal."

Impermanence also has other valences, suggesting the mutability of gender and sexuality as identity constructs. Joanne Meyerowitz's (2002) meticulously researched *How Sex Changed: A History of Transsexuality in the United States* provides readers with a wonderful history, not just of transsexuality, but of how sex, sexuality, and gender have changed in meaning over the last 100 years. Of particular note for bi/trans intersections is Meyerowitz's provocative claim that "biological sex has a history"–one that can be traced, analyzed, and understood as bearing the weight of a lot of cultural baggage about what it means to be male and female (p. 21). In other words, our understanding of what actually comprises biological maleness and biological femaleness has changed over the course of history, much as ideas, values, and "standards" for masculinity and femininity have changed. Meyerowitz's tracing of this history reveals some curious constructions–and intersections–of sexuality and gender. For instance, some prominent late nineteenth- and early twentieth-century sexologists, such as Otto Weininger, believed that all humans were "physically bisexual," with sex existing on a "continuous spectrum" (p. 24). Others such as Magnus Hirschfeld proposed the notions of "sexual intermediaries" and a "third sex" to encompass hermaphrodites, androgynes, homosexuals, and transvestites (p. 26). Meyerowitz's unpacking of this work suggests that our culture's rigid gender/sex dichotomies (male and female, gay and straight), and the sexual orientations and gender identities upon which they rest, are capable of continued revision. In many ways, we feel that bisexuality and transgender prompt us to re-examine the way we construct gender and sexuality.

Trans identities in particular are challenging for more "mainstream" queers. In a recent article, "Transgender and Les/Bi/Gay Identities," Alan Sinfield (2000) has suggested that LGB politics has had a hard time understanding and welcoming trans lives and issues underneath its sociopolitical umbrella because trans (whether its transgenderism or transsexuality) works at the level of "gender," not "sexuality": "The issue is whether one sees oneself, *first*, in terms of sexuality or gender" (p. 153). For Sinfield (2000), trans queries the way we've constructed LG/queer history and politics:

In gay liberation, it is lesbians and gays who could pass who gained the option of coming out, because now they were defined fully as homosexuals. In other words, sexual orientation became prior, and gender identity was subsumed, more or less uneasily, into it. Transgender demands reconsideration of that model. (p. 157)

Part of our interest in bringing together trans and bi identities, even if they are at times "identities in motion," is to capture part of that critique, that reconsideration. More fundamentally, in terms of fostering positive and healthy relations among members of our community, we feel that being judged for claiming a provisional identity doesn't feel good, and further, adds to the suffering caused by identity politics. Bi/trans people are judged in another way as well, described in the next intersection.

Full-Disclosure Intersection

Trans and bi people are expected to disclose their "full" identities (past and present genders, or past and present partners' genders, if it varies). Bs and Ts are expected to provide a "warning" to potential lovers (or friends even) of what they're getting into before proceeding with the relationship. While "honesty is the best policy" and is certainly healthy for relationships, shouldn't disclosure be up to the individual to determine for his/her/hirself? Again, who has the power to deem what is "necessary" to disclose? Simply *wanting* to know something about others doesn't make us entitled to *their* information. We have consumed the oppressor's values when we disrespect individuals' rights to privacy and then try to take away their own legitimate agency. Obviously, these actions are based upon fear: of being hurt, deceived, or betrayed. We hope that our discussion of bi and trans issues and intersections will help *all* of us better understand one another and avoid reactions based on fear.

Intersecting Identities Intersection

While confusion lingers about the differences between gender and sexual identities, transgendered individuals make it clear that these are different; hence, people–should they be so inclined to adopt labels–are either transgendered or traditionally gendered *and* straight, gay/lesbian, or bisexual. For example, Martin-Damon, whom we mentioned earlier, speaks of her experiences as a *bisexual transsexual*. Initially, we found ourselves missing this obvious intersection, even after reading about her struggle to come out both as bi and trans.

Obviously, we are not alone. For some reason, the desires of trans people have yet to really be addressed by either the straight or the LGB community. Is this because it's too difficult, given our limited (and exclusionary) language? Is it all still too overwhelming and new? Or is it that trans folks don't want to lose the only community they have by making their desires an issue, given their (already) fragile relationship with the LGB community? Hopefully this is not true, though it would be understandable. After all, trans individuals see how "real" lesbians and gays have struggled to accept bisexual women and men, respectively. Should the transgendered assert their sexuality in addition to their gender (re)configuration, will they jeopardize the tiny foothold they have within the seemingly gated LGBT community by seeming just a little too complex, even illegitimate? For instance, we know that transwomen who desire other women have often been excluded from "lesbian-only" forums, events, and communities; they are not "real" women. Would addressing their lesbian desires provoke productive discussion, or incite further exclusion, as the boundaries of "lesbianism" become more clearly defined and policed to exclude those who make too much gender trouble? Or should transwomen simply except the minimal acceptance they are gaining in the broader gay community?

In our experience, we have found that this minimal acceptance (mere tolerance) of the transgendered seems eerily similar to what women of color experienced for so long (and still do, we imagine, in some settings) within the (White) women's movements of the "first" and "second" waves of feminism? Essentially the mindset was, "We'll accept your presence–quite frankly we could use your numbers–but don't push your own (colored, or in this case, gendered) agenda." Lesbians experienced the same thing during the second wave as well, being referred to as the "lavender menace." Shared stigma is acceptable to organize around in activism, but unfortunately, "additional" differences tend not to be; in other words, bi and transgendered people, not unlike all the other double and triple minorities before them (e.g., Latina lesbian women), have all been told "go create your own group for that."

REVIEW OF CONTENTS . . .

These were some of *our* initial thoughts about BT intersections; our contributors, writing from a variety of perspectives and forwarding a diversity of views, brought us many more to consider. Part of the challenge of their work lies not only in the content but in the *style* with which our writers chose to express themselves. While some produced essays in a recognizably academic vein, others offered reflections in narratives, opinion pieces, and even manifestoes and poetry. We have decided to "mix" these genres, organizing the pieces around intersecting themes.

Another challenging aspect of our contributors' work is that we found ourselves periodically disagreeing with some of the views forwarded. Over the course of the last year, we've had numerous e-mail discussions with our writers, who have consistently and provocatively challenged our theories and positions, just as we have tried to challenge (productively!) their views and beliefs. In some cases, we might not agree with a particular point made–but the goal of this collection is not to "streamline" thinking about bi- and trans-intersections. Rather, the goal is to open ourselves to learning from and sharing with one another about our experiences of sexuality and gender. And, collectively, these pieces have taught us much about bisexuality and transgenderism; they have helped bring our thinking to another level of depth and insight.

The first section introduces the notion of intersecting identities, communities, practices, and experiences among bi and trans people. In addition to this introduction, in which we have offered some of our own thoughts on the intersections between bisexuality and transgenderism, we include Jill Weiss's magnificently thorough and provocative essay detailing gay and lesbian history alongside bisexual and transgendered history.

While Weiss reviews biphobia and transphobia more generally, in the next section, "Intersecting Communities: B/T Concerns in Common," several other contributors detail various bi- and trans-difficulties or dis-ease with/in the so-called LGBT "community." Edwards' piece for example warns us of the dangers of creating identifiable communities for the sake of consumerism. Allies offers an astute essay regarding the harm inherent in the concept "pomosexual play." Cooper's piece highlights isolation within and amongst LGBT individuals and swingers, and, in a scientific study, Mathy's research confirms the dangers of lumping all queers together when trying to understand differential suicidal intentions within the LGBT community.

The next section, "Real(izing) Lives: Personal and Theoretical B/T Identity Formations," offers several narratives of bi/trans individuals who provide insights into their multifaceted lives. Chase takes the reader on an intimate journey through the "unfolding" of his life "so far," paying his respects to the many drag queens that took him under sequined wings. Seabrook, another bi/trans individual, echoes the struggles to be honest with all of one's emerging selves. Both speak eloquently about their unique journey toward self-realization. Alexander conducted a group interview of a trans support group, providing a forum for transsexual individuals to reflect upon fascinating aspects of transition, such as the influence of hormones on emerging bi-desires. Lastly, sociologist Michaela Meyer offers a theoretical framework for both bi and trans identity formation, filling a significant gap in the research literature.

Continuing the exploration of B/T lives, contributors in the fourth section, "Reel Lives," take a look at B/T pop cultural icons such as Angelina Jolie and Sandra Bernhard. While contributors do not necessarily identify either star as bi or trans, they do note the ways in which these pop icons provoke productive discussion about bisexuality and transgender issues. Just as Chase and Seabrook speak about the multiplicity of their identities beyond being bi and trans, Stasia and Rosenberg highlight aspects of the stars, for example, Jolie's knife fetish and Berhnard's Jewish identity, that challenge simple or reductive notions of gender and sexuality identity. In this way, then, the stars are transgender in the broadest sense, even when not specifically trans identified. Ultimately, both writers remind us that popular culture provides many opportunities to examine emerging images of both bi-eroticism and transgendering–frequently at the same time.

In section five, "Western Intersections, Eastern Approximations," we see how our Western constructions of gender and sexuality do not easily translate to all cultures. McLelland and Graham do an excellent job of taking such Western constructions and approximating them to trans and bi experiences within Japanese and Indonesian cultures. This section serves as a reminder of how concepts such as gender and sexuality, often treated as so "naturally" occurring, are really subject to much cultural interpretation.

The collection concludes with "Steering Queer of LGBTI Identity Politics," which offers some speculative pieces that attempt to map out some further directions for thinking about bisexuality, transgenderism, their intersections, and, indeed, the future consideration (and construction) of desire, identity, and community. In this last section, Kailey, Drechsler, and Green each argue for an alternative, i.e., queer, perspective in their provocative pieces.

AFTER THIS PUBLICATION . . .
WHAT THEN? BEYOND INTERSEXIONS . . .

As we've concluded working with our contributors and finished our own work in writing this introduction, our attention turns, inevitably it seems, to what *now*? If the pieces included in this book argue collectively for mutual understanding and appreciation, then how might the future challenge our expanding sense of understanding, of appreciation, of *valuing* each other?

Hopefully, we can learn from all these various "turf" wars and be mindful of the next others who seek a community, a place where they have a sense of belonging. We see intersexuals as the next possible group to "test" our ability to practice inclusivity and demonstrate acceptance of diversity. Some LGBT groups, in places such as Australia, have already tacked on "I" to their LGBT label. Hopefully, the incorporation of transgendered individuals may have paved the way for inclusion of intersexuals, since both challenge the binary notion of sex/gender, albeit in different ways. Attempting to include intersexuals might push our understanding of the intersections between gender and sexuality/sexual orientation to the breaking point; or, it may offer us completely new ways of articulating desire, identity, and community.

How so? Let's look briefly at some of the possibilities. To start, given that physicians have been (re)constructing intersexed individuals for the past fifty years, one *could* argue that doctors are in the business of creating transgendered people out of intersexuals. They hormonally and surgically make intersexuals either male or female; the difference of course–and a significant one it is–is that it is not at the request of the "patient." The power to decide one's fate lies outside the person. While there is no medical necessity in most cases, the medical "industry" acts upon beings too young to understand, and therefore unable to give their informed consent. The cover story, of course, is that physicians and psychiatrists/psychologists are all doing their part to ease the pain of individual after individual after individual, while unnecessary gender-based laws and social mores continue to go unchecked.

Intersexual surgeries are framed as helping the child (and perhaps more truthfully, the family) be more comfortable in society. Intersexuals who have just begun to organize politically are now asking, "For whose benefit, exactly, are these surgeries?" Answering their own question, they contend it is for *society* as much as–if not more than–for the intersexed child. We pose the question, "Whose society?" The heteronormative one or the LGBT/queer one as well? The lives of the intersexed remind us of the constructedness of gender, and consequently, sexual orientation. We, as queers, ask, who holds the power to reconstruct these two classification systems? Do *we*? *Can* we? What does it take to challenge the discriminatory status quo?

Looking even *further* down the road with respect to intersexuality, two thoughts come to mind: one, if biologically born women and men were to "come out" and request to transition from single-sexed to intersexed, will the mental and physical health professions honor their desires, feelings, or creativity? Two, *should* the powers that be respect this request, will it be important, i.e., meaningful, to distinguish between those who transition from one single-sex category to another (i.e., MtF and FtM) and those who transition from single to intersexed? If so, will these individuals be classified as something other than trans (or a special type of trans)? Perhaps if (or once) a "third gender" concept is adopted, it will remove the bizarreness of desiring to transition to a place that has yet to be "built"–that is, officially recognized and legitimized.

While that is one way to approach the future, there may be other ways (better ways?) to go. Will identity politics become so complex and cumbersome that labels will no longer be shortcuts to knowing someone, but rather, neverending signifiers that become meaningless due to the sheer number of them? While these speculations are beyond the purview of this collection, they are provocative nonetheless–particularly when we consider that gender was not initially the organizing principle for understanding and *knowing* one's sexual identity (Katz, 1995). For quite some time in the West, the primary distinction made was between procreative sexual activity (penis-vagina penetration) and non-procreative sexual activity (i.e., everything else by everyone else–two men; two women; a man and a woman engaging in oral or anal sexual behaviors; an individual engaging in masturbation). In other words, male-female couples who were engaging in sex for pleasure were viewed similarly to same-gender couples; both, of course, were "perverts." When did gender take over, and why?

As we've considered this question, it occurs to us that sexual orientation and gender labels describe but two aspects of the colorful spectrum of desire. Will it take other dimensions of the spectrum "coming forth" or "coming out" for gender (and sexual orientation)–as dominant modes of human classification, categorization, and hence control–to "go away"? Perhaps it comes down to this: if power and control were no longer linked to sexuality, would anyone really care about labeling people based upon their desires?

If we continue to highlight gender (of mate or lover choice), then it seems only fair that the classification systems of gender and sexual orientation be expanded to include categories of, and attractions for, trans and intersexed individuals. Of course, acknowledging these groups will complicate matters, demanding that lesbians, gays, and perhaps even bisexuals make explicit exactly what it is they find desirable. To the scientists (and linguists) interested in taking this (re)construction project on, we say, "Good luck trying to reach consensus on an operational definition of 'desire.'" One thing we have learned from this project is just how diversely interpreted and expressed desire is within the LGBT/queer community.

One remaining question haunts us: how long will it take for those diverse expressions of desire to be accepted, appreciated, and *valued*–not just within the LGBT/queer community, but in the "larger" world as well? History might provide some answers, or at least guideposts.

In the United States, it took 100 years to go from emancipation of a 300 year old system of slavery to the beginnings of desegregation. In only half that amount of time, the country evolved to a place where, if a Black man such as Colin Powell were to run for office, he might possibly be the first African-American President of the United States. We ponder, if in only half that time again, will the inalienable right to "life, liberty, and the pursuit of happiness" finally be fully realized for Blacks, and perhaps all people of color, in "the land of the free"? Similarly, during that same time period, women went from being disenfranchised, patriarchal property to obtaining a position on the highest court and members of the President's Cabinet. Although the equal rights amendment has yet to pass, there have been significant strides in women's right to live in a just society (e.g., rape is no longer a property crime, nor a crime of passion). While discrimination at both the institutional and interpersonal levels continues, there has been an observable progression in society's treatment of both women and people of color.

Putting "queer" rights into perspective vis-à-vis these other fights for equality and justice, how long will it take before *we*, whether L, G, B, T, I, Q, or any combination thereof, enjoy untrammeled rights to "life, liberty and the pursuit of happiness"? We are optimistic. The U.S. Supreme Court ruling (of Lawrence v. Texas) on June 26, 2003, which overturned all sodomy laws in the country, gives us hope that we are finally carving out a place in our supposedly democratic society. As reported by Rostrow (2003) in PlanetOut.com, the ". . . Lambda Legal Defense said Thursday's high court ruling 'starts an entirely new chapter in our fight for equality for lesbians, bisexuals, transgenders, and gay men.'"

Now more than ever we need to dialogue about our continued strategy for liberation. Do we dive into the assimilationist, erroneous "melting pot" of America? Or, do we strive to be tossed into the "salad" of a truly pluralistic society, where each group (or individual) adds its own unique *and recognizable* flavors? Realistically, as diverse as we are, we will surely advocate for–and argue the merits of–both.

But what will guide our discussion? Recently, academics and activists have been talking about a politics of value replacing a politics of identity.[2] In *Pomosexuals,* an anthology of articles "challenging assumptions about gender and sexuality," D. Travers Scott (1997) argues that "Homosexuality's over," and, with its demise, it's time to open up "the philosophical playroom for much more exciting possibilities, such as *choice* and *freedom*. These ideas, in turn, necessitate exploration and articulation of *values* and *responsibilities*." Or, to sum up, "The issue [facing queer contemporary queer activists] isn't identity; it's ideology. It's about freedom, responsibility, and values" (p. 68). Scott argues against an identity politics that suggests we must first "understand" or "know" one another before we can accept one another and fight for each other's rights. We have come to the same conclusion; what is important is not that we "get it" but rather that we value each other without–or before–"getting it."

More provocatively, we believe it is important to challenge ourselves to reach across chasms that we may think are unbridgeable. As such, *we value precisely those who call into question our very existence.* Even though it can be unsettling at times, and quite frankly, down right exhausting, we find it necessary for our continued growth. Too much comfort can cause stagnation, and even more dangerously, restrictive dogma. It is with this in mind that we invite you to read our provocative collection of essays on the interSEXions of the "others." We hope that you will find them stimulating, challenging, and encouraging. Bisexuals and the transgendered often symbolize "identities in motion," and many find this unsettling. At the very least, it seems transgressive to embrace the impermanence of our social world. As we ourselves have grown in our own exploration of bisexuality and transgenderism, both professionally and personally, we have found that such motion is both transgressive and, ironically, quite normal.

NOTES

1. Rust (1995) explains how bisexuals are no more (or less) likely to *choose* their sexual desires than monosexuals.
2. See in particular the special issue of *The Journal of Gay, Lesbian, and Bisexual Identity,* "Queer Values, Beyond Identity." Volume 4, Number 4. October 1999.

REFERENCES

Alexander, J. (1999). Beyond identity: Queer values and community. *Journal of gay, lesbian, and bisexual identity,* 4(4), 293-314.
Bornstein, K. (1998). *My gender workbook.* London: Routledge.
Butler, J. (1993). *Bodies that matter: On the discursive limits of "sex."* New York: Routledge.
D'Emilio, J. (1999). The gaying of America. *The Harvard gay and lesbian review,* 6(1), 48-49.
Feinberg, L. (1998). *Transliberation: Beyond pink or blue.* Boston: Beacon Press.
Franek, H. (2003). Talking about the iSsues no onE's eXpressing: Telling it like it is in the world of bi-trans romance [online]. *Anything that moves.* Available: http://www.anythingthatmoves.com/ish17/issues-no-ones-expressing.html
Garber, M. (1995). *Vice versa: Bisexuality and the eroticism of everyday life.* New York: Simon & Schuster.
Gays and lesbians have 'gender-bender' brains [online]. Available: (http://breaking.examiner.ie/2003/03/25/story93076.html).
Hemmings, C. (2002). *Bisexual spaces: A geography of sexuality and gender.* New York: Routledge.
Katz, J. N. (1995). *The invention of heterosexuality.* New York: Dutton Books.
Lano, K. (2003). Bisexuality and transgenderism [online]. *Anything that moves.* Available: (http://www.anythingthatmoves.com/ish17/report-from-uk.html).
Martin-Damon, K. (1995). Essay for the inclusion of transsexuals. *Bisexual politics.* New York: Harrington Park Press.

Meyerowitz, J. (2002). *How sex changed: A history of transsexuality in the United States*. Cambridge, MA: Harvard University Press.

Prosser, J. (1998). *Second skins: The body narratives of transsexuality*. New York: Columbia University Press.

Rostrow, A. (2003). Supreme Court strikes down sodomy laws [online]. June 26, 2003. Available: (http://www.planetout.com/pno/splash.html).

Rust, P. C. (1995). *Bisexuality and the challenge to lesbian politics: Sex, loyalty, and revolution*. New York: New York University Press.

Scott, D. T. (1997). Le freak, c'est chic! Le fag, quelle drag! In C. Queen and L. Schmeil (Eds.), *Pomosexuals: Challenging assumptions about gender and sexuality* (pp. 62-68). San Francisco: Cleis Press.

Sinfield, A. (2000). Transgender and les/bi/gay identities. In D. Alderson and L. Anderson (Eds.), *Territories of desire in queer culture: Refiguring contemporary boundaries* (pp. 150-163). Manchester, UK: Manchester University Press.

Valerio, M.W. (April 26th, 2003). The joker is wild: Changing sex + other crimes of passion. *Anything that moves* [online]. Available: (http://www.anythingthatmoves.com/ish17/jokers-wild.html).

Yescavage, K. (1999). Oppressed oppressor: Fighting for queer values while fighting to value queers. *Journal of gay, lesbian, and bisexual identity*, 4(4), 357-368.

GL vs. BT:
The Archaeology
of Biphobia and Transphobia
Within the U.S. Gay and
Lesbian Community

Jillian Todd Weiss

http://www.haworthpress.com/web/JB
Digital Object Identifier: 10.1300/J159v03n03_02

[Haworth co-indexing entry note]: "GL vs. BT: The Archaeology of Biphobia and Transphobia Within the
U.S. Gay and Lesbian Community." Weiss, Jillian Todd. Co-published simultaneously in *Journal of Bisexuality* (Harrington Park Press, an imprint of The Haworth Press, Inc.) Vol. 3, No. 3/4, 2003, pp. 25-55; and: *Bisexuality and Transgenderism: InterSEXions of the Others* (ed: Jonathan Alexander, and Karen Yescavage) Harrington Park Press, an imprint of The Haworth Press, Inc., 2003, pp. 25-55. Single or multiple copies of this article are available for a fee from The Haworth Document Delivery Service [1-800-HAWORTH, 9:00 a.m. - 5:00 p.m. (EST). E-mail address: docdelivery@haworthpress.com].

SUMMARY. Heterosexism against bisexuals and transgenders exists not only in the straight community, but in the gay and lesbian community as well. Are "biphobia" and "transphobia" examples of "phobias"–irrational fears? No, such heterosexist attitudes are all too rational, mirroring social tensions, which only appear to be an ahistorical psychological phenomenon. Rather, as the GLBT community developed, power relations arose which resulted in the four different groups (G/L/B/T), assigning them different social locations. Prejudice in gay and lesbian communities against bisexuals and transgenders is heterosexism because it is, among other things, an accommodationist attempt to disavow these more "radical" forms of sexuality. *[Article copies available for a fee from The Haworth Document Delivery Service: 1-800-HAWORTH. E-mail address: <docdelivery@haworthpress.com> Website: <http://www.HaworthPress.com> © 2003 by The Haworth Press, Inc. All rights reserved.]*

KEYWORDS. Biphobia, transphobia, heterosexism, prejudice, discrimination

What will it take
for the gayristocracy to realize
that bisexual, lesbian, transgender and gay people
are in this together?
We can and will
move the agenda forward.

But this will not happen
until public recognition
of our common issues is made,
and a sincere effort to confront
biphobia and transphobia is made
by the established gay and lesbian leadership
in this country.

–Lani Ka'ahumanu
(Speech delivered at the March on Washington
for Lesbian, Gay and Bi Equal Rights and Liberation, 1993)

I am reminded of my first, puzzling experience with "transphobia." Having grown up as a very straight and narrow white heterosexual male, I had no experience with the "GLBT (gay, lesbian, bisexual and transgender) community." Until I came out at the age of 35, I viewed my longstanding transsexual impulses as a sick fantasy that had to be contained at all costs, and assumed (and hoped) that it would go away at some point. When my marriage broke up in 1997, I realized it was time to transition. I looked for a new place to live. A friend of ours, a gay man, offered his apartment as a place to stay until I found a place of my own. I liked him, and thought myself very lucky to have him as a friend. Who better to speak to about these very difficult issues? I was rather incautious. Having someone to listen (who would not run out of the room screaming) was an aphrodisiac. I told him freely of my plans, not dreaming of anything other than ecstatic acceptance, and was surprised to see shock register in his face. He was gracious about it, but clearly he thought he was offering his apartment to a straight man. The idea of hosting "a transsexual" in his fashionable New York City apartment building, who would parade around in women's clothes, was not at all what he had in mind. I slowly realized that my presence was embarrassing to him, that he did not wish to know me, and that the sooner I was out of there, the better.

Years later, someone told me of his disparaging description of me displaying my new-found femininity "proud as a peacock." After a number of minor humiliating incidents, I left, and my attempts to contact him were not returned. I still like him, and wish it weren't this way, but this was to be only the first of a number of unsatisfactory contacts and misunderstandings with the "GLBT community." One could say that he had a "problem" (meaning, in common parlance, a psychological problem) with "transphobia" (fear of transgenders). To locate this issue within the psychology of an individual, however, is wholly unsatisfactory to an understanding of this phenomenon. This is not a bad person. He is urbane, witty and intelligent, and went out of his way as best he could to avoid insult or injury to me at a very difficult time in my life. I say without irony that he saved my life. The two of us, however, were in the grip of social forces far beyond our comprehension. When a significant portion of the population start to have the same "psychological problem," it is time to call out the sociologists.

THE NATURE OF BIPHOBIA AND TRANSPHOBIA

The Myth of "GLBT Community" Togetherness

The "GLBT community" appears monolithic. The quadratic formula of "GLBT," adding together several second-order elements to create a single, defined community, suggests communal interests. This is the understanding that most heterosexuals in the U.S. seem to have. Such a community of interest makes sense because homosexuals have long been subjected to heterosexist prejudice. Yet, like most social phenomena, the situation is far more complex than it seems at first glance. The very creation of the "GLBT" acronym suggests that gay and lesbian and bisexual and transgender are each clearly defined, separate and mutually exclusive categories–not one and the same. When one begins to examine this "community," one finds evidence of this separateness, for internecine struggles seethe beneath the surface, calling into question the idea of a "GLBT community." While many gays and lesbians feel that "bisexual" and "transgender" are simply names for parts of their own community, others actively reject the idea that bisexuals or transgenders are part of their community, seeing them as entirely separate and distinct. Heterosexism against bisexuals and transgenders exists not only in the straight community, but in the gay and lesbian community as well. Some feel, as we shall see, that bisexuality and transgenderism are detrimental to the social and political acceptance of gays and lesbians. This curious phenomenon has been called "internalized homophobia" by some, meaning an irrational fear and dislike of other homosexuals (Fone 2000:6, Sears and Williams 1997:16). This presumes, of course, that bisexuals and transgenders are, in fact, "homosexuals." Others use neologisms such as "biphobia" and "transphobia," meaning an irrational fear and dislike of bisexuals and transgenders. The need for such terms belies the idea that there is a single monolithic "GLBT community."

The difference between "homosexual" and "GLBT" is elusive to many U.S. Americans. The above paragraph and its plethora of specialized terms would have made little sense to most U.S. Americans (except a few specialized psychiatrists and psychologists) in 1950. I suggest that most U.S. Americans, even today, do not understand. When I ask how many students in my college sociology classes know what the acronym "GLBT" means, I find that less than 50% of the students admit to such knowledge. Many are unaware of any significant distinction between "GLBT" and "homosexual." Yet within the GLBT population itself, these distinctions mark intense personal and political struggles. The divisions between gay and lesbian and bisexual and transgender are far deeper and more significant to each other than to those outside. Where do these divisions come from?

Until the 1990s, there was little need to distinguish between different groups within the homosexual movement. The differences between gay/lesbian and bisexual/transgender were of no practical consequence until the attempt came in the late 1990s to marry them together in a "GLBT" marriage of convenience. The purpose of this marriage, of course, was political advantage through a community of interests. Bisexuals and transgenders, however, include all sorts of groups with radically unconventional lives: polyamorites, pansexuals, sadomasochists, Radical Faeries, drag queens, she-males, hetero-sexual crossdressers, working-class transvestite prostitutes, gender benders, genderqueers. Many of these bisexual and transgender people have little in common with the modern construction of middle-class gay and lesbian identi-ties. When leaders of the U.S. GLBT movement began to confront the incon-sistent interests of the bisexual and transgender people with whom they were now allied in the "GLBT movement," they were faced with a political prob-lem. Having included bisexuals and transgenders in the coalition, how could they at the same time argue that GLBT people are "just like you," wanting the same middle-class lives as other U.S. voters (with the single exception of a same-sex partner) while being required to politically embrace polyamory and a man in a dress?

The placement of bisexuals and transgenders last in the GLBT acronym (or LGBT, as many prefer) is not accidental. It is frequently thought that gays and lesbians are natural allies with bisexuals because all share victimization from a narrow view of sexuality. Some gays and lesbians, however, have a narrow view of sexuality themselves, along with the rest of society. Questioning whether a photographer can capture on film a "bisexual wedding" or "bisexual family" as easily as a "lesbian wedding" or a "gay family," one writer noted that bisexuality challenges our monosexual culture's assumption that sexual-ity can be identified by appearance or by the gender of one's partners (Trnka and Tucker 1995). When I attended a bisexual women's support group at the New York City Lesbian and Gay Community Center in 1999, I learned for the first time of the mythology of bisexuals amongst the gay and lesbian commu-nity. I was shocked to discover that bisexuals are looked down upon by gays and lesbians, that it is thought that they enjoy same-sex encounters as a tempo-rary diversion, that they will return to their "real" heterosexual orientation sooner or later, deserting same-sex partners, and that they are getting the best of both worlds by denying their gayness to avoid societal prejudice.

One could argue that only a small portion of the gay and lesbian communi-ties have heterosexist ideas about transgenders and bisexuals, that these are not sufficiently serious issues about which to speak, and that we should con-centrate on our alliances. While there is no data of which I am aware regarding the size of the problem, there are serious personal and political consequences for bisexuals and transgenders, as we shall see. We will not repair our divi-sions by ignoring them and attributing them to psychological aberration. In this article, I examine the concepts of "biphobia" and "transphobia," attempt-ing to begin an "archaeology" of the concepts. I specifically refer to archaeol-ogy in the Foucauldian sense. C. G. Prado describes such "archaeology" as an investigation of professional disciplines and expert idioms. It discounts re-ceived wisdom and reconstructs the obvious and natural as suspect. It then searches out the discontinuities that mark shifts between conceptual frameworks. It is not a search for "Truth" but for what counts as truth in particular fields of knowledge (Prado 1995:29). Such a study allows us to look at two specific concepts, "biphobia" and "transphobia," to see how they came to be used to describe intra-group prejudice within the GLBT population in the early 21st century United States, and to demonstrate the social forces and historical meanings that allowed and required such usage. "Biphobia" and "transphobia" not only offer an inadequate understanding of contemporary events, but also contribute to the internecine conflicts of those who might otherwise be standing shoulder to shoulder in a heterosexist world that grants them but little quarter.

Discrimination as Disease

"Biphobia" and "transphobia" sound like psychological problems. "Phobia" is a Greek word meaning "fear" or "flight." Merriam-Webster's Online Dictionary defines "phobia" as "an exaggerated, usually inexplicable and illogical fear of a particular object, class of objects, or situation." As a combining noun-form, it is also defined as "intolerance or aversion for," giving the example of "photophobia," an intolerance to light (Merriam-Webster 2003). Merriam-Webster's Online Dictionary does not include "biphobia" or "transphobia." It does, however, define "homophobia" as "irrational fear of, aversion to, *or discrimination against* homosexuality or homosexuals" (italics supplied). In fact, the term may first have been used in print in a psychological context. The word was used in 1971 in an article entitled "Homophobia: A Tentative Personality Profile," in Psychological Reports (Fone 2000:5). A year later, George Weinberg's book *Society and the Healthy Homosexual* defined it as "the dread of being in close quarters with homosexuals." The term has been integrated into the social sciences, used by activists, policy makers and the judiciary (Sears and Williams 1997:15). Yet its current usage has expanded it far beyond the coiner's initial intent, so that it is applied to any act that discriminates against homosexuals, in stark contrast to other phobias in the dictionary, such as "agoraphobia" and "claustrophobia," which are defined as "abnormal dread of" being in open or public places, or closed or narrow spaces.

Some have divided homophobia into several parts, such as personal, interpersonal, institutional and cultural (Ochs 1996:221). Homophobia's origins, motivations, functions and measurement have been studied (Sears and Williams 1987). Yet conflating fear, prejudice and discrimination and medicalizing it into a "phobia" seems to give it a legitimacy that "racism" and "sexism" could never have. How did a disease descriptor come to characterize discriminatory conduct? Clearly, "biphobia" and "transphobia" are different from what we commonly refer to as "phobias." Speaking of them as "phobias" is as inappropriate as calling racism "racephobia." Such a usage changes prejudice, the attribution of negative characteristics to a group, and discrimination, the exclusion of such a group from the benefits of society, into a psychiatric illness, a sickness over which the sufferer has little control. It contributes to such injustices as the "gay panic defense," in which a defendant accused of murder defends on the grounds that the victim's homosexual advances frightened the defendant, thereby excusing the killing.

"Biphobia" and "transphobia" are unrelated to psychiatric and psychological definitions of "phobias." Phobias are a significant medical and social phenomenon. According to a study by the National Institute of Mental Health (NIMH), between 5.1 and 12.5 percent of Americans suffer from phobias (American Psychiatric Association 1992). This means that between 13 million and 32 million people in the U.S. had phobias in 1992, of a U.S. population of approximately 250 million in 1992. Psychiatrists and psychologists have developed a number of treatments for victims of phobias. The following paragraph describes the position of the American Psychiatric Association Joint Commission on Public Affairs and the Division of Public Affairs on treatments for phobias. (I note that the pamphlet from which it is drawn, "Let's Talk Facts About Phobias," states that it is not necessarily the position of the American Psychiatric Association.) The following surreal thought exercise demonstrates the distinction between medical definition of "phobias" and "biphobia" or "transphobia." Imagine this as a treatment for biphobia or transphobia:

> Psychiatrists find the most effective and longlasting treatment for specific phobias is a behavior therapy called exposure, which relies on exposing the person to the feared object or situation. The two most common methods of exposure are systematic desensitization and "flooding." In both, the patient meets with a trained therapist and confronts the feared object or situation. By confronting rather than fleeing the object of fear, a person becomes accustomed to it and can lose the terror, horror, panic and dread he or she once felt. Systematic desensitization is a more gradual form of exposure therapy. In a series of steps, the patient first learns relaxation to control the physical reactions of fear. Then he or she imagines the feared object, works up to looking at pictures that depict the object or situation, and finally actually experiences the situation or being in the presence of the feared object. During "flooding," on the other hand, the person is exposed directly and immediately to the most feared object or situation. He or she stays in that situation until his or her anxiety is markedly reduced from its previous level. In general, this requires about two hours per session. (American Psychiatric Association 1992)

Is the answer to biphobia and transphobia no more than a simple matter of people going off to therapy to spend a couple of hours with a bisexual and a transsexual to overcome their irrational fears? I suspect not. Biphobia and transphobia are not good descriptions of the phenomenon of heterosexist prejudice against bisexuals and transgenders, and are particularly inappropriate in the case of heterosexist prejudices within the GLBT community. I suggest that gays and lesbians who discriminate against bisexuals and transgenders are reacting to political and social pressures, not psychological ones.

Political Consequences

At this point in the argument, the conflict appears to be nothing more than a disagreement about names and categories: how are bisexuals and transgenders related to gays and lesbians? Yet this dispute has serious real-world consequences. In several years up to and including 2003, a bill entitled the Employment Nondiscrimination Act ("ENDA") had been proposed a number of times in the U.S. Congress, the goal of which is to prohibit job discrimination. Its principal organizational backer, the Human Rights Campaign ("HRC"), a D.C. lobbying group, now estimates that there are enough favorable votes in Congress to make passage possible in the near future. It is more likely a matter of when, rather than whether, such a bill will pass. Gay activists are ecstatic about getting to this stage of political development.

Not all GLBT people are so ecstatic. Some are concerned because the legislative protection is phrased in terms of "sexual orientation," rather than "sexual preference," and deliberately does not include "gender identity." "Sexual orientation" applies to one's choice of sexual partner, and does not apply to one's gender presentation. Thus, it is not clear whether the "sexual orientation" language would protect a transgender person who has been fired for wearing the clothing of the opposite sex. Furthermore, the term "sexual orientation" implies that one is oriented in a particular sexual direction by a force or forces outside the will of the individual. It stands in direct opposition to the term "sexual preference," which implies that sexuality is a matter of choice. The displacement of "sexual preference" by "sexual orientation" is not a matter of linguistics, but of politics. When bisexuals, lesbians, gays and heterosexuals are placed under the rubric of "sexual preference," sexual *choices* are represented. When placed under the rubric of "sexual orientation," then bisexuality stands out as a failure of orientation or a dual orientation, a product of confusion, promiscuity or indecision.

At the same time, it is assumed that there is no need to demarcate the social space held by bisexuals in political figurings. "Gay political groups often protest that there are no 'bisexual issues,' that bisexual rights are subsumed under gay rights, and that bisexuals will be liberated and accepted fully once gay rights are won" (Hutchins 1996:241). In fact, although bisexuals share many issues of discrimination concerning their same-gender relationships with lesbians and gay men, they are also discriminated against because they are bisexual–specifically because they upset the dichotomies in a polarized world. In addition, it needs to be understood that polyamory (multipartner relations), pansexuality (openness to all forms of sexuality) and other forms of responsible nonmonogamy are being pioneered by bisexuals. While bisexuality cannot be equated with polyamory and pansexuality, if bisexuality were to be valued as distinct from gay and lesbian issues, this dimension would then need to be added to the current social debate about domestic partnership and same-gender marriages (Hutchins 1996:241).

Bisexuals are also subject to community exclusion and invisibility. The addition of the term "bisexual" to "gay and lesbian" in the titles of political groups, community centers, pride marches and other arenas is often a subject of bitter debate. For example, Northampton, Massachusetts, has long had a parade for the gay and lesbian community, but the suggestion that bisexuals be included in the parade caused several years of strife during which the Northampton gay and lesbian community, like many others around the country, fought over whether to include "bisexual" in its Pride March title. In fact, it was added in one year, and was so controversial that it was deleted the next year (Hutchins 1992).

The political conflict between gays/lesbians and bisexuals/transgenders can also be found in the attempts to claim historical territory. Prior to 1890, the terms "homosexual," "gay," "lesbian," "transgender," "transsexual," and "transvestite" did not exist. Can past historical figures correctly be described as "gay" or "bisexual" or "transgender"? Who gets to say whether a cross-dressing man who had sex with both men and women was "gay" or "bisexual" or "transgender" or whatever? Marjorie Garber notes that Sappho, Socrates, Alexander the Great, Julius Caesar, King James I of England, and Marie Antoinette had liaisons with both women and men (Garber 1995:14). Joan of Arc, Queen Christina of Sweden and King James cross-dressed. Even today, there are questions as to what marks a bisexual or transsexual person versus a gay or lesbian person. Why does this matter and what is its social meaning? These are not issues of phobia–these are issues of politics and political consequences.

Thus, we begin to see the nature of the problem: there are social and political forces that have created a split between gay/lesbian communities and bisexual/transgender communities, and these forces have consequences for civil rights and community inclusion. "Biphobia" and "transphobia" are a result of these social and political forces, not psychological forces causing irrational fears in aberrant individuals.

ROOTS OF THE CONFLICT

How did "biphobia" and "transphobia" begin in the gay and lesbian community? Undoubtedly there are psychological elements, but a purely psychological, ahistorical explanation ignores the longstanding context of the issue that allows for the phenomenon. The GL vs. BT split is especially surprising because distinctions between gays, lesbians, bisexuals and transgenders developed rather recently in history. Until the 1950s, those now called "transgender" were classified as homosexuals by everyone, including the physicians who specialized in their treatment, and it is only in the past fifty years or so that transgender has been theorized as different in kind from homosexuality. "Bisexuality" as a concept (though not as a practice) began in the 1960s and emerged as a recognizably separate identity in the 1970s, but it is still subsumed within the larger context of "sexual orientation," today's phraseology for "homosexuality." Many in U.S. society today still consider bisexuals and transgenders to be homosexuals, no different from gays and lesbians. Yet sometime in the past century, bisexuals and transgenders started to become separate from homosexuals, being gay or lesbian became more acceptable than being bisexual or transgender, and a split developed between gay/lesbian and bisexual/transgender. When one looks at the specific ways in which homosexuality was constructed in the West, these results are clearly foreshadowed.

The Construction of Homosexuality

While a basic sexual drive seems to exist instinctually in most human beings as a matter of nature, the forms of sexuality seem to be socially constructed. Foucault is famous for championing the idea that, as of the 19th century, "the sodomite had been a temporary aberration; the homosexual was now a species" (Foucault 1980:43). This insight is useful (albeit strongly contested, e.g., Karras 1999a, b), but insufficient to explain why we now have four separate species (gay, lesbian, bisexual and transgender) in the homosexual community, and why there is a fault line between gays/lesbians and bisexuals/transgenders. For this, we must look into the specific historical context of the construction of homosexuality in the West.

Early texts, including Greek and Roman sources, speak of same-sex desire, but do not categorize persons solely by the sex of their partners. There was no single identity, which linked all men who engaged in same-sex acts. Indeed, adult patrician males were expected to have sex with both boys and women, who were passive and expected to be so. Homosexual behavior was not limited to some subculture that had distinct tastes for men only (Cantarella 1992:216). Significantly, mirroring the distaste for effeminacy of much of modern gay male and patriarchal culture, and the separation of what we now call "transgender" culture, Greek texts satirized effeminate males, and both literary and legal texts suggested it was unmanly behavior to accept a passive role in sexual intercourse after passing a certain age (Fone 1998:11-15). Also in keeping with patriarchal culture, women were believed not to have sexual feelings, and with the exception of the poetry of Sappho, little was written or understood about female same-sex acts. It was assumed not to exist; its various forms were secret and did not inform the public perceptions of same-sex relations (Cantarella 1992:78, Traub 1994:62, Spencer 1995:8, Fone 2000).

By the fourth century, the male same-sex acts that had been so public were forced to go underground, creating a tension between secret identity and public identity, between "passing" or "assimilating" (as a non-sodomite or non-homosexual) versus being open about one's sexuality, either to potential partners or to the public, by declaration or behavioral style. Those who wished to engage in such practices risked strong social condemnation and severe judicial punishment. In keeping with earlier ideas, it was believed that any man could be led astray, rather than a distinct subgroup of men who had inclinations towards men only. However, there is evidence that, beginning in the twelfth century, this belief began to change, and the contrasting belief that there was a certain type of man who engaged exclusively in same-sex behaviors slowly began to arise. Those who engaged in same-sex behaviors were beginning to be designated as "sodomites" (Fone 1998:92). Nonetheless, it was "passive" homosexuals who received the brunt of the condemnation, leaving in place an ethic in favor of the masculine (Cantarella 1992:221). Passing as the opposite sex occurred fairly frequently, however, and while it was also forbidden, it was rarely punished, as it was not considered, in and of itself, a sexual crime (Dekker and van de Pol 1989). It does not appear that there was any necessary linkage in the public mind between cross-dressing and sodomy until the eighteenth century.

By the eighteenth century, the public understanding was that same-sex acts were connected with effeminacy and cross-dressing, that those who engaged in same-sex acts did so exclusively, that same-sex acts were confined to a specific group of people, and that the propensity towards such acts was inborn (Fone 2000:232, Norton 1992:9). Despite this linkage between male same-sex behavior and effeminacy in the public mind, most men who engaged in same-sex behavior rejected effeminate practices and role-playing (Fone

1998:198). The public conception of homosexuality coincided with a growing concern with effeminacy that appeared in England in the eighteenth century (Greenberg 1988:388). Boys typically wore girl's clothing until they were sent away to boarding school. Men's clothing was frilly in the Elizabethan Age. However, clothing became more sharply differentiated from the 1770s on (Greenberg 1988:390). There were diatribes against fops and dandies. By the nineteenth century, men no longer dared embrace in public or shed tears. Concerns about effeminacy periodically boiled over during the ensuring years with regularity (Greenberg 1988:490).

The nineteenth century scientific crusaders, Ulrichs and Hirschfeld, furthered the linkage between homosexuality and gender by theorizing homosexual men as "hermaphrodites of the mind," with male bodies and female souls, though not without opposition (Fone 1998:440). In 1910, Magnus Hirschfeld coined the term "transvestite" to refer to one who prefers to wear the clothing of the opposite sex, to distinguish it and separate it from the phenomenon of homosexuality. Hirschfeld first mentioned "psychic transsexualism" in passing in 1923, but it was not accepted until popularized by Dr. Harry Benjamin in the 1960s (Pfäfflin and Junge 1998).

Thus, from the nineteenth century unitary conception of homosexuality there developed two concepts: "sexual orientation" (sexual object choice) and "gender identity" (sexual self-identification as male or female). This scientific rationalism and medicalization of homosexuality confirmed it as a unitary, monolithic phenomenon. This created a monosexist (exclusively same-sex) "homosexual identity," and a corresponding tension between identification as homosexual, on the one hand, and passing as heterosexual and/or engaging in heterosexual relationships.

The sex/gender dichotomy was deepened when, in the mid-twentieth century, homosexuality was separated into distinct male and female forms, each of which had different stylized behavioral styles, and distinguished from cross-dressing and effeminacy. This formed a gender divide, and corresponding tensions with bi-gender intermingling and gender ambiguity. After World War II, there were furtive movements towards political action, but these were largely separated along gender lines. The Mattachine Society, an organization for gay men, was established in 1950. The first openly lesbian organization in the U.S., the Daughters of Bilitis, was established in 1955. These accommodationist groups encouraged gay people to "act normal" and fit in (lesbians belong in dresses, gay men don't), and recruited prominent "experts" like psychiatrists and psychologists to comment on homosexuality (Wikholm 2000).

In the context of the counterculture of the 1960s United States, the "sexual revolution" permitted these separate populations to exist openly and to enter into the arena of state politics. The struggle to obtain social acceptance and civil rights pitted these groups against one another. Gays and lesbians campaigned for acceptance by suggesting that they were "just like you," but with the single (but extremely significant) exception of partners of the same sex. This fueled the tensions between accomodationist tendencies in the gay/lesbian community and gender ambiguity. It was perceived that gender ambiguity (echoing the Greek disdain for passivity) channeled the stigma of illegitimacy. It was not surprising, therefore, that some homosexuals sought to lessen the stigma of homosexuality by rejecting the stigma of "inappropriate" gendered behavior.

These historical circumstances led to four areas of tension: monosexism versus bisexism, gender accommodationism versus gender ambiguity, open homosexual identity versus passing as heterosexual, and a gender divide versus bi-gender intermingling. Transsexuals and bisexuals violated the tacit social understandings of the homosexual community in the U.S. both by failing to pass and passing too much. Bisexuals were disparaged because some were "passing" as straight through embrasure of heterosexual practices and heterosexual privilege, thus violating the monosexist idea of a "homosexual identity" and the idea that being gay or lesbian was an organic and/or psychological orientation towards only the same sex. They were also looked down upon because they violated cultural norms of sexual behavior through such practices as polyamory and pansexuality, thus violating the monosexist idea that they are "just like you." Transsexuals, and later transgenders, were disparaged because some were "passing" as straight through embrasure of stereotypes of gendered behavior, i.e., effeminacy for MTFs and hyper-masculinity for FTMs, and embrasure of heterosexual practices and privilege by identifying their same-sex practices as heterosexuality, thus rejecting homosexual identity. They were also looked down upon because they violated cultural norms of sexual behavior through gender ambiguity, visible androgyny and genderqueerness, thus violating the accommodationist idea that they are "just like you." The resulting split has been attributed to "biphobia" and "transphobia," rather than social and political forces.

The History of Transphobia

When the story of Christine Jorgensen was published in 1951, debates began as to the proper response. In the first case study of Jorgensen, published in 1951 by her endocrinologist, he referred to her "homosexual tendencies" (Meyerowitz 2002:171). Jorgensen herself, however, specifically distinguished her condition from homosexuality, referring to the prevalent theory of transsexuality as "nature's mistake," in which a woman is trapped in a man's body (Jorgensen 1967, 2000:114). She takes pains to distinguish her situation from "a much more horrible illness of the mind. One that, although very common, is not as yet accepted as a true illness, with the necessity for great understanding." This "horrible illness of the mind" is a reference to homosexuality. In this way, she attempts to avoid the severe mid-century stigma of homosexuality, as did many transsexuals of the time (Meyerowitz 2002:183-184). Jorgensen's endocrinologist later changed his mind, deciding that Jorgensen's condition differed fundamentally from homosexuality, and many other prominent scientists and doctors agreed, provoking intense controversy (Meyerowitz 2002:171). The importance of this controversy can only be understood in reference to the extreme intensity and pervasive ubiquity of the stigma of homosexuality up to the 1950s. Such extremis provokes compassion for Jorgensen's attempts to distinguish herself from homosexuality, and empathy for those who saw her as an opportunist who condemned homosexuals in order to earn the acceptance of straight society.

There was a vigorous debate in the U.S. homophile movement of the 1950s as to whether homosexuals should embrace Jorgensen. Some gay men and lesbians denounced those who felt themselves to be of the opposite sex, criticizing them for acting like "freaks," bringing disrepute to those gays and lesbians trying to live quietly within heterosexual society (Meyerowitz 2002:179). Such attitudes were prevalent within the gay and lesbian community at the time (Meyerowitz: 2002:185). Meyerowitz relates one such debate from 1953:

> In 1953, for example, *ONE* magazine published a debate among its readers as to whether gay men should denounce Jorgensen. In the opening salvo, the author Jeff Winters accused Jorgensen of a "sweeping disservice" to gay men. "As far as the public knows," Winters wrote, "you were merely another unhappy homosexual who decided to get drastic about it." For Winters, Jorgensen's story simply confirmed the false belief that all men attracted to other men must be basically feminine, which, he said, "*they are not.*" Jorgensen's precedent, he thought, encouraged the "reasoning" that led "to legal limitations upon the homosexual, mandatory injections, psychiatric treatment–and worse." In the not-so-distant past, scientists had experimented with castrating gay men. (Meyerowitz 2002:177)

Meyerowitz portrays the tension between homosexuals and transsexuals as based upon the tension between passing and openness, what she terms "gender transgression," suggesting that it may have derived from class differences and differing class tolerances for "swish" and "butch" (Meyerowitz 2002:178). She notes that some gays and lesbians associated gender transgression with undignified and low-class behavior, while "fairies" and "butches" were more readily accepted in working class communities. She also relates a survey from the 1960s that found that more than two-thirds of a sample of almost 300 gays and lesbians in the homophile movement considered those who asked for sex-change surgery to be "severely neurotic" (Meyerowitz 2002:183).

Kay Brown of Transhistory.org ("Transsexual, Transgender and Intersex History") has set forth a long chronology of the ejection of those whom we now know as "transgendered" from gay organizations starting in the 1970s, and the following material is drawn from her Website (Brown 2001). She notes that transgendered people played pivotal roles in gay organizations of the late 1960s and early 1970s, including the Gay Liberation Front and the Gay Activists Alliance ("GAA"). While the original goals included complete acceptance of sexual diversity and expression, by the early 70s the gay men's community returned to the assimilationist strategy as the lesbians turned to separatism and radical feminism. There seemed to be no room for transgendered people in either camp (Brown 2001). For example, in 1971 the GAA wrote and introduced a bill to the New York City Council to protect homosexuals from discrimination. The bill did not include any explicit protection for transsexuals.

In early 1970s, Beth Elliott, a founder and active member of a number of gay and lesbian organizations, was Vice-President of the San Francisco chapter of the Daughters of Bilitis. Brown describes the events as follows:

> Late in her term of office her transgender status became a point of contention at the West Coast Lesbian Conference, where she was outed and vilified for being a MTF transsexual. The complaint was that Beth Elliott had insinuated herself into a position of power over women as a patriarchal man, a propagandist ploy that was to become common when attacking other transgendered people. At the conference she was forced to stop her music concert due to the catcalls from the audience by women that knew nothing more about her than that she was transsexual. She was required to sit through a popular vote of the attendees to determine whether they would let her finish her set. In the weeks and months to follow she was further vilified and even betrayed by women who had once called her friend.

In 1973, during a gay rally, a well-known transgender activist was followed on the stage by a lesbian separatist who denounced transgenders as men who, by "impersonating women," were exploiting women for profit. Later in the 70s, lesbian separatists made an issue of the presence of lesbian-identified transsexual women in their movement. Central to the conflict was a transsexual recording engineer working at Olivia Records. Lesbian separatists threatened a boycott of Olivia products and concerts. On the edge of profitability, the company eventually fired the engineer. Attempts to exclude transsexuals also characterized the 1977 San Francisco Gay Pride Parade.

Two years later, Janice Raymond, a lesbian academic, wrote *The Transsexual Empire*, a book based on her doctoral dissertation (Raymond 1979). Raymond argued that the phenomenon of transsexuality was created by fetishistic males who sought to escape into a faux stereotypical femininity, with the connivance of male doctors who thought that femaleness could be medically created and homosexuality medically vitiated. Although "male to constructed female" transsexuals claimed to be against the stereotyped gender system by virtue of their escape from stereotypical masculinity, they in fact added force to the binary system by merely escaping from one stereotype to another, or at most mixing together different stereotypes, rather than advocating true gender freedom. They were not political radicals, as they claimed, but reactionaries seeking to preserve a stereotypical gender system that was already dramatically changing due to the political action of 60s and 70s feminists and gays. Transsexuals were, according to Raymond, sheep in wolf's clothing.

Henry Rubin argues that the creation of a separate transsexual identity and community emerges in the 1970s in the U.S., when it was made clear that butch lesbians were no longer welcome within the lesbian feminist movement (Hemmings 2002:92).

The blatant lack of regard for transgendered identities can also be found in gay rewriting of history. For example, Dr. Alan L. Hart was born October 4, 1890, as a female named Alberta Lucille Hart. After graduating from the University of Oregon Medical College in 1917, Hart consistently presented a male persona to the world for four and a half decades. In the 1920s, Hart consulted a psychiatrist, underwent a hysterectomy and changed name to Alan L. Hart. The majority of Hart's biographers insist upon viewing the doctor as a woman in disguise, without regard for Hart's self-identification as a man, medical treatment and legal documentation (O'Hartigan 2002).

In his 1976 book, *Gay American History*, for example, Professor Jonathan Ned Katz categorized Hart as "clearly a lesbian, a woman-loving woman [who] illustrates only too well one extreme to which an intelligent, aspiring Lesbian in early twentieth-century America might be driven by her own and her doctor's acceptance of society's condemnation of women-loving women." O'Hartigan also refers to Pat Califia's statement that "Katz's book is unfortunately tainted with a heavy dose of transphobia." She also brings up Katz's footnote in his *Gay/Lesbian Almanac* about an unpublished paper, *"Transsexualism": Today's Quack Medicine: An Issue for Every Body*, noting his statement "An historical study needs to be made of the medical and autobiographical literature on 'transsexualism'; it will, I think, reveal the fundamentally sexist nature of the concept and of the associated medical treatments." O'Hartigan also sets forth, disapprovingly, an explanation for referring to Hart as female by Susan Stryker: "As an historian favoring 'social construction' approaches to questions of identity, I have reservations about using the word 'transsexual' to refer to people before the mid-20th century who identify in a profound, ongoing manner with a gender that they were not assigned to at birth."

It is against this backdrop that, in the early 1990s, the term "transgender," a neologism with an unclear meaning, began to be included in the GLB coalition. The term was used as an umbrella term referring to transvestites, cross-dressers, transsexuals, and other gender-variant people, who seemed to have similar and interlocking interests with gay men and lesbian women, and that had caught the imagination of the public through sympathetic portrayals of transsexuals such as Christine Jorgensen, Renee Richards and Wendy Williams. Originally, the term "transgender" was intended by its coiner to refer only to certain non-operative transsexuals, but later mutated to refer to anyone whose gender performance varied from the norm. This more open meaning, however, conflicted with the goals of the coalition builders, which was to capture public sympathy by appealing to an image of homosexuals as people "just like" the majority of U.S. voters, middle-class people (or people with middle-class yearnings), who held steady jobs, had long, loving relationships with partners of the same sex, and who wanted the same lives that the majority of U.S. voters wanted. As a result, some gays find themselves agreeing with straights who see in transgenders an assault on normative reality, as in the following diatribe thinly veiled as humor:

> There's something a little annoying about transgendered people insisting that they be called whatever sex they want to be called . . . Like so many transgendered people, Califia is like a bush resenting the grass for not calling it a tree. Well, if you've got bush and no trunk, are you really a tree? Before all the MTF (male-to-female) transgendered people flick their compact mirrors shut and take up their pitchforks (with matching handbags, of course), I'd like to point out that there's a reality that exists outside of ourselves. If you wear brown and insist that I call it red because you say so, then you're asking me to skew an objective reality to your liking. Enrolling people into in an illusion unsupported by facts seems manipulative to me . . . So for all the Pattys, Pats and Patricks out there, you go boys/girls/TBA. Just don't back over us with your whoop-ass mobile because we didn't get your pronoun right. (Alvear 2003)

At the same time, some transgenders pass as heterosexuals and reject homosexual identity by calling their sexual relations heterosexual. The reaction of the gay and lesbian community, predictably, has been an attempt to limit the inclusion of transgenders. This reaction, which is often called "transphobia," is not a result of a psychological "phobia," but a result of the previously identified tensions between accomodationism and gender ambiguity, and between homosexual identity and "passing."

The History of Biphobia

In the 1960s, homosexuality began to be referred to by a number of terms, including "alternative lifestyles," "sexual preference" and "sexual orientation." Each of these had political connotations. "Alternative lifestyles," a term connected with the counterculture of the 60s, connoted sexual freedom, if not free-for-all. "Sexual preference" connoted the right to choose one's sexuality, rather than having it imposed by a heterosexist and monosexist society. "Sexual orientation" implied that one's sexuality was inborn or fixed early in life, and is not subject to change. Furthermore, as noted in the introduction, the term "sexual orientation" implies that one is oriented in a particular sexual direction by a force or forces outside the will of the individual. It stands in direct opposition to the term "sexual preference," which implies that sexuality is a matter of choice. When bisexuals, lesbians, gays and heterosexuals are placed under the rubric of "sexual preference," sexual *choices* are represented. When placed under the rubric of "sexual orientation," then bisexuality stands out as a failure of orientation or a dual orientation, a product of confusion, promiscuity or indecision.

Until the 1970s, however, there was little need to define the precise boundaries of "homosexuality." While the groups had different origins, their common goals united them despite the differing interests that militated for separation:

> The gay movement, heady with the sense of liberation following Stonewall, could afford to be utopian, and pronounced the goal of "free[ing] the homosexual in everyone." Gay theorist Dennis Altman argued that the gay movement would bring "the end of the homosexual because 'gay liberation will succeed as its *raison d'etre* disappears.'" Such language and priorities created a climate in which bisexuality was not particularly problematized, though the only people calling themselves bisexual at that point were swingers and free love advocates. (Udis-Kessler 1995)

However, the balance changed, narrowing the homosexual movement to gays and lesbians. A separate category was needed, and "bisexuality," first discussed as a concept in the 1960s, was employed to demarcate the space (Highleyman 2003). Though pockets of bisexual organizing were visible as early as the 1970s, and the "National Bisexual Liberation Group" was founded in New York in 1972, local groups did not begin connecting regionally and nationally until the 1980s (Tucker 1995:3, 11). The bisexual movement of the 1970s to early 1980s organized around the principles of visibility and support (Tucker 1995:1).

During the 1970s, with the advent of feminism, some lesbians were dissatisfied with the growing reference to and acceptance of the "gay" lifestyle, which appeared to and in many instances, did refer to male homosexuality. Many lesbians left the gay movement fairly early on in frustration over gay male sexism and turned to the burgeoning feminist movement (Udis-Kessler 1995:19). This gender divide is reflected in the understanding of "gay" as males, and "lesbian" as females. Thus, the "gay and lesbian" (or "lesbian and gay," as many prefer) movement was born with a gender divide. Bisexuals, who comprised both men and women, desiring both men and women as sexual partners, represented a problem in this schema.

Udis-Kessler also notes that bisexual movements are often gender specific. Much of bisexual history is bisexual women's history, many bisexual activists are women who formerly identified as lesbian feminists, and bisexual women's groups often have mailing lists ten times the size of bisexual men's groups. Tensions between lesbian and bisexual women are understood as much more problematic than tensions between gay and bisexual men, caused by the politics of lesbian separatism (Udis-Kessler 1995).

Bisexuality was seen as a sexual libertinism, politically and emotionally uninvested, rather than a political choice (Hemmings 2002:74). Bisexuals were seen as privileged as nonhomosexuals and stereotyped as amoral hedonistic disease carriers and disrupters of families, indecisive and promiscuous (Ochs 1996:217). In 1987, bisexuality emerged in the mainstream press as a symbol of unbridled promiscuity, threatening heterosexuals with the "gay plague" of AIDS. The bisexual was portrayed as "a homosexual posing as a heterosexual," as "amoral as regards sexual candor," less apt to feel the guilt that a gay man might "going both ways." *Newsweek* featured "bisexuals" on its cover, suggesting that bisexuals were becoming the "ultimate pariahs of the AIDS crisis" (Weinberg 1995:205).

In the gay and lesbian community, it was widely assumed that bisexuals were confused about their sexual identity, and that bisexuality was a pathological state. From this point of view, "confusion" is literally a built-in feature of "being bisexual." As expressed in one study:

> While appearing to encompass a wider choice of love object . . . [the bi-
> sexual] actually becomes a product of abject confusion; his self-image is
> that of an overgrown young adolescent whose ability to differentiate one
> form of sexuality from another has never developed. He lacks above all a
> sense of identity . . . [He] cannot answer the question: What am I?

There was persistent pressure on bisexuals from the gay and lesbian community to relabel themselves as gay or lesbian and to engage in sexual activity exclusively with the same sex. It was asserted that no one was *really* bisexual
(Weinberg, Williams and Pryor 1995).

In addition to this invalidation of bisexual identity, bisexuals face invisibility (Tucker 1995). It is very difficult to find historical sources documenting bisexual history in any detail. Bisexuality doesn't really exist, bisexuals are
really gay, and yet they are confused, can't make commitments or have mature
relationships (Sumpter 1991). As a middle ground, bisexuality is frequently
demonized for supporting and generating fixed oppositional structures of sexuality and gender, and is dismissed in both epistemological and ontological
terms (Hemmings 2002:1). Within the gay and lesbian community, there are
many monosexist assumptions:

- Assuming that everyone you meet is either heterosexual or homosexual.
- Automatically assuming romantic couplings of two women are lesbian,
  or two men are gay, or a man and a woman are heterosexual.
- Assuming bisexuals would be willing to "pass" as anything other than
  bisexual.
- Expecting a bisexual to identify as heterosexual when coupled with the
  "opposite" gender/sex.
- Expecting a bisexual to identify as gay or lesbian when coupled with the
  "same" sex/gender.
- Thinking bisexual people haven't made up their minds.
- Believing bisexuals are confused about their sexuality.
- Using the terms "phase" or "stage" or "confused" or "fence-sitter" or "bi-
  sexual" or "AC/DC" or "switchhitter" as slurs or in an accusatory way.
- Feeling bisexuals just want to have their cake and eat it too.
- Thinking bisexuals only have committed relationships with "opposite"
  sex/gender partners.
- Assuming that bisexuals, if given the choice, would prefer to be within
  an "opposite" gender/sex coupling to reap the social benefits of a "heterosexual" pairing.
- Expecting bisexual people to get services, information and education
  from heterosexual service agencies for their "heterosexual side" (sic)
  and then go to gay and/or lesbian service agencies for their "homosexual
  side" (sic).

- Thinking that bisexual people will have their rights when lesbian and gay people win theirs.

–Ka'ahumanu and Yaeger (2000)

A particularly striking example of biphobia occurred in the late 1980s and early 1990s in Northampton, Massachusetts, a town renowned for its large concentration of lesbian and gay people and its atmosphere of sexual freedom. The town had held a lesbian and gay pride march for many years when, in 1988, members of the Valley Bisexual Network approached the Northampton Lesbian and Gay Pride March Committee, requesting that the name be changed to the Lesbian, Gay and Bisexual Pride March. The five or six members of the committee unanimously agreed to change the name for 1989. The overall community response was overwhelmingly negative. A vote was again held for the 1990 march, which retained the name change. The vote was denounced in the local lesbian press. An announcement was circulated in the lesbian community, making it clear that one was expected to choose between the lesbian "we" who have "created a community we care deeply about and are in danger of seeing . . . made invisible" and the bisexual interlopers. At the next meeting, attended by forty or fifty people, a clear majority confirmed the decision to revert to the former name, omitting "bisexual" from the title (Hemmings 2002:66).

Hemmings underlines the fact that the debates about the inclusion of the term "bisexual" in the march emerged as a result of a conflict within the lesbian and gay community, not outside it. In the view of those who wished to include the term, its inclusion demonstrated that bisexuals were considered part of the core of lesbian and gay community, in need of allies, rather than being allies. In the alternate view on which its later exclusion was premised, the attitude towards bisexuals demonstrated a policy of "political affiliation," based on the assumption that they are not part of the community. Bisexuals are then seen as claiming lesbian space that is not theirs. In the words of one writer, "We lesbians have worked long and hard to create safe communities for ourselves. Bisexuals are welcome to, and should do, the same. But do not try to grab what we have created." Yet those arguing for the inclusion of *bisexual* in the title of the march do so on the basis of "group unity inclusion," rather than the desire to create a bisexual community separate from the lesbian and gay community. This has created an ambiguity in the use of the often-used term *community*. For example, one committee member stated, after the 1990 march "The lesbian and gay community gets on very well with the rest of the community." Does this refer to bisexuals, or heterosexuals? Does reference to "bisexuals" demarcate a space inside the lesbian and gay community, or outside it? (Hemmings 2002:71).

Another issue that must not be overlooked regarding biphobia is the fact that the term "bisexual" is not gendered. Bisexuals comprise both men and women. The lesbian "reclaiming" of the 1990 march was consistently viewed in terms of territorial rights, where lesbian territory is understood as a space free from men. A triumphant editorial in the local lesbian press was entitled "Take Back the March Night." A connection was clearly being drawn between violence against women protested in Take Back the Night marches and bisexuals. This link was made more explicit in a "note to the editors" of the Valley Women's Voice that read, "The following statement on lesbian occupied territory was in part sparked by the recent controversy in Northampton, MA surrounding the 1990 Gay/Lesbian Pride March." The authors linked the Pride March debates with the rape of a woman following the Take Back the Night march in the same year, arguing that both marches will remain symbolic until the community becomes "LESBIAN OCCUPIED TERRITORY," which is the only space that "can offer long-term protection from men, and create alternative women's culture free from the violence of heterosexuality." In the context of this lesbian separatist spirit, the inclusion of bisexuals was seen as intrusion (Hemmings 2002:77).

The experience of Northampton was not unique. Hemmings notes that the lesbian and gay community in San Francisco marginalized bisexuals by omitting bisexual involvement in events, publishing letters of complaint from bisexuals under disparaging headings such as "Bis *Feel* Left Out." In 1984, the San Francisco Bisexual Center closed. According to Hemmings, this was centrally because of its continued emphasis on nonmonogamy, group sex and SM (sadomasochism, now often called the "leather" lifestyle) as political expressions. The crowd booed the bisexual contingent in the 1985 San Francisco Lesbian and Gay Freedom Parade (Hemmings 2002:157-159).

Concerns about bisexuals and bisexuality remain alive and well in the gay and lesbian community. In speaking about a recent survey about the disclosure of homosexuality by patients to physicians, a gay columnist noted that bisexuals disclosed less often than the gays and lesbians:

> That leads to the conclusion that for some purposes, it can be important to disaggregate gays, lesbians and bisexuals (to say nothing of transsexuals) and not talk of them as if they were a unitary "community" or have more in common than they actually do . . . In other words, bisexuals face discrimination only because they sometimes behave like homosexuals.

But despite the identity of interests, there are important differences at the psychological and personal identity level. It seems clear from survey research that bisexuals understand their sexuality far differently from lesbians and gay men, and handle disclosure and relationship issues far differently, as the medical survey mentioned earlier suggests . . . The question gays may then ask is how seriously these self-described bisexuals take their same-sex tricks, dates and relationships, or more fundamentally, how seriously they take the homosexual component of their sexuality.

Such findings suggest troubling obstacles for gay activists on a range of issues, from efforts to reach bisexual men with HIV information to attempts to solicit bisexual support for same-sex marriage. They also remind us that in many ways the recently coined "GLBT community" is more a semantic artifact or political term-of-art than anything like an actual community. (Varnell 2003b)

Such views reveal great discomfort in the gay and lesbian community with bisexuality and bisexual inclusion. Nonmonogamy, polyamory, pansexuality, and SM conflict with the middle-class gay/lesbian claim of being "just like you." At the same time, bisexuals comprise two sexes, unlike the gay community or the lesbian community, threatening to homogenize and dilute homosexual identity. Many bisexuals also have social privileges because they can pass as straight. The reaction of the gay and lesbian community, again predictably, was an attempt to limit the inclusion of bisexuals. This "biphobic" reaction is not a result of a psychological "phobia," but a result of the historical tension between homosexual identity and passing, between monosexism and bisexism.

CONCLUSION:
TOO QUEER AND NOT QUEER ENOUGH

Are biphobia and transphobia examples of phobias–irrational fears? No, because such heterosexist attitudes are all too rational, and they mirror the social tensions inherent in the historical formation of the U.S. homosexual identity. The gay and lesbian communities have worked long and hard to have same-sex desire be seen as an orientation, rather than a preference, a viable, open and healthy identity alternative to heterosexuality, rather than a stigma to be hidden. The path to this end has largely been gender appropriateness and accommodationism, with the significant but single exception of same-sex preference. Political progress has been won by the argument that gays and lesbians are "just like you," albeit with the minor exception of sexual orientation. Bisexuality, with its escape hatch marked "heterosexual desire," is viewed as assuming that homosexuality is something to be avoided, constituting a step back into the closet. Thus, in this view, being bi is a way of being gay or lesbian in denial. Ochs describes this as the "aristocratization" of gay and lesbian identities, and cites as reasons for this phenomenon the psychological difficulties of coming out as gay or lesbian and the need to fight heterosexism (Ochs 1996). She attributes biphobia to prejudice and invisibility, similar to Garber (Garber 1995:89). Such a heterosexist view would analyze a bisexual man's identity by saying, "you are not bisexual, you are a gay man who has not yet reconciled with his gayness, who thinks he needs an out into the safety of the straight world." Thus, gay men and lesbians, who have been designated "queers" by a world unforgiving of social difference, find bisexuals insufficiently willing to step out of the closet, stop "passing" for straight, take the consequences of being "queer," and in so doing recoup the rewards of changing society to accept people of nonheterosexual orientations. Bisexuals must learn to accept their essential "queerness."

Marjorie Garber notes her discussion with a gay male theorist regarding her work on bisexuality, *Vice Versa*. This theorist expressed some concern about what a fully theorized bisexuality would do to the project of gay and lesbian studies. Gay and lesbian studies have sought to describe homosexuality not as the "other" of heterosexuality, but as a locus for cultural critique, social re-evaluation and change, but now perhaps bisexuality would repolarize hetero- and homosexuality. Gay and lesbian studies have also famously claimed the cultural production of figures such as Virginia Woolf, Oscar Wilde, and Anne Rice–what if we now had to recontextualize them as bisexual? (Garber 1995: 28). Yet they had both opposite-sex and same-sex relationships. Both Harry Hay, founder of the Mattachine Society, and Patricia Ireland, president of the National Organization for Women, had long relationships with opposite-sex partners as well as same-sex partners, but are rarely considered bisexuals (Garber 1995:74). Reconceptualizing gay history as bisexual history could erase homosexual identity.

Transgenders, too, have stepped into the safety of the closet. They also erase gay and lesbian identities by becoming, literally or figuratively, the opposite sex, creating or attempting to create heterosexual identities by their inconvenient insistence that "gender identity" has nothing to do with "sexual orientation." One lesbian writer described transsexuality this way: "Gays and Lesbians have struggled for decades to be able to name ourselves and to BE ourselves. But now in our own community we are expected to applaud Dykes rejecting womanhood and embrace men taking it over" (Dobkin 2000). To a transsexual man, it would say, "you are not a transsexual man, you are a lesbian woman who has mutilated herself in order to change a woman-loving woman into a more acceptable figure." Some within the bisexual and transgender community see in these attitudes an attempt to reconfigure bisexuals and transgenders into gays and lesbians gone wrong, to erase bisexual and transgender identities, and to absorb the differences into a greater gayness.

An example of this attitude can be found in the recent reaction of some gays to two recent court rulings in favor of transsexual marriage. Here is one gay columnist's reaction:

> Both cases will be cited as gains for GLBT rights. The *New York Times* quoted Lynne Gold-Bikin of the American Bar Association as saying of the Florida case, "This is a major victory for alternative lifestyles." But you have to wonder.
>
> It is not clear how the Florida ruling affirms any "alternative life-styles." The whole focus of the case was the effort by a transsexual male to prove that he should not be viewed as a woman in a same-sex relationship, but a nice, normal heterosexual guy in a heterosexual marriage—in short, that there was nothing "alternative" about his life or his lifestyle at all.
>
> And far from benefiting gays and lesbians in any way whatso-ever, the ruling conspicuously reaffirmed opposite-sex, heterosexual marriage as normative and exclusionary.
>
> Ironically, the Florida transsexual's case was argued by the Na-tional Center for Lesbian Rights (NCLR) which won by convincing the court that its client, although born a woman and married to a woman, was not female and therefore not a lesbian. How this supports lesbian rights is obscure.
>
> . . . So gay and lesbian people gain nothing from heterosexual transsexuals being able to marry. But transsexuals, all transsexuals, would gain from gay marriage. (Varnell 2003a)

There is another problem with bisexuals and transgenders in addition to be-ing insufficiently queer; they also are "too queer." The mainstream gay and les-bian political organizations, attempting to create political legitimacy, seek to convince the heterosexual majority that gays and lesbians are "just like you," *i.e.*, just like mainstream America. Bisexual Websites, however, teem with non-mainstream positions, such as polyamory and polysexuality. Transgenders in-clude many flamboyant drag queens, drag kings, male and female impersonators, androgynes, gender benders and genderqueers. These elements contradict the claim that gays and lesbians are "just like you," and must be culled, in the opinion of many, in order to have a successful campaign of ac-ceptance by the larger society.

As "homosexuality" became increasingly more accepted, freeing itself from shame with the 1968 Stonewall Riots, and the 1974 declaration of the American Psychiatric Association ("APA") that homosexuality was not a mental disorder, the more accepted homosexual elements began to agitate for more social tolerance and civil rights in law. In order to do so, like any political creation, it had to drop the lead weights represented by the less accepted and frankly unacceptable elements of the group, particularly effeminate transsexuals and promiscuous bisexuals. Transsexuality and transgenderism are still considered mental illnesses by the American Psychiatric Association. Homosexual rights groups, while committed in principle to inclusion of all homosexuals, including bisexuals and transgenders, began to be led by the more politically savvy gays and lesbians to espouse a platform that, consciously or unconsciously, served the interests of the normative homosexual elements, but not necessarily bisexuals or transgenders. Over time, the "GL" portion of the platform became increasingly acceptable to the population at large, both through increased education and desensitization of the public and by disavowing the more unacceptable elements of the movement. At the same time, this political success fueled a separatist culture, which bisexuals and transgenders threatened to dilute and homogenize.

The movie *Flawless*[1] (1999) contains a fictional scene in which drag queens and transsexuals confront gay Republicans regarding the gay pride parade. While fictional, the scene accurately portrays the tensions described here.

> Gay Republican #1: Thanks for meeting with us, gentlemen. We've been discussing this year's gay pride parade, and we felt that it would be important, well, a good idea, to show a united front . . .

> Gay Republican #2: Synthesis I believe.

> Gay Republican #1: Right, we felt as gay republicans, we thought it would be a really good idea if we could all come together and show the world our *likenesses*, not our differences. To celebrate the, um . . .

> Gay Republican #2: . . . synthesis . . .

> Gay Republican #1: . . . right, synthesis . . .

> Transsexual #1: You're very good. Sorry, go ahead.

> Gay Republican #1: We could march together as a united brotherhood . . .

Transsexual #2: What about the sisterhood, honey?

Gay Republican #2: . . . march on foot, no floats.

Transsexual #3: Yeah, you think if you have no floats we won't do drag because we can't march in heels. Well, let me tell you something, honey. We can march to Lake Titicaca and back in stilettos.

Gay Republican #1: Hey let's just calm down then.

Transsexual #1: Aren't you guys the same group that raised a shitload of money and gave it to Bob Dole's campaign and he sent it back, didn't he?

Gay Republican #2: No, no, that's because he would have lost support of the Christian right.

Transsexual #1: Exactly, because you're gay. You're gay, that's why he sent it back. Aren't you ashamed? All right, listen, you are right. We *are* different, but not in the way that you mean. We're different because you are all ashamed of us, and we are not ashamed of you. Alright, because as long as you get down on those banana republican knees and suck dick, honey, you're *all* my sisters and I love you, I do. God bless you and fuck off.

As Hemmings notes, bisexuality and transsexuality are both abstracted as the middle ground of sexual and gender culture. "Within contemporary queer and feminist terrain, both are understood to embody both the worst aspects of heterosexuality and the best of queerness." They are seen, on the one hand, as heterosexual apologists, and, on the other hand, as transcending stereotypical oppositions. They are traitors, insufficiently feminist or queer, yet also positioned at the cutting edge of debates about gender, sexuality and political meaning (Hemmings 2002:99).

From these historical circumstances, one can begin to see the outlines of the emerging split between "GL" and "BT." It involves a classic case of political conflict of interest, which nonetheless appears to us, looking ahistorically at individual experiences, to be a psychological phenomenon specific to certain aberrant individuals within the gay and lesbian community, called "biphobia" or "transphobia." This is not to deny that florid phobias never have as their subjects bisexuals and transsexuals, but it is my instinct to restrict such terms to the far end of the spectrum where, along with fear of germs or public places, one starts wearing gloves and a mask and stays home to avoid contact with the open sky.

As we have seen, the historical circumstances of the construction of homosexuality in the U.S. created power relations, which called both for a more inclusive grouping and, at the same time, for a more exclusive grouping. These power relations created the four different groups of which the homosexual community are composed, assigning them different identities, different resources, different spaces in the political sphere. It is these social constructions that created the environment for identity politics within the homosexual community. To the extent that this identity politics has created prejudice and discrimination within the community, it might be more accurate to call it "heterosexism" or "internalized heterosexism" rather than dividing the community even further by referring to "biphobia" and "transphobia," as if bisexuals and transgenders are outside of the community. I understand the argument that "biphobia" and "transphobia" are useful terms because they label phenomena as different in some ways from "homophobia." However, to so define them is to demarcate different spaces inhabitable only by those who are thereby indelibly marked as "not one of us." I prefer to go with Rust's understanding: "Heterosexism refers to the whole constellation of psychological, social and political factors that favor one form of sexuality over another" (Rust 1996:26). Prejudice in gay and lesbian communities against bisexuals and transgenders is heterosexism because it is an accommodationist attempt to disavow these more "radical" forms of sexuality. As Riki Anne Wilchins (1997:15-17) has noted of this phenomenon of identity politics:

> Alas, identity politics is like a computer virus, spreading from the host system to any other with which it comes in contact. Increasingly, the term has hardened to become an identity rather than a descriptor . . . The result of all this is that I find myself increasingly invited to erect a hierarchy of legitimacy, complete with walls and boundaries to defend. Not in this lifetime . . . But at some point such efforts simply extend the linguistic fiction that real identities (however inclusive) actually exist prior to the political systems that create and require them. This is a seduction of language, constantly urging you to name the constituency you represent rather than the oppressions you contest. It is through this Faustian bargain that political legitimacy is purchased.

REFERENCES

Alvear, M. (2003). She Said, He Said. *Southern Voice*, May 9, 2003. Retrieved May 27, 2003, from *http://www.southernvoice.com/forum/columns/index.php3?pub=atl*

American Psychiatric Association (1992). Let's Talk Facts About Phobias. Retrieved May 26, 2003, from *http://www.psych.org/public_info/pdf/phobias.pdf*

Brown, K. (2001). Transsexual, Transgender and Intersex History: Gay, Lesbian and Feminist Backlash. Retrieved May 26, 2003, from *http://www.transhistory.org/history/index.html*

Brown, M.L. and Rounsley, C.A. (1996). *True Selves: Understanding Transsexualism.* San Francisco: Jossey Bass Publishers.

Cantarella, E. (1992). *Bisexuality in the Ancient World.* New Haven: Yale University Press.

Dekker, R.M. and van de Pol, L.C. (1989). *The Tradition of Female Transvestism in Early Modern Europe.* New York: Macmillian.

Dobkin, A. (2000). Come Back, Little Butches. *Outlines,* January 26, 2000. Retrieved May 26, 2003, from *http://www.suba.com/~outlines/alix12600.html*

Fone, B.R.S. (1998). *The Columbia Anthology of Gay Literature: Readings from Western Antiquity to the Present Day.* New York: Columbia University Press.

Fone, B.R.S. (2000). *Homophobia.* New York: Metropolital Books.

Foucault, M. (1980). *The History of Sexuality, vol. 1,* (trans. Hurley, R.) New York: Vintage.

Garber, M. (1995). *Vice Versa.* New York: Simon & Schuster.

Greenberg, D.F. (1998). *The Construction of Homosexuality.* Chicago: University of Chicago Press.

Hemmings, C. (2002). *Bisexual Spaces: A Geography of Sexuality and Gender.* New York: Routledge.

Highleyman, L. (2003). *A Brief History of the Bisexual Movement.* Retrieved May 26, 2003, Available: http://www.binetusa.org/bihistory.htm.

Hutchins, L. (1992). *Speech to the Northampton, MA Lesbian/Gay/Bi Pride March.* Retrieved May 26, 2003, from *http://www.lorainehutchins.com/noho.html*

Hutchins, L. (1996). Bisexuality: Politics and Community. In B.A. Firestein (Ed.), *Bisexuality: The Psychology and Politics of an Invisible Minority* (pp. 240-255). Thousand Oaks: Sage Publications.

Jorgensen, C. (1967). *A Personal Autobiography.* San Francisco: Cleis Press.

Ka'ahumanu, L. (1995). It Ain't Over 'Til the Bisexual Speaks. In N. Tucker (Ed.), *Bisexual Politics: Theories, Queries and Visions* (pp. 1-5). New York: Harrington Park Press.

Ka'ahumanu, L. and Yaeger, R. (2000). *What Does Biphobia Look Like?* Retrieved May 26, 2003, from *http://www.biresource.org/pamphlets/biphobia.html*

Karras, R.M. (1999a). Prostitution and the Question of Sexual Identity in Medieval Europe. *Journal of Women's History,* 11(2), 159-167.

Karras, R.M. (1999b). Response: Identity, Sexuality and History. *Journal of Women's History,* 11(2),193-214.

Merriam-Webster (2003). Merriam Webster Online Dictionary. Retrieved May 26, 2003, from *http://www.merriam-webster.com* (q.v. "homophobia").

Norton, R. (1992). *Mother Clap's Molly House: The Gay Subculture in England 1700-1830.* London: GMP Publishers Ltd.

Ochs, R. (1996). Biphobia: It Goes More Than Two Ways. In B.A. Firestein (Ed.), *Bisexuality: The Psychology and Politics of an Invisible Minority* (pp. 218-225). Thousand Oaks: Sage Publications.

O'Hartigan, M. D. (2002). Alan Hart. In D. Kotula (Ed.), *The Phallus Palace* (pp. 157-165). Los Angeles: Alyson Publications.

Pfäfflin, F. and Junge, A. (1998). Sex Reassignment. Thirty Years of International Follow-up Studies After Sex Reassignment Surgery: A Comprehensive Review, 1961-1991 (trans. Jacobson, R.B. and Meier, A.B.). Retrieved May 26, 2003, Available: *http://www.symposion.com/ijt/* (q.v. "Book Collection").

Prado, C.G. (1995). *Starting with Foucault: An Introduction to Genealogy.* Boulder: Westview Press.

Rust, P.C. (1996). Managing Multiple Identities: Diversity Among Bisexual Women and Men. In B. Firestein (Ed.), *Bisexuality: The Psychology and Politics of an Invisible Minority.* Thousand Oaks: Sage Publications.

Sears, J.T. and Williams, W.L. (1997). *Overcoming Heterosexism and Homophobia.* New York: Columbia University Press.

Spencer, C. (1995). *Homosexuality in History.* New York: Harcourt, Brace & Co.

Sumpter, S.F. (1991). Myths/Realities of Bisexuality. In L. Hutchins and L. Ka'ahumanu (Eds.), *Bi Any Other Name: Bisexual People Speak Out* (pp. 12-13). Boston: Alyson Books.

Traub, V. (1994). The (In)Significance of "Lesbian" Desire in Early Modern England. In J. Goldberg (Ed.), *Queering the Renaissance* (pp. 62-83). US: Duke University Press.

Trnka, S. with Tucker, N. (1995). Overview. In N. Tucker (Ed.), *Bisexual Politics: Theories, Queries and Visions* (pp. 5-11). New York: Harrington Park Press.

Tucker, N. (1995). Introduction. In N. Tucker (Ed.), *Bisexual Politics: Theories, Queries and Visions* (pp. 1-4). New York: Harrington Park Press.

Udis-Kessler, Amanda. (1995). Identity/Politics: A History of the Bisexual Movement in Naomi Tucker (Ed.), *Introduction, in Bisexual Politics: Theories, Queries and Visions.* New York: Harrington Park Press.

Varnell, P. (2003a). Trans Marriage: No Gain For Gays. *Boston Bay Windows,* February 27, 2003, p. 8.

Varnell, P. (2003b). Do Bs really fit in 'GLBT'? *Southern Voice,* March 20, 2003. Retrieved May 27, 2003, Available: *http://www.southernvoice.com/forum/columns/030321ndex.php3?pub=atl*

Weinberg, M., Williams, C.J., and Pryor, D.W. (1995). *Dual Attraction: Understanding Bisexuality.* New York: Oxford University Press.

Wikholm, A. (2000). *A Glossary of the Words Unique to Modern Gay History.* Retrieved May 26, 2003, from *http://gayhistory.com/rev2/words/homophile.htm*

Wilchins, Riki Anne. (1997). *Read My Lips: Sexual Subversion and the End of Gender.* Ithaca: Firebrand Books.

"Tieresius"

David Clowers

http://www.haworthpress.com/web/JB
Digital Object Identifier: 10.1300/J159v03n03_03

[Haworth co-indexing entry note]: "Tieresius." Clowers, David. Co-published simultaneously in *Journal of Bisexuality* (Harrington Park Press, an imprint of The Haworth Press, Inc.) Vol. 3, No. 3/4, 2003, pp. 57-61; and: *Bisexuality and Transgenderism: InterSEXions of the Others* (ed: Jonathan Alexander, and Karen Yescavage) Harrington Park Press, an imprint of The Haworth Press, Inc., 2003, pp. 57-61. Single or multiple copies of this article are available for a fee from The Haworth Document Delivery Service [1-800-HAWORTH, 9:00 a.m. - 5:00 p.m. (EST). E-mail address: docdelivery@haworthpress.com].

Tieresius was a seer from the Greek city of Thebes. As a young man, he had walked in a garden sacred to a god, and when he spied two snakes coupling, he killed the female with his stick, whereupon he was changed into a woman. For seven years he lived this way until one day he saw once more two snakes mating and slew the male, thereby restoring his manhood. When Hera and Zeus argued about who, the male or the female, had the greatest pleasure during the sex act, they called on the one person able to speak from experience. When Tieresius told them the woman, Hera became furious and blinded him. Acts of the gods may not be undone, so Zeus gave Tieresius the ability to foretell the future. But when he told Oedipus that he would kill his father and marry his mother, Oedipus fled to avoid his fate, only to meet it on the road to Colonus and in his mother's bed. When Oedipus learned of his fate, unable to see the truth, he blinded himself. Similarly, Tieresius told Narcissus's mother that her son would live a long life, "If he did not come to know himself." These and other prophecies made him sought after, though feared, for his advice.

TIERESIUS

A sudden blow of my staff broke
two mating snakes asunder: she died,
who in the god's holy grove was loved
and the god's fury became my fate:
I stood amid the flowering trees
amazed at my softening limbs,
my rounding breasts, and smooth cheeked face–
my manhood scooped from my loins,
and my fearful crying became a shrill lament.
As woman, then, for seven years I lived
knowing how gods change lives as they will,
until I killed another snake–the male this time–
and found my normal form restored.
When Zeus and Hera asked me who
had more pleasure from their sex, I said, "Woman"–
and Hera blinded both my woman and my man.
Zeus gave me the gift of future sight,
and my bi-nature saw and told.
But with Narcissus dead
and Oedipus blinded,
I learned neither the gods nor men
would hear their truth.

My father worked for the YMCA, an organization devoted to the triangular virtues of spirit, mind, and body. The first two were easy enough to keep abstract and out of the everyday life, but the body part–given the Y's emphasis at the time on service to men and boys–posed a dilemma, since the body could be both a good thing and a bad thing. The heterosexual norm of sex and marriage was the accepted ideal; its opposite was a fearful secret. For example, after being arrested for a solicitation for sex in a men's room, my father's married boss hung himself. Thus, a secret fear of the body's difficult impulses pervaded my childhood. My father pointed out the holes drilled in men's room stalls and told me what they were for. Being six or seven years old, I couldn't imagine that peeking at someone using the toilet could be exciting, but the dark, fetid toilet stalls made an impression on me. To be open, bright, and masculine was prized. To be secretive, dark, and differently masculine was feared.

Given my upbringing, therefore, imagine my shock, after functioning as a casually heterosexual teenager, when I woke up at age twenty stuck to my sheets, having experienced a homoerotic dream. Was I one of those persons who so horrified my father? I read everything that I could find on the subject of homosexuality in an attempt to explain to myself how such feelings could have happened in me, because when I thought about the etiology of my dreams, I realized that if I allowed myself to do so, I did have erotic feelings about men. How could this be, I wondered? I felt confused because I also had erotic thoughts about women.

Fortunately, I soon found a counselor who showed me that it was mistaken to view sexuality in Puritanical either-or terms. Sexual impulses and attributes, he taught me, were a continuum. If latent homosexuality exists, then latent bisexuality and heterosexuality must exist also. But in spite of my intellectual willingness to admit my attraction to both sexes, thereby breaking the narrowly defined sexual role that previously I had assigned to myself–and also sanctioned by both gay and straight cultures–emotionally it still was not easy for me. I was no longer permitted the easy certainty of a socially acceptable, safe self-definition. I was still afraid.

I surmise that, for many of us, fear is the glass through which we see others, darkly. Rather than probing deeply into who we are, we define themselves by who we are not. And there is a socially accepted benefit: by joining with others in expressing fear or hate for another person or group, it is possible to merge back within a comfortable perception of ourselves. "We aren't_____!" (fill in the blank); "We're_____" (fill in your peer group of choice). Defining others by exclusions that are crafted out of fear, however, creates that feared entity, "the other." And "the other" makes us feel comfortable with ourselves again, because, "We ain't him." It is possible, however, to see things differently.

I had to choose, therefore, either to see myself as flawed because I did not fit, or to see myself as merely different but equally valuable. By accepting the aspects of myself that did not fit societal norms, I thereby gained an understanding of "the other." The other was me. When I realized that truth, I had to abolish the concept of "the other" and to stop defining myself by who I was not. If I was different and I could accept myself, then it followed that if someone else was different, I could accept them as well. If society said part of my nature was aberrant, then others who society had so classified must be my brothers and sisters.

I took my insight even further. If I had to accept who I was, I asked myself if there is anyone for whom I could not feel a sense of community. Gradually I opened to the possibilities for inclusiveness. I might not approve of someone's behavior, but since I shared their humanity, I could not condemn them as inhuman, as the "Other."

Thus, the recognition of my bi-nature has led me to tolerance. I know myself to be the best and the worst of everyone. My brothers are Gandhi as well as Hitler, Sheriff Bull Connon, and Martin Luther King, Jr.

INTERSECTING COMMUNITIES: B/T CONCERNS IN COMMON

Yeah, Yeah, Oh-Yeah, Just Dropped in to See What Condition My Condition Was In

kari edwards

[Haworth co-indexing entry note]: "Yeah, Yeah, Oh-Yeah, Just Dropped in to See What Condition My Condition Was In." edwards, kari. Co-published simultaneously in *Journal of Bisexuality* (Harrington Park Press, an imprint of The Haworth Press, Inc.) Vol. 3, No. 3/4, 2003, pp. 63-69; and: *Bisexuality and Transgenderism: InterSEXions of the Others* (ed: Jonathan Alexander, and Karen Yescavage) Harrington Park Press, an imprint of The Haworth Press, Inc., 2003, pp. 63-69. Single or multiple copies of this article are available for a fee from The Haworth Document Delivery Service [1-800-HAWORTH, 9:00 a.m. - 5:00 p.m. (EST). E-mail address: docdelivery@haworthpress.com].

SUMMARY. how to consider situating without signifying, or maybe how to place another without them becoming a commodity. are we to assume one mode fits all with within academic dioramas, or is it one size will get you by as the standard for excellence in scholarly production units? what is it to exclude types of writing, or limit inclusion of certain types into journals? why do we continue to believe in the failed fairy tale of definitional identity as an answer, when all that happens is the reinforcement of the other? *[Article copies available for a fee from The Haworth Document Delivery Service: 1-800-HAWORTH. E-mail address: <docdelivery@ haworthpress.com> Website: <http://www.HaworthPress.com> © 2003 by The Haworth Press, Inc. All rights reserved.]*

KEYWORDS. Identity, transgender, bisexual, liberation, radical

Yeah, yeah, oh-yeah, Just Dropped In
To See What Condition My Condition Was In[1]

–or what position my position is in, or how to position my position machine, or how to consider situating without signifying, or maybe how to place another without them becoming a commodity.

there is this phenomena in this (queer) community (is there a community that I do not know about?) that creates an insurable hunger to situate and name, to volley up to the Act Up power bar with (wall streetish) slogans like "SILENCE = DEATH," or the universal "I am queer and I am proud," or "I'm proudly queer," or . . . "gay power" . . . all good at creating an identity and a situation that becomes a media campaign, with side order products and glossy magazines, to be pierced/perceived and tattooed. We have queer or (reallY) GAY & LESBIAN "getaways." what are we getting away from may be a bigger question? what are we being or what are we living in that makes it necessary to get away? we create the multiplicity of multiple positions and multiple tracking systems to situate the multiple positions to a singularity with a few hand picked letters from the alphabet, then we create dramatic discourses on each letter. no wonder there's a need for holiday getaways.

by now you have realized this is not your typical academic paper. are we to assume one mode fits all with within academic dioramas, or is it one size will get you by as the standard for excellence in scholarly production units? What is it to exclude types of writing, or limit inclusion of certain types into journals? more of the same, a time magazine for queers? oh, that's right, we already have those . . .

this is not some universal absolute doctrine to rally the troops around and march to a future tense perfection written all over our utopian dreamscape, or some miracle to bring about greater acceptance by those others in the alphabet soup . . . (the can of soup I am a part of but not sure I want to join). this is a question and proposition. what are we doing here by trying to bring in more and more discussions around "bi" and "trans"? what does it truly accomplish? is it a further exercise in creating a defense against the oppression, against heteronormative perspectives, all the while reinforcing that perspective? why are we not talking of ways of disrupting this codification economy, instead of further situating already oppressed groups?

one of the questions ought to be, is; what is it when there is an act of piracy by the privileged using academic writing within a logocentric context, to speak of or about queers or "bi" or "trans" issues and or individuals? inherently this seems like a problem, situating those who have already been doubly situated by the medical, psychological, and academic community with further discourse; as if we could write ourselves out of this economy with the speech that created the situation in the first place. this is not to say critical theory and a deconstruction of social lies are not beneficial, but I do think there has to be a critic of the critics. without a diversity of voices it becomes a monotone of re-sistance and an act of doubly situating the already multiply signified.

no one has ever written, painted, sculpted, modeled, built, or invented except literally to get out of hell.[2]

QUESTIONS:

1. whose writing are we using to get out of hell?
2. have we forgotten Audre Lorde's (1996) provocative statement: "The master's tools will never dismantle the master's house" (110)?

WHAT IS NOT THE MASTER'S TONGUE, TOOL, SWORD, AND OR GUN?

Allen Ginsberg's *Howl*, Anne Waldman's *Fast Speaking Woman*, Leslie Fineberg's *Stone Butch Blues*, Radcylffe Hall's *The Well of Loneliness*, Rachel Blau DuPlessis's *Drafts*, Eileen Myles's *Maxfield Parish* use either poetic or fictional positioning/nonpositioning, with at least mild disruption of the father tongue through content or major disruption of syntax. without theory, these text have been the rally point of a queer community in different times and different spaces. would it not make sense then to give these texts equal weight in the discourse? the problem is these text tend to be more phenomenological and less analytical, so there is no measuring stick to judge them by, but isn't that the point?

yet, even this partial list is segregated when it comes to the types of writing accepted by academia, which does nothing but create a hierarchy of one text form over another, institutionalizing a certain privilege for those that can afford a certain type of education, or privileges of a certain type of speaking . . .

enough!!

is it not the content and expression we should be worried about . . . not the form it takes? isn't that the whole question; what form are you? should we not hear the mode of expression of one's being, or the content that one carries to the moment?

so how does this relate to a transgender/bisexual intersections/conception or conscription? it is important to stay on track, be reproducible, predictable, same time every time, part of the assembly line, a repetitive pattern, to be seen and read, punch the clock, life in a cube, and transport our bodies in sheltered environments where ever we go . . .

and I desire rights . . . the right to not be a thing.

> *in a society where no one is any longer recognizable by anyone else, each individual is necessarily unable to recognize his [sic] own reality.*[3]

the option then is to be super-situated, super-signified with special laws to protect us from the gross inequities of this society. even then we are not recognizable to each other, and passing becomes of yearning hunger of privilege. yet, we want to be seen, so we create a special day where we are all together, even then we are invisible . . . so we try harder, be more of that which is thought to be our own unique position, that that is shared by a thousand others with labels like "trans" and "bi" . . . I am this, I am special . . . look at me, feel me, touch me . . . I am not you, but I am in your parade . . . you have to accept me now.

that will not happen, or who cares if it happens, or it will happen in time . . . time I do not have. I am a stranger in my own land, but that's fine. I do not want to be a contributing member of the GNP . . . we have to stop situating and create a potential future. Krishnamurti (1989) said; "the future is now," yet we have this desire to conceptualize the past/present, instead of future/present (no page number).

so, one of the questions is what does the life of someone who is "trans" or "bi" have to do with politics? as Kate Bornstein said so beautifully during one of the many times I have seen Kate perform, "there are not words that can describe me" . . . or something like that . . . (if I damaged the flow, Kate, I do

apologize) . . . but the deeper I go into the understanding of language and social construction, the further away I get from a need for an inevitable body, or a
recognizable figure or a situated constraint. I say we open our bodies to desire
without language, eroticize without shame.

and what is the meaning of the words "trans" and "bi" when it emanates
from a bankrupt system bent on violence and subjugation?

yes, it's true, I identify with those "trans" individuals brutally murdered. I
also identify with those in Bosnia, Afghanistan, United States of America and
where ever individuals are denied their freedom of desire and are forced by violence to conform . . .

does this mean I try to pass and fit in? . . . hardly . . . I am not a thing, or I am
everything. I am never a thing, but a verb, that works and lives to do what I can
to protect others against the silent violence of the state, such as naming, time,
and product placement.

let's face it, any definition does harm . . . instead of speaking of this or
that, who cares if you are "bi" and you a truck driver, and/or what that means?
or if you are "trans," can you wear other things? the problems we are facing are
so much bigger than what kind of doll does a "bi" (person) pick, as compared
to a "trans" (person). we have only disconnected islands of natural forests left,
the oceans' levels are rising and threatening indigenous people on the islands
in the pacific. we are in the middle of a world sports match with live weapons,
losing rights left and right, increasingly told to buy more, spend more, be patri-
otic, which is an evil unto itself. this is a nation of excess; ten billion hamburg-
ers sold daily and we are worrying about what kind of vibrator "trans" and "bi"
people choose. . . . this is a world in crisis, and yes, it includes violent discrimination against those who do not pass the state sponsored car buying and baby
making test . . . hundreds of those that use labels to protect themselves are murdered each year . . . so there are bigger questions . . . why are we allowing murder in the name of the state? why do we continue to believe in the failed fairy
tale of definitional identity as an answer, when all that happens is the reinforcement of the other?

we need to consider that even in the name of progress, signifying through discourse is based on knowledge, which is equal to power. so the question then is
who is discussing what for whom? I do not need any one describing for me my
general sense of the world and reiterating through repetition what may or may not
be my worldview. I need a personal fiction that sings like poetry and is
crossdressed in the night. I need creative writing that becomes philosophical
drag in an all night sex scene where revolution is the scream of ecstasy. becoming is an ever-evolving voice, that is killed by the need to constantly situate as a
thing.

NOTES

1. Mickey Newbury, "Just Dropped In (To See What Condition My Condition Was In)," recorded by Kenny Rogers (1968). Lyrics available at: http://www.lyricscafe.com/r/rogers_kenny/krog12.html.
2. (Artaud, 1976, p. 497)
3. (Debord, 1994, p. 152)

REFERENCES

Debord, G. (1994). *The society of the spectacle.* New York: Zone Books.

Krishnamurti. (1989). *The future is now: Last talks in India.* New York: Harper Collins.

Lorde, A. (1996). *Sister outsider: Speeches and essays.* Freedom, California: The Crossing Press.

Sontag, S. (Ed.). (1976). *Antonin Artaud: Selected writings.* Berkeley: University of California Press.

Pomosexual Play:
Going Beyond the
Binaristic Limits
of Gender?

Jennifer C. Ailles

[Haworth co-indexing entry note]: "Pomosexual Play: Going Beyond the Binaristic Limits of Gender?"
Ailles, Jennifer L. Co-published simultaneously in *Journal of Bisexuality* (Harrington Park Press, an imprint of
The Haworth Press, Inc.) Vol. 3, No. 3/4, 2003, pp. 71-85; and: *Bisexuality and Transgenderism: InterSEXions
of the Others* (ed: Jonathan Alexander, and Karen Yescavage) Harrington Park Press, an imprint of The
Haworth Press, Inc., 2003, pp. 71-85. Single or multiple copies of this article are available for a fee from The
Haworth Document Delivery Service [1-800-HAWORTH, 9:00 a.m. - 5:00 p.m. (EST). E-mail address:
docdelivery@haworthpress.com].

SUMMARY. Jennifer Ailles examines the limitations imposed by the strict binary gender system and the attempt to subvert that system through pomosexual play. Using Kate Bornstein, a transgendered transsexual pomosexual, as a case study, she argues that pomosexual play is a theoretical oxymoron that is not sufficient to re-write the cultural construction of gender. Ultimately, pomosexual play relies on the same artificial binary alignment that normative gender relies on. Instead, it is the material existence of pomosexual bodies, particularly the bodies of the intersex, individuals who are genetically distinct from male and female, and the multiplicity of ethical positions that they inhabit, who present a real challenge to the binaristic limits of gender. *[Article copies available for a fee from The Haworth Document Delivery Service: 1-800-HAWORTH. E-mail address: <docdelivery@haworthpress.com> Website: <http://www.HaworthPress.com> © 2003 by The Haworth Press, Inc. All rights reserved.]*

KEYWORDS. Pomosexual play, pomosexuality, Kate Bornstein, transgender, transsexual, genital reassignment surgery, intersex, signification

There's a real simple way to look at gender: Once upon a time, someone drew a line in the sands of a culture and proclaimed with great self-importance, "On this side, you are a man; on the other side, you are a woman." It's time for the winds of change to blow that line away. Simple.

Kate Bornstein
Gender Outlaw: On Men, Women, and the Rest of Us (1995, p. 21)

"SENDING OUT AN S.O.S...."[1]

In contemporary western society gender is a contentious subject. Gender is often posited as the culturally scripted ideological social roles that men and women are supposed to fulfil as opposed to an individual's natural biological sex, which just "is" and which people just "are." The major work of feminist praxis has been to reveal the limitations, many of them inherently violent, that have historically resulted from gender differentiation. For those who do not accept the two traditional genders (female and male) as essential, immutable, trans-historical, categorical truth(s), the systemic societal imposition of strict genders results in restricted liberty and, often, the foreclosure of individual potentialities. These potentialities range the full scope of human affairs from the seemingly insignificant, such as who can/should paint their toenails or use a particular bathroom, to experiences of national/international importance, such as who can/should fight and die for their country, let alone lead their country in political and religious matters. At the heart of the protest against the limitations of signification and related practices is the belief that social roles and their associated constraints are in conflict with the natural biological state of the body. But, as Judith Butler has argued, biological sex is also a socially demarcated and artificially constructed category. Sex and gender are not oppositional, as they both constitute the body as *always already* culturally constructed and therefore *always already* limited in potentiality.[2] As Kate Bornstein signals with the phrase "Once upon a time" in my epigraph, the cultural coding of individuals as either male or female is part of a grand, fictional, culturally constructed fairy tale that has nothing to do with individual realities. And, as Bornstein declares, the fairy tale needs to be re-written.

One way of re-inscribing the culturally scripted fairy tale of gender is through the manipulation of bodies and gender roles that is a part of pomosexual play. Pomosexual play involves using the material reality of bodies and the *assumed* division between "gender roles" and "natural sex" to purposefully demonstrate the arbitrariness of both that categorical division and of gender itself. Furthermore, play involves taking pleasure in this act of cultural enlightenment. In this paper I will delineate some of the issues surrounding pomosexual play using Kate Bornstein, a transgendered transsexual pomosexual, as a case study from which to launch my enquiry. Specifically, I will argue that pomosexual play is a theoretical oxymoron that ultimately leads to anything but libratory pleasure and that, while useful, it is not sufficient to re-write the fairy tale of gender. Ultimately, pomosexual play relies on the same artificial binary alignment that Normative[3] gender relies on. Instead, it is the material existence of pomosexual bodies, particularly the bodies of the intersex, individuals who are genetically distinct from male and female, and the multiplicity of ethical positions that they inhabit, who present a real challenge to the binaristic limits of gender.

"YOU MAKE ME FEEL LIKE A NATURAL WOMAN"[4]–NOT!

Kate Bornstein, a North American transgendered transsexual, transformed her body and her identity from male to female in the mid 1980s through "genital reassignment surgery" (*Gender Outlaw*, 1995, p. 15). A few years ago, I had the pleasure of hearing and seeing Bornstein talk about her experiences as a male to female transgendered transsexual. According to Bornstein she began her life as a Normative male but she had her body surgically altered to appear like that of a woman's. But how much of a woman's body does Bornstein actually have? How much of a man's does she retain? And how much of her is something entirely new and different? Some of Bornstein's bodily alterations included passing as a woman before her surgery, taking hormones, having a "penile inversion" to remove his penis and create her vagina, growing breasts, and changing the texture of her skin to make it softer. She even suffers from "raging PMS" because of all the hormones she has had to take, though she notes that she does not "have cramps or bleed. But I get the water retention, the mood swings, and all that" (*Gender Outlaw*, 1995, p. 19).

Beyond her materially altered reality, Bornstein openly states that she enjoys "*playing* with people's perceptions of gender" as she works ultimately to dismantle society's need for gender categorization ("Talk," 2000). Bornstein states that "Real gender freedom begins with fun. Here, you get what might be called The Gender Blender, a sort of whirling confusion of leather and rhinestones" (*Gender Outlaw*, 1995, p. 87). Bornstein's usage of play on the road to liberation coincides with pomosexuality and "its" stressing of the pleasure and fun involved in transgressing societal limits, particularly the limits of gender and sexuality. Carol Queen and Lawrence Schimel note in the introduction to their book *PoMoSexuals: Challenging Assumptions About Gender and Sexuality*, for which Bornstein wrote the preface, that

> Pomosexuality lives in the space in which all other non-binary forms of sexual and gender identity reside–a boundary-free zone in which fences are crossed for the fun of it, or simply because some of us can't be fenced in. It challenges either/or categorizations in favor of largely unmapped possibility and the intense charge that comes with transgression. It acknowledges the pleasure of that transgression, as well as the need to transgress limits that do not make room for all of us. (1997, p. 23)

Transgression, crossing over and moving beyond limits, is a major part of the pleasure involved in pomosexual play. But what exactly is the nature of this play? How is play manifested in the real world?

Play can take on many forms since there are multiple individuals who refuse to accept Normative gender. Those who engage in camp, S/M, sex-play, "gender terrorism" (Bornstein, *Gender Outlaw*, 1995, p. 69), taking on various alternative personas, and/or parodying gender roles, are all examples of those who reject the Norm and engage in the project of pomosexual play. Camp, in particular, demonstrates pomosexual play's subversive nature in that it "thumbs its nose at the straight world, lampooning and violating its rituals. Camp points out the silliness, exaggerates the roles, shines big spotlights on the gender dynamic" (Bornstein, *Gender Outlaw*, 1995, p. 136). As well, Queen and Schimel note "one of the strange twists of postmodern sexual culture, [is that] just as scores of gay men have 'gone lesbian' . . . scores of queer women have 'gone fag'" (1997, p. 113)–which may or may not be done as a form of play. Bornstein, as an example of one who actively resists the gender Norm, plays "with people's perceptions of gender" ("Talk," 2000) primarily through the taking on of identity roles through various forms of drag–particularly, "femme drag" ("Talk," 2000). Drag requires the individual to act according to the performative requirements of the "opposite" gender, or a specific identity, by cross-dressing, enacting mannerisms, and replicating physicality, whereas passing requires the individual to do the same things in order to substantiate one's "own" supposed gender. Bornstein's "femme drag" is really a mix between passing and drag since she is a "woman" who used to be a "man" trying to be a "woman" who is excessively "womanish" and "femme." Bornstein's mix of passing and drag amounts to a sl(e)ightly complicated engagement of gender since she is trying to satisfy cultural gender roles while also working to dismantle them.

Pomosexual play thus works to challenge essentialist notions of gender by demonstrating that the boundary between male and female can be crossed and that men can play and be women and that women can play and be men along with being multiple identities and engaging in multiple actions in between simultaneously. Pomosexual peoples reveal the material and social mutability of seemingly essentialized genders–that gender is not natural since it can be disrupted so easily. Bornstein's attempts at libratory subversion are echoed by Leslie Feinberg, who self-describes as "a masculine, lesbian, female-to-male cross-dresser and transgenderist" (Feinberg, 1998, p. 19). Feinberg states "We, as cross-dressers–gay, bisexual, and straight–and our partners, have a stake in challenging restrictive attitudes toward human behavior and self-expression" (1998, p. 25). Feinberg reinforces both the openness of pomosexuality and the need to contest the artificial boundaries that restrict all individuals regardless of gender and sexual orientation.

As Queen and Schimel state, the realm of the pomosexual is one of "transgress[ing] limits" where there is "pleasure" in the act of "transgression" (1997, p. 23). That pleasure though, comes at a price. The whole motive behind pomosexuality, of "fence . . . cross[ing]" (Queen and Schimel, 1997, p. 23), is to escape the tyranny, the violence (psychological, physical, and symbolic), that results from the dual-gender imperative and systemic signification. Signification, the alignment of signs and signifieds, is tyrannical and oppressive because it imposes artificial limits on the potentially unlimited. Whenever a label, a sign, is designated it necessarily restricts and contains that which is labelled. Signification relies on the binary system of Norm/Other for differentiation. Though signification is a process of continual social construction, signifieds are often assumed to be concrete, essentialized, and immutable. When the signifier applies to a "rock" or a "piano" this essentializing *may* not be harmful, but when the same assumptions are applied to individuals as part of their identity, especially in relation to gender and sexuality, the results can be, and often *are*, brutal and destructive.

I would argue that pomosexual play is just as violent as the heterosocial system it wishes to subvert and that any pleasure gained is ultimately undermined by the violence that is recreated against the self. Those who engage in pomosexual play desire the pleasure that comes from escaping pain and violence and it is unfortunate that their means of play actually leads to recreating the system they wish to subvert. Ironically, and sadly, Bornstein presents a sketch of one of the "enemies" of gender liberation, "The Gender Defender," without realizing that she, herself, acts in the same manner as the "enemy." According to Bornstein, "The Gender Defender is someone who actively, or by knowing inaction, defends the status quo of the existing gender system, and thus perpetuates the violence of male privilege and all its social extensions. The gender defender, or gender terrorist, is someone for whom gender forms a cornerstone of their view of the world" (*Gender Outlaw*, 1995, p. 74). Since pomosexual play depends on "the existing gender system" to subvert, gender, for any pomosexual activist, is necessarily a "cornerstone of their view of the world."

The violence of pomosexual play also derives from the reality that any form of identity, including the nascent and reclamatory queer and pomosexual identities, that subscribes to a nominal signifier imposes boundaries even as it challenges old signifiers. Thus, the performative options of any new identity, even of "non-identity" pomosexuals, are necessarily as ascribed and limited as the old. An individual cannot play with someone else's expectations simply by being the new–the individual must position and label the new identity in relation to the old so that both parties are aware of the "fences" that are being "crossed"–the zone is anything but "boundary-free" (Queen and Schimel, 1997, p. 23). Furthermore, the realm of pomosexual play and the assumed freedom to subvert and transgress Normative social roles actually supports the hegemonic by substantiating the oppositional binary of Norm/Other in society since any playing or "crossing" requires fixed markers (genders) to cross/trans-/play with/over/in opposition to. Using the title of Bornstein's book, one cannot be an "outlaw" without maintaining the law–without maintaining the three distinct categories of "man, woman, and the rest of us." For example, drag depends on and reinforces the two strict Normative genders since drag requires the recognition by the "audience" that a crossing over is occurring, that there is a discrepancy between the supposed Normative gender state and the one being played.

Pomosexual play thus cannot occur without the Normative existing as something to subvert and though the goal of pomosexual play is the transgression of the Normative, pomosexual play can never accomplish this goal without re-substantiating the system and all of its inherent violence. Therefore, to avoid the self-inflicted violence involved in perpetuating systemic signification, the pomosexual cannot play, the pomosexual cannot take "pleasure" in any transgression, the pomosexual cannot privilege the Otherness of being Other, the pomosexual cannot subscribe to the label of "pomosexual" even if it is seemingly the most libratory and least ascribed of the performative signifiers. Playing is, therefore, not a productive form of ethical practice if one's goal is liberation from the tyranny of signification. Though pomosexual playing *may* be useful in disrupting people's perceptions, it is not sufficient to totally change the binaristic gender system.

"WE ARE LIVING IN A MATERIAL WORLD AND I AM A MATERIAL GIRL"[5]

So what can an individual do if pomosexual play does not work to break down and end the tyranny of Normative gender? Since the primary idea behind pomosexual play is to demonstrate the assumed discrepancy between physical bodies and perceived/performed identities, a more direct return to material pomosexual bodies may offer a way out of the dichotomy between female and male. Rosalyn Diprose states in her article "A 'Genethics' That Makes Sense," that

> To be located in space, which we all are, and to locate others, which we all do, requires embodiment. To be positioned, and to take up a position (even if this involves sitting on the fence) is a question of ethics. "Ethics" is derived from the Greek word *ethos*, meaning dwelling, or habitat–the place to which one returns . . . Taking up a position, presenting oneself, therefore requires . . . awareness of temporality and location. And, the intrinsic reference point for temporarily, spatial orientation and, therefore, difference, is one's own body. That location and position are concepts easily interchangeable, illustrates the co-incidence of embodiment and ethics which necessarily come together by virtue of our spatio-temporal being-in-the-world. (1991, p. 65)

The body maintains an ethical position by virtue of its material existence. If one is aware of the body and its "spatio-temporal being" then one can more readily confront the arbitrary and nonmaterial conventions that are enforced by society. Pomosexual bodies challenge the status quo by their very existence. The transgendered, those who have altered or transformed their gender from the gender that they were medically and socially ascribed at birth without the use of surgery, and the transsexuals, who, like Bornstein, have surgically altered or transformed their gender from the gender that they were medically and socially ascribed at birth, present ethical positions that work to subvert social Norms.

Neither the transgendered nor the transsexuals can physically escape what they were before they "trans-ed"; thus, they are always the gender that they were originally ascribed as well as the gender they have chosen to become. Pomosexual bodies are therefore a complex mixture of genders; they are, by their very physicality, *always already* multiply gendered. Thus, pomosexuals, particularly transgendered and transsexuals, can never posit a unified pure traditional gendered habitat from which to play in the first place. Pomosexuals are also *always already* Other since the "new" transformed physical body is neither a Normative male nor a Normative female. Thus, the far from heterogeneous "group" of pomosexuals ethically challenge the Normative heterosocial binary of male and female with their material multigendered bodies or "habitats." These ethical beings occupy particular positions that cannot be as readily negated as positions that are merely products of pomosexual play. Bornstein, once again, serves as an example of the materially altered pomosexual body. At her lecture, Bornstein stated that now, fourteen years after she had the "surgery," she is "neither a man nor a woman." Leslie Feinberg is also in a similar material state of Otherness in that sie[6] has also altered hir body by removing hir breasts. Feinberg states that sie "had the chest surgery last spring (1997) after many years of binding my chest to look male but not having the [sic] 'lop 'em offa me'" (1998, p. 77).

Bornstein and Feinberg had to undergo surgery to satisfy sociomedical beliefs that dictated which body parts could belong to particular identities. The option to be a "girl with a penis" or a "male lesbian transvestite," among many other "combinations," was not a part of the performative options open to either Bornstein in the 1980s or Feinberg in the 1990s. These performative options are only now, at the start of the new millennium, beginning to be positioned as part of the new queer realm of pomosexuality. For the most part, the linguistic signifiers of these new options are combinations of "known" performative realities since their particular individual "hybrids" have yet to be subsumed into the tyranny of the signification system and given their own labels. As Bornstein notes in *Gender Outlaw*,

> [T]ranssexuality in this culture is considered an illness . . . [W]e're taught that we are literally sick, that we have an illness that can be diagnosed and maybe cured. As a result of the medicalization of our condition, transsexuals must see therapists in order to receive the medical seal of approval required to proceed with any gender reassignment surgery. Now, once we get to the doctor, we're told we'll be cured if we become members of one gender or another. (1995, p. 62)

The doctors believe that once the "sick" individual has had "genital reassignment surgery" (*Gender Outlaw*, 1995, p. 15), that the person will be *fixed* and that the internal and external realities will match up, thereby allowing the individual to become a "healthy" Normal participant in Normative society. But, as Bornstein and all transsexuals demonstrate, the interior and the exterior can not really be matched up: even if the psychological interior sees itself as a "female" the physical exterior of a transsexual, in a male to female case, will never be the same as those traditionally assigned to the category of female at birth. The discrepancy between a transsexual individual's interiority, the psychological reality, and the person's external material existence cannot be resolved by present medical and surgical practices. Contemporary surgery can only manipulate the body in an attempt to approximate the Norm; to make the transsexual's body *look like* the Norm rather than *be* the Norm that the individual has internalized.

The inability of medial science and other authoritative social institutions to perfect the alignment of psychological and physical realities brings up questions about the demarcation between the interior and the exterior. Without getting into the elaborate arguments surrounding the existence of a privileged site of identity such as a mind, soul, or ego since they are beyond the scope of this paper, I am going to focus on the material aspects of gender and the phenomenological assumption that we are our "own body" (Diprose, 1991, p. 65), that we are our "habitats." There can be no real separate recognition of internal psychology of gender: the ethical realm of our materiality cannot be separated from phenomenal reality. Further, the illusory "internal" can only be "expressed" or "known" in its opposition to the performative options of the society and the differentiation that occurs when one set of options rubs up against another set–often without an individual's awareness–thus creating a habitat that is seemingly "out of place" in the phenomenal world.

* * *

One group of non-Normative individuals whose internal and external habitats have the potential to match up is the intersex. The intersex, by their material existence, move beyond pomosexuals who have modified their bodies to offer the greatest ethical challenge to the fairy tale of gender ascription. The intersex are those who used to be classed as hermaphrodites–those born transgendered without having to "trans." Hermaphrodites were seen as mythical forerunners of heterosocial gender; Plato describes the original three sexes (male, female, and hermaphrodite) in the *Symposium*. According to Plato, the hermaphrodites were punished by Zeus and materially split apart into the two now traditional genders because they were "arrogan[t], [and] that they actually tried–like Ephialtes and

Otus in Homer–to scale the heights of heaven and set upon the gods" (1973, p. 543). Plato's hermaphrodites, like those who engage in pomosexual play, refuse to accept the rule of the gods, of Normative society. Hermaphrodites were also seen as "mistakes," as aberrations from Normative gender. Subsequently, hermaphrodites were, and still are, destroyed, mutilated, physically altered in many of the same violent ways as transsexuals are, to force their bodies to match the two restrictive genders of male and female. An example of how insidious this violence can be is revealed in the case of Herculine Barbin whom Bornstein incorporated as a character in her play "Hidden: A Gender" (in *Gender Outlaw*). Barbin, a hermaphrodite who lived life in nineteenth-century France as a girl, was forced to become a man when her physicality was found to differentiate from her lived gender. Herculine found that s/he was socially unprepared to suddenly live as a man and, in response, s/he committed the ultimate violence against the self: suicide. Michel Foucault notes in his introduction to Barbin's memoirs that, historically, it was "[c]hanges of option, not the anatomical mixture of the sexes [sic], [that] were what gave rise to most of the condemnation of hermaphrodites" (1980, p. viii). Or, to return to Plato, it is the assumed "arrogance" of those whose bodies are already in play, and their ability to challenge the status quo, that is really threatening to the Normative.

The intersex, on the other hand, go beyond Plato's mythical dichotomy and consist of at least five distinct sexes or genders. Anne Fausto-Sterling, in her article "The Five Sexes: Why Male and Female Are Not Enough," comments on reality by stating "Western culture is deeply committed to the idea that there are only two sexes. Even language refuses other possibilities" (1993, p. 20). She elaborates:

> if the state and the legal system have an interest in maintaining a two-party sexual system, they are in defiance of nature. For biologically speaking, there are many gradations running from female to male; and depending on how one calls the shots, one can argue that along that spectrum lie at least five sexes–and perhaps even more. (1993, p. 21)

Fausto-Sterling classifies the intersex into three primary groups: "the so-called true hermaphrodites, . . . herms" (1993, p. 21), "the male pseudohermaphrodites (the 'merms')" (1993, p. 21) and the "female pseudohermaphrodites (the 'ferms')" (1993, p. 21). John Money agrees with Fausto-Sterling but he increases her five categories of intersex gender to seven in his study *Venuses Penuses: Sexology, Sexosophy and Exigency Theory.*[7] Add Normative male and Normative female to Money's list and there are at least NINE genders! The intersex thus challenge the mutually exclusive gender dichotomy of male/female by presenting biologically classed material beings that are neither Normative male nor Normative female. Each of the herms, merms, and ferms, along with Money's groupings, have their own distinct genetic codes and yet the intersex are still nominally troped, via the use of the prefix *inter*, as part of a continuum or "relatively discontinuous series" (Grosz, 1996, p. 60) between Normative whole females and Normative whole males. The effort of science to classify the intersex actually results in the Normalization of the various genders that are neither strictly male nor strictly female.

The nascent, yet growing, sociomedical recognition of the intersex as Normative categorical material beings has significant implications for those whose genders are not Normative male or Normative female. First, the fact that the intersex expands gender beyond the two traditional genders increases the performative options in society; namely, that people have more categories to play with. Second, as the intersex gain Normative value, the less individuals will be violently forced to alter their bodies to fit either of the two Normative genders of female and male. Arguably, people could be forced to fit one of the nine intersex genders rather than just one of two traditional genders since each specific Normalized gender will have its own set of "expectations" to "meet," and, presumably, the same violent means of attainting/enforcing them. But, the possibility of restrictive enforcement of gender is tempered by the reality that if the herms, merms, ferms, et al., can be sanctioned then there is no telling how many other genders will someday be deemed Normal. As the genetic make-up of material bodies continues to be mapped, it is yet to be determined how many "biological" genders exist and remain to be classified some day. At the present moment though, general societal knowledge has yet to catch up to scientific knowledge of the intersex; as Bornstein notes, "Unless you're an athlete who's been challenged in the area of gender representation [to see if one actually is male or female and can participate in a particular sport and/or keep a hard-earned medal], you probably haven't had a chromosome test to determine your gender. If you haven't had that test, then how do you know what gender you are, and how do you know what gender your romantic or sexual partner is?" (*Gender Outlaw*, 1995, p. 56).

Basically, without full genetic testing and ascription, the extent and range of intersex peoples cannot be known. Though, as the history of hermaphrodites makes explicit, the intersex have not suddenly appeared on the planet as a new part of human experience. The intersex have always been around but they have been subsumed, for the most part, into the two traditional gender signifiers of Normative "male" and Normative "female" and thus made virtually and performatively invisible. It is quite possible that those who have felt internally at odds with the gender that they have been ascribed may actually be intersex individuals who have never been allowed their own systemic legitimacy in the first place. In fact, with the existence of the intersex, the male/female female/male transgendered/ transsexual becomes more of a logical impossibility since the individual requires a unitary fence that necessarily only has two sides to cross-over and trans. With the realization of the multiplicity of the intersex, the fences can no longer exist in binary form of either/or. Arguably, the new configuration of material habitats could create an endless chain of fences with each fence representing another Normative intersex space for individuals to cross-over and play with. But as the number of fences increases, as more ethical positions become recognized as materially viable, the greater the challenge to linear systems that privilege male and female gender. Ultimately, the sheer number and variety of different genders opens up the possibility of the "boundary-free" (Queen and Schimel, 1997, p. 23) zone that is central to the quest of pomosexual play.

"I'M ONLY HUMAN, OF FLESH AND BLOOD I'M MADE"[8]

The sociomedical recognition of the intersex brings up other issues related to the materiality of gender. Namely, the physical and medical intervention and alteration of the body, beyond the mutilations that frequently occur at birth (circumcision, genital (re)construction), present larger questions about what is human, let alone male or female. Diprose notes that "biomedical practice can *alter* the texture of the body" (1991, p. 68) and further, that "biomedical manipulation can institute an irreversible change to one's habitat [ethics]" (1991, p. 69). For example, amputees (including breast cancer survivors who have undergone partial or whole mastectomies), cyborgs (those with mechanical or non-human "parts" such as penile inserts, silicon breast implants, robotic limbs), and inter-specials (recipients of non-human organs transplants, or, potentially anyone whose body now incorporates viral anti-bodies), are all products of biomedical manipulation. All of these unique material bodies create new habitats and associated nascent ethics that further challenge and problematize societal limitations with their multiplicity that has *yet* to be subsumed within the tyranny of differential signification. It is only a matter of time, though, before each of these new positions becomes classified and demarcated.

The final question we are left with is whether differential signification is necessarily bad. And the answer, I believe, is a problematic "no." Classification is not necessarily evil and violent, rather it is the systemic valuation that is almost always assigned to it that is bad. Description does not necessarily lead to prescription though it almost always does. If valuation, where the binary like/same is good/Normative and Other/different is bad/non-Normative, could be eradicated and difference could just be accepted as is then there would be no problem. But the binaristic line of valuation does exist and, unfortunately, we will have to wait a little longer till the fictional fairy tale of gender is re-written and "the winds of change blow that line away" (Bornstein, *Gender*, 1995, p. 21) forever.

ACKNOWLEDGMENTS

This paper was revised with the assistance of the Social Science and Humanities Research Council of Canada. I would like to thank Elizabeth Grosz and April Miller for their insightful comments on earlier versions of this paper. Thanks, too, to Kate Bornstein for daring to play in the first place and challenging people, including myself, to think further about the multiplicity of boundaries and possibilities in the world.

NOTES

1. The Police. (1978). "Message in a Bottle."
2. In this paper I am using the term "gender" to refer to both socially constructed roles and to biological "sex" since both labels refer to the socially demarcated, oppositional, and artificial categories of male and female. Arguably, "sex" could be employed to represent both terms instead, but "gender," in its current usage, is more clearly associated with the non-naturalness of the categories than "sex" which is still often positioned in opposition to "gender" as the naturalized and "truthful" base state of material being.
3. I have capitalized "Normative" as part of a writing practice that seeks to render the differential signification process more visible. Traditionally, only the "Other" is marked with a capital letter thus emphasizing "its" difference from the "Normative." The "Norm," since it is seemingly everywhere, is virtually invisible; therefore, I have chosen to mark the "Norm," removing some of its hegemonic privilege and signalling "its" relational dependency on the "Other."
4. King, Carole. (1971). "(You Make Me Feel Like) A Natural Woman."
5. Madonna. (1984). "Material Girl."
6. "Sie" and "hir" are Feinberg's chosen alternatives to "she" and "him." Feinberg calls "sie" and "hir" "gender-neutral pronouns" (1998, p. 1) but I would question how gender neutral they are since they are used as direct replacements for similar sounding gender-specific pronouns.
7. According to Money, the seven intersexes are: "Female Pseudohermaphrodites with Hyperadrenocorticism," "Female Pseudohermaphrodites with Phallus, Normal Ovaries, and Normal Mullerian Structures," "True Hermaphrodites," "Male Pseudohermaphrodites with Well-Differentiated Mullerian Organs," "Stimulant Females with Feminizing Testes," "Cryptorchid Hypospadiac Males with Feminizing Testes," and "Cryptorchid Hypospadiac Males" (1986, pp. 135-136).
8. Human League. (1986). "Human."

REFERENCES

Barbin, H. (1980). *Herculine Barbin: Being the Recently Discovered Memoirs of a Nineteenth-Century French Hermaphrodite.* (Michel Foucault, Intro.). (Richard McDougall, Trans.). New York: Pantheon Books. (Original work written 1868).

Bornstein, K. (2000, October 18). "Talk" (Lecture/Discussion). Rochester: University of Rochester.

Bornstein, K. (1995). *Gender Outlaw: On Men, Women, and the Rest of Us.* New York: Vintage Books. (Original work published 1994).

Bornstein, K. (1993). *Bodies That Matter: On the Discursive Limits of "Sex."* London: Routledge.

Butler, J. (1990). *Gender Trouble: Feminism and the Subversion of Identity.* London: Routledge.

Diprose, R. (1991). A 'Genethics' That Makes Sense. In Rosalyn Diprose and Robyn Ferrell (Eds.), *Cartographies: Poststructuralism and the Mapping of Bodies and Spaces* (pp. 65-76). Sydney: Allen and Unwin.

Fausto-Sterling, A. (1993, March/April). The Five Sexes: Why Male and Female Are Not Enough. *The Sciences*, 33, 20-25.

Feinberg, L. (1998). *Trans Liberation: Beyond Pink or Blue.* Boston: Beacon Press.

Grosz, E. (1996). Intolerable Ambiguity: Freaks as/at the Limit. In Rosemarie Garland Thomson (Ed.), *Freakery: Cultural Spectacles of the Extraordinary Body* (pp. 55-66). New York: New York University Press.

Human League. (1986). Human. *Crash.*

King, C. (1971). (You Make Me Feel Like) A Natural Woman. *Tapestry.*

Madonna. (1984). Material Girl. *Like a Virgin.*

Money, J. (1986). *Venuses Penuses: Sexology, Sexology, and Exigency Theory.* Buffalo: Prometheus Books.

Plato. (1973). Symposium. In Hamilton and Cairns (Eds.), *Plato: The Collected Dialogues* (pp. 526-574). Princeton: Princeton University Press.

Police, The. (1978). Message in a Bottle. *Outlandos D'Amour.*

Queen, C., and L. Schimel (Eds.). (1997). *PoMoSexuals: Challenging Assumptions About Gender and Sexuality.* San Francisco: Cleis Press Inc.

Swing It Baby!

Charlotte Cooper

http://www.haworthpress.com/web/JB
© 2003 by The Haworth Press, Inc. All rights reserved.
Digital Object Identifier: 10.1300/J159v03n03_06

[Haworth co-indexing entry note]: "Swing It Baby!" Cooper, Charlotte. Co-published simultaneously in
Journal of Bisexuality (Harrington Park Press, an imprint of The Haworth Press, Inc.) Vol. 3, No. 3/4, 2003,
pp. 87-92; and: *Bisexuality and Transgenderism: InterSEXions of the Others* (ed: Jonathan Alexander, and
Karen Yescavage) Harrington Park Press, an imprint of The Haworth Press, Inc., 2003, pp. 87-92. Single or
multiple copies of this article are available for a fee from The Haworth Document Delivery Service
[1-800-HAWORTH, 9:00 a.m. - 5:00 p.m. (EST). E-mail address: docdelivery@haworthpress.com].

SUMMARY. This essay argues that swingers who practice bi and trans behaviour are a significant part of the BT population but are often marginalized by traditional LGBT players. It discusses some of the reasons for their exclusion in an attempt to create a more open, flexible, honest and welcoming notion of what it is to be B, T, L or G. *[Article copies available for a fee from The Haworth Document Delivery Service: 1-800-HAWORTH. E-mail address: <docdelivery@haworthpress.com> Website: <http://www.HaworthPress.com>*

KEYWORDS. Contact advertisements, identity, belonging, "real" homosexuality, bisexual, transgendered

For a couple of years I worked part time for an adult contact magazine, first as a packer sending out thousands of things to mail-order clients, and then as a sub-editor. I got to know the readers' submissions and personal advertisements very well and built up quite a picture of the sexual interests of middle England, the readership at whom the magazine was pitched.

Most of the advertisements were placed by couples looking for sex with other couples, groups, and individuals. Certain sets of behaviour recurred in almost every ad. These included: femme drag, high heels, stockings, corsetry worn by men and women; women fucking other women whilst their husbands watch; strap-ons worn by women and used to fuck submissive men or other women; a substantial contingent of transvestites, wannabe maids, assorted masochists and bitchy tops.

I'm not going to go into detail here about the implications of these activities; suffice it to say that drag, dildo-play, multiple partners, underground sex parties, hot girl-on-girl action, the erotic gaze and SM are staples in discourses on transgressive sexuality and transgendered experience. In short: these folks are queering it up with bi and trans behaviour that goes beyond theory and debate. It just is.

Indeed, if I were a writer submitting a paper about the relationship between bisexuality and transgender, I'd say this group occupies a significant spot within that particular Venn diagram. They are a huge population that regularly feeds and plays off bi and trans experience. In addition, this group is hardly marginal in its outlook. These are mainstream people, the backbone of the country, the managers, personnel assistants, retail staff, administrators, teachers, office clerks, civil servants and local government workers living in the Oburbs, satellite towns and provinces.

But what concerns me is that, despite their size and prevalence, this group is hidden and marginalized by LGBT players.

It's not surprising that the big, starchy, lesbian and gay dinosaurs of the scene wouldn't want to include those queers who brought the dignity of homosexual identity into disrepute with their salacious behaviour. Swingers simply do not figure on the radar of the Human Rights Campaign, the National Gay and Lesbian Task Force, or, in Britain, Stonewall. But their exclusion carries on into smaller organizations and groups who are reluctant to take this demographic on board, where swingers are frequently the butt of jokes, where single-gender spaces are the order of the day (try taking your tranny husband to a women-only queer space), and where dykes express horror that a boyfriend might want to watch them get it on.

It must be said that there are Bi and Trans groups that are more open to swingers, possibly out of a necessity for constituents rather than a real embrace of them. Often those swingers who get involved have learnt the language and conventions of the LGBT movement. Rarely does it happen the other way around; in fact, I can't think of a single occasion when LGBT representatives learned the language and conventions of swinger culture. Of course it depends on the context too; you're more likely to encounter swingers at a bi/trans-friendly play party than at a Lesbian Avengers meeting. For many bi and trans people living away from established communities and media, swinger life is the only place you can be.

But despite these interactions, swingers don't really figure highly within the LGBT scene, and here's why I think that is.

Swingers are not considered real LGBT people. They are regarded as heterosexual dilettantes who just want to spice up their sex lives with a bit of homosex. So? The sex is still homo! Many swingers refer to themselves as "bi-curious" which comes with the assumption that being bisexual and not having had a same-sex experience renders that sexual identity as invalid. Similarly, some of my colleagues laughed at the male transvestites in the adverts I worked on because they didn't pass and looked weird and funny. So? You don't have to pass in order to be transgendered, neither do you have to have surgery or take hormones. It is unbelievable that the turf war over who can be queer is being perpetuated, not least by some bi and some trans people who have fought so hard to be included and acknowledged by lesbians and gay men.

Many swingers enact bi and trans behaviour but are unlikely to take on bisexual or transgendered identity. Sometimes this is regarded along the lines of having not "paid one's dues" by those who do identify as LGBT, and used as a reason for ignoring the group. Some swingers consider LGBT people and politics as beneath them, overly "politically correct" or just irrelevant. The LBGT world does not have the monopoly on nonheterosexual, transgendered experience. However, whilst those who enact queer behaviour can't join in if they don't identify in a certain way, the inadequacy of a BT, or LGBT, label is rarely questioned.

In the whole time I worked at the magazine, handling thousands of adverts, maybe about five single gay men and lesbian personal ads passed by my keyboard. Certainly no gay/lesbian couples, triads or groups placed adverts. This leads me to think that lesbian and gay and, by extension, bisexual and transgendered–people don't consider the sexual realm of the swinger as a place where they can pick up some easy trade–a tragedy when one considers how many queers spend their lives suffering sexual loneliness and frustration. It's not that those to the right of the Kinsey scale are unwelcome in swinger circles, but there are good reasons why some LGBT people might not seek membership in those spaces unless they are forced to because of isolation.

Same-sex sex, for want of a better term, is highly exoticized by many swingers. I've noticed that the dyke sex sought by this group is often a fantasy version of it rather than that behaviour which, in my experience, "real dykes" do. Is anyone likely to want to be part of a scene where they constantly have to educate people about what it means to be a dyke? To be transgendered? To be both?

When one group of people are exoticized by another the reverse side of the coin is usually ignorance. Many of the swingers I encountered during my time at the magazine were totally unaware of queer conventions and language. Same-sex sex was the interest, not the wider culture, and the adverts suggested that some swingers were happy to play on stereotypes or believe in wildly outmoded notions of what it is to be queer. For example, the double standard that it is fine for women to fuck each other for male pleasure but that sex between men is somehow demeaning.

Can swingers accept challenges to traditional ideas about gender and sexuality by a new generation of politicized bi and trans people? Does the taboo about men fucking men extend to FtM transsexuals, or intersexed people? Is it acceptable for a bio man to fuck a MtF tranny? And what about those hokey notions concerning sex between women? What if those bi chicks don't want their men to be involved?

Perhaps the main reason that swingers who enact bi, trans and queer behaviour are problematic members of LGBT communities is because sex is their primary focus, and that this is limiting in terms of generating gender and sexual identities that can be politicized. Swinging culture often occurs within a framework that is frequently sexist, and arguably racist, certainly not within the context of liberation politics. Moreover, participants might regard liberation politics as a killjoy and actively discourage support of those perspectives.

Perhaps they don't even need to consider the wider sexual and gendered politics of their experience. It seems that although swingers are isolated from LGBT politics, they are functioning well at the moment and are happy to remain closeted from the rest of society.

It's a real shame that LGBT, and especially the already marginalized BT, people and the global swinging contingent share so much experience but exist in isolation of one another. Here is a chance to embrace a lot of people with common experience, whose position in the mainstream offers other LGBT people a way in to create considerable social change. But if LGBT communities are going to make efforts to reach out to swingers then they must acknowledge that not everybody is going to be hip and have the right kind of politics. And if swingers are going to drag themselves into a new century, attract new participants and survive, they have to recognize and celebrate their queerness. Haven't we all got things to learn from each other? It's corny, but it's true.

Bisexual and Transgender Identities in a Nonclinical Sample of North Americans:

Suicidal Intent, Behavioral Difficulties, and Mental Health Treatment

Robin M. Mathy
Barbara A. Lehmann
Deborah C. Kerr

http://www.haworthpress.com/web/JB
Digital Object Identifier: 10.1300/J159v03n03_07

[Haworth co-indexing entry note]: "Bisexual and Transgender Identities in a Nonclinical Sample of North Americans: Suicidal Intent, Behavioral Difficulties, and Mental Health Treatment." Mathy, Robin M., Barbara A. Lehmann, and Deborah L. Kerr. Co-published simultaneously in *Journal of Bisexuality* (Harrington Park Press, an imprint of The Haworth Press, Inc.) Vol. 3, No. 3/4, 2003, pp. 93-109; and: *Bisexuality and Transgenderism: InterSEXions of the Others* (ed: Jonathan Alexander, and Karen Yescavage) Harrington Park Press, an imprint of The Haworth Press, Inc., 2003, pp. 93-109. Single or multiple copies of this article are available for a fee from The Haworth Document Delivery Service [1-800-HAWORTH, 9:00 a.m. - 5:00 p.m. (EST). E-mail address: docdelivery@haworthpress.com].

SUMMARY. We hypothesized that a higher proportion of bisexual females ($n = 792$) and transgender individuals ($n = 73$) than bisexual males ($n = 1,457$) would self-report suicidal intent, behavioral difficulties, and mental health treatment. Relative to bisexual males, bisexual females and transgender individuals had significantly higher prevalence rates of suicidal intent, mental health difficulties, and mental health services. Prevalence rates among transgender participants did not vary by sexual orientation. The findings suggest that sexism and heterosexism have an interactive effect that compounds the social weight of oppression and increases risks for overwhelming sexual minorities' adaptive functioning. *[Article copies available for a fee from The Haworth Document Delivery Service: 1-800-HAWORTH. E-mail address: <docdelivery@haworthpress.com> Website: <http://www.HaworthPress.com> © 2003 by The Haworth Press, Inc. All rights reserved.]*

KEYWORDS. Transgender, bisexual, suicide, mental health, discrimination

Lesbian, gay, bisexual, and transgender identities are often referred to with the acronyms GLBT or LGBT. These acronyms convey a sense of homogeneity and unity. For many bisexual and transgender members of this ostensibly unified, homogeneous group, the consistent placement of the letters B and T at the end of the acronyms belies their relatively low salience and the marginalized status they are afforded relative to gays and lesbians. Clinically as well as statistically significant differences among bisexuals, gays, lesbians, and transgender individuals may require reconsideration of the 'GLBT' acronym–at least in research concerning sexual orientation and mental health, including suicide ideations and attempts.

To date, most researchers conducting research on the topic of sexual orientation and suicidal intent (ideations and attempts) have combined gay, lesbian, and bisexual participants into an aggregate group (McDaniel, Purcell, & D'Augelli, 2001). Sometimes, in fact, sexual minorities of both sexes have been grouped together. Some researchers have compressed questioning youth into this aggregate group. Aggregating these disparate groups may have seriously confounded research concerning sexual orientation and suicidal intent. The possibility of confounded samples is suggested the varying weights of social oppression related to gender, sexual orientation, or both (Mathy, 2001, 2002a). Like lesbians, transgender individuals must cope with both sexism and heterosexism (cf. Herek, 1990). Gay males and heterosexual women must cope with either heterosexism or sexism, respectively. Only heterosexual males escape sexist and heterosexist forms of oppression, with the notable exception of effeminate heterosexual males, because they are prone to being misperceived as gay or transgender.

Mathy (2001, 2002a) found that the proportion of transgender individuals who have had mental health difficulties is significantly greater than both heterosexuals and gay males, but not lesbians. Unfortunately, Mathy's work neglected to consider the possibility that the proportion of transgender individuals with mental health difficulties is significantly greater than that of bisexual males but not bisexual females. To complement the gay, lesbian, and heterosexual data and correct the oversight endemic to excluding bisexuals, we reexamined Mathy's hypothesis by comparing transgender individuals to bisexual females and males. We examined their self-reported histories of (a) suicide ideations and attempts, (b) difficulties excessively using alcohol, drugs, and sex, and (c) their prior and current treatment with psychotherapy and psychiatric medications.

Although researchers studying sexual orientation and suicidal intent often use variations on the GLBT acronym, the T is usually neglected altogether. Few researchers studying sexual minorities have examined suicidal intent and transgender identity per se (Mathy, 2001). There are important reasons to question whether there are differences in the constituent groups included in the GLBT aggregate. Diversity between each constituency of the gay, lesbian, bisexual, and transgender groups is at least as great as that between heterosexuals and each of the other sexual minority identities. In fact, to date, no study has evaluated risks of suicidal intent among bisexuals relative to transgender individuals. This is unfortunate, in part, because some recent research (Jorm, Korten, Rodgers, Jacomb, & Christensen, 2002; Robin, Brener, Donahue, Hack, Hale, & Goodenow, 2002) suggests that risks of suicidal intent among bisexuals are higher than among gay males and lesbians as well as heterosexuals. Using data from a longitudinal study being conducted in Canberra, Australia, Jorm et al. (2002) reported that bisexuals had worse mental health than both heterosexuals and gays and lesbians. Gays and lesbians had scores intermediate between bisexuals and heterosexuals. Robin et al. (2002) found differences in suicidal intent by sexual orientation (as measured by exclusively and eclectically same-sex sexual behaviors) when they reexamined cross-sectional data from four large representative, population-based high school surveys (N between 3,982 and 8,636 in each) conducted in 1995 and 1997 in Massachusetts and Vermont. They reported that the prevalence of suicide attempts was significantly higher among students who indicated that they had engaged in sexual behaviors with both female and male partners rather than one or the other.

Grossman, D'Augelli, and O'Connell (2001) did not find a difference in suicidality by bisexual and lesbian or gay sexual orientation among participants aged 60 to 91 years ($N = 416$). These authors evaluated self-administered surveys collected from a national sample of 416 sexual minorities aged 60 to 91 years. Participants were drawn from social, recreational, and support groups. Bisexuals did not differ from heterosexuals *vis-à-vis* gays and lesbians on measures of mental health, self-esteem, loneliness, suicidality, or problems associated with alcohol or drug use. Using a convenience sample drawn from community-based social and recreational groups, Hershberger, Pilkington, and D'Augelli (1997) found that bisexual-identified participants aged 14 to 21 years ($N = 194$) were more than 5 times more likely than heterosexuals as well as gays and lesbians to report that they had attempted suicide more than once. However, D'Augelli and colleagues did not report a similar finding 5 years later despite a sample collected from similar sources by the same authors (D'Augelli, 2002), with a larger sample ($N = 542$) of participants who were also aged 14 to 21 years.

Moreover, there is *prima facie* evidence to suggest that creating aggregate groups of gay males and lesbians or bisexual females and males is problematic. There is a plethora of rigorous research on suicidal intent that shows risks of suicide attempts and ideations as well as completions vary by sex. Although rates of suicide completions are higher among males than females everywhere except China (Eisenberg, Desjarlais, & Good, 1995), suicide attempts are more prevalent among females than males in the U.S. (Mościcki, 1994). Data from the nationally representative National Comorbidity Survey conducted between 1990 and 1992 ($N = 5,877$, aged 15-54 years) found that the lifetime odds of a suicide attempt were 2.2 times greater among females than males, even after controlling for other potentially confounding, covarying variables (Kessler, Borges, & Walters, 1999). Using similar statistical controls, the study also found that the odds of suicide ideations were 1.7 times greater among females than males. Another population-based study (Weissmann et al., 1999) reported that the odds of lifetime prevalence of suicide attempts among females were more than 3 times greater than males, and the odds of suicide ideations among females were 1.5 times higher than those of males. This suggests that studies of sexual orientation and suicidal intent that have combined females and males into an aggregate group may have inadvertently confounded their data. In fact, it appears that a substantial number of peer-reviewed studies on this topic (McDaniel et al., 2001) have done so.

This is the first study of sexual orientation and suicidal intent to compare bisexual females and males to transgender individuals. The biological sex of the self-identified transgender participants is unknown and probably unknowable (Mathy, 2001, 2002a). The development of a priori hypotheses was limited by the paucity of preexisting data. Theoretically, however, the assignment of bisexuals (as well as transgender individuals) to the end of the GLBT or LGBT community's acronym symbolically represents a somewhat devalued, "add-on" identity (Weinberg, Williams, & Pryor, 1995). As Weinberg et al. noted, self-identified bisexuals are often treated with suspicion by gays and lesbians as well as with contempt by heterosexuals. Garber (1996) dispels the myth that bisexuality is a developmental phase in the process of becoming a self-identified gay or lesbian. Instead, bisexuality is a sustainable identity that generally has been unsupported by either mainstream heterosexual or gay and lesbian cultures. Recent research has shown considerable fluidity in self-identification of sexual orientation among females during early adulthood (Diamond, 1998, 2000), even as same-sex attractions persisted among participants who subsequently identified as heterosexual (Diamond, 2003).

To examine risks among self-identified bisexual females and males relative to transgender individuals, we conducted a secondary analysis of a community-based sample collected in June 2000 via the Internet Website of an international news organization (Cooper, Scherer, & Mathy, 2001). That study was designed to study human sexuality, including online sexual behaviors. Altogether, the study collected data on 76 items from 40,935 participants. The present study examined suicide ideations and attempts, behavioral control difficulties, and current or previous mental health treatment. Following Mathy (2001, 2002a), we tested the null hypotheses that there are no differences between (a) bisexual females or males when compared to (b) transgender individuals. Following the work of Cochran and Mays (2001) concerning the relation between stress-related disorders and sexual minority status, Mathy hypothesized that the combined effects of heterosexism and sexism are greater than either form of oppression alone. Transgender individuals and bisexual females are both subjected to sexism and heterosexism, and bisexual males are subjected to heterosexism but far less sexism. Therefore, as with Mathy's findings that transgender individuals had higher prevalence rates of suicidal intent and mental health difficulties than heterosexuals and gay males but not lesbian females, we would expect that transgender individuals have higher risks of mental health problems, including suicide ideation and attempts, than bisexual males but not bisexual females.

METHODS

Data Analysis Strategy

Secondary data analyses were conducted of a large dataset ($N = 40,935$) used in six prior peer-reviewed papers addressing Internet research methods

(Cooper, Scherer et al., 2001), online sexual activities (Cooper, Griffin-Shelley, Delmonico, & Mathy, 2001; Cooper, Morahan-Martin, Mathy, & Maheu, 2002), sexual orientation and suicidal intent cross-culturally (Mathy, 2002b), transgender identity and suicidal intent (Mathy, 2002a), and transgender identity and stress-related disorders (Mathy, 2001). All analyses reported here are unique to the present study and have not been published previously. We used the same 73 transgender participants as did Mathy (2001, 2002a) to address the neglected comparison between these individuals and bisexuals. The study was approved by the Institutional Review Board at the University of Minnesota–Twin Cities, at which the first author had an affiliation at the time data analyses were conducted.

Two subsamples were collected in June 2000. They included a convenience sample, with which to oversample sexual minorities, and a selected random sample to ensure heterogeneity among participants. For the present study, we examined data from all self-identified transgender and bisexual participants, regardless of subsample, in order to increase the statistical power of our analyses. The null hypothesis of between-group equality was rejected if $p < .05$. We did not assume equality of variances when conducting independent sample t-tests of the null hypothesis.

Participants

A community-based sample of 40,935 Internet users was obtained via the Website of a major (anonymous) news organization between June 1 and June 30, 2000. The specific sampling design has been well articulated elsewhere (Cooper, Scherer et al., 2001). Briefly, every 1,000th visitor to the news organization's Website was invited to participate in a study of human sexuality. Using this selected random sampling design, we obtained 7,544 participants. A convenience sample was collected simultaneously, via an Internet link imbedded in the news organization's Health Information section. The convenience sample was advertised by other news media and word of mouth. We obtained 33,391 participants in the convenience sample.

Initially, these two samples were drawn simultaneously to evaluate the hypothesis that implementation of rigorous research methods could effectively eliminate unreliable cases when research is conducted via the Internet. The hypothesis was supported by the data, with the exception of questions directly related to online sexual behaviors (i.e., sampling on the dependent variable), as we had predicted. No Internet usage questions appear in the present study. The 76-item survey instrument administered via the Website included 10 items (13.16% of total) specifically designed to lead to a priori exclusion from the study. Three subscales consisting of two sets of four items each as well as two other items were randomly distributed throughout the questionnaire. The subscales assessed participants' predispositions to narcissism and neuroticism (i.e., overly positive or overly critical self-evaluations). Participants who made affirmative responses to all four items on either scale were eliminated from the study. Cronbach's alpha for the scales were 0.34 for narcissism and 0.37 for neuroticism. Two items designed to identify misrepresentation or carelessness were also randomly distributed. These items included, "I have spent more than 5,000 hours engaged in online sexual activity this year" and, "I have spent more than 8,000 hours engaged in online sexual activity this year." These are equivalent to 13.7 and 22 hours per day online, every day. Participants who responded affirmatively to either of these items were eliminated from the study.

Several post hoc criteria were used to further increase reliability. Although there was a normal attenuation in frequency of participants until age 80 years, there was a suspicious increase in frequency among participants aged 81 and older. Therefore, we eliminated from the data any participant who gave an age older than 80. Post-hoc data analyses also revealed a statistically significant difference between participants who failed to answer more than two questions *vis-à-vis* those who left only one or two items unanswered. Therefore, we eliminated participants with more than two items unanswered. A total of 6.5% of the convenience sample and 6.8% of the selected random sample was eliminated. The between-sample difference in percentage of cases eliminated was not statistically significant. Elimination of these cases and combining the samples resulted in a total $N = 38,204$ (94.6% of original combined samples). The selected random sample included 5,925 males and 1,112 females. The convenience sample included 25,306 males and 5,776 females. Self-identified transgender participants ($n = 14$ in selected random sample; $n = 70$ in convenience sample) were included. Comparisons of transgender participants to gays, lesbians, heterosexual females and males, and psychosocially matched females and males can be found elsewhere in the peer-reviewed literature (Mathy, 2001, 2002a). Due to the complexity of analyzing a multinational sample as well as the administration of the survey only in English, participants from countries other than the U.S. and Canada were not included in these analyses.

The total sample included 2,322 participants, consisting of 1,457 bisexual males (62.7%), 792 bisexual females (34.1%), and 73 transgender individuals (3.1%). On average, bisexual males were aged 36.22 years ($SD = 11.82$), bisexual females had a mean age of 29.53 years ($SD = 8.85$), and transgender participants had an average age of 36.88 years ($SD = 9.96$). Analysis of variance revealed that bisexual females were significantly younger than transgender participants (6.68 years, SE 4.78) and bisexual males (7.34, SE 1.33), F (2,

2319) = 100.35, $p < .001$. Sexual minority females often experience multiple stages of the coming out process simultaneously during middle adulthood (Diamond, 2003). Thus, the age differences in the sample are consistent with existing literature regarding ages of bisexual females and males.

Instrument

The survey contained 76 items. A total of 17 questions were added to a previous survey administered by the same (anonymous) international news organization (Cooper, Scherer, Boies, & Gordon, 1999). The survey has been appended *en toto* in a prior peer-reviewed publication (Cooper, Morahan-Martin et al., 2002). As in the study from which the survey was adapted, age was a continuous variable: "My age is: ___." Four new questions queried participants about their history of suicidal intent and prior mental health treatment. These included (a) "In the past, I have been on medications for a psychiatric condition," (b) "In the past, I have been in psychotherapy," (c) "I am currently on medications for a psychiatric condition," and (d) "I am currently in psychotherapy." Response categories included "Yes" and "No." Suicidal intent (ideations and attempts) was assessed with two questions, including (a) "I have had serious thoughts of suicide," and (b) "I have made a serious suicide attempt or gesture." Response categories included "Yes" and "No." Previous history of behavioral difficulties was assessed with several categorical responses to the following item: "In the past, I have excessively used or had difficulties controlling (check all that apply)," with response categories including alcohol, drugs, gambling, food, sex, work, and shopping or spending money. Current history of behavioral difficulties was evaluated with the following item: "At present I PRIMARILY have difficulties with:" Response categories were identical to those in past behavioral difficulties. Prior behavioral difficulties assessed items likely to be included as part of a comprehensive mental assessment. Current primary behavioral difficulties are important because they may cause or contribute to the reasons for seeking treatment. Items evaluating mental health treatment were included at the beginning of the survey. Items assessing behavioral difficulties were included at the end of the survey.

Procedure

Participation was voluntary. Prior to beginning the survey, participants were asked to give their informed consent and acknowledge that they were aged 18 years or older. Institutional Review Board approval for the study was granted by the Pacific Graduate School of Psychology, with which one of the

Co-Principal Investigators had an affiliation. The University of Minnesota–Twin Cities, with which another Co-Principal Investigator has an affiliation, subsequently approved the secondary analyses reported here. Agreement to participate in the study and acknowledgment of majority age status were required to gain access to the questionnaire. The news organization's systems analysts enabled a program that proffered an invitation to participate in the selected random sample at each 1,000th unique visitor to the Website. The overall response rate in the selected random sample was 25% without replacement and 75% with replacement, a percentage comparable to random digit dialing (Cooper, Scherer et al., 2001). Global User Identification Numbers (GUIDs) and electronic cookies ensured mutually exclusive participation in either the selected random sample or the convenience sample. Only participants using browsers set to accept electronic cookies could respond to the survey. The GUID assigned a unique number that maintains anonymity while tracking username, Internet Service Provider, and computer.

The final sample was not representative of all users of the Website in June 2000. The results cannot be generalized to all Internet users. Although a national sample, it is not representative of the U.S. population. However, the sampling design enabled us to gather a large and heterogeneous, community-based sample of sexual minorities from a nonclinical source entirely independent of formal or informal gay, lesbian, bisexual, or transgender-related organizations and institutional infrastructures. It did not rely upon knowing any other gay, lesbian, bisexual, or transgender person (as in snowball methods), membership in any organization (as in social or recreational activities), or potentially confounding educational structures (as in university support groups). Although neither probabilistic nor representative, the sampling method attempted to address key criticisms concerning prior research about sexual orientation and suicidal intent (Muehrer, 1995; McDaniel et al., 2001).

RESULTS

Suicidal Intent

We show results of our analyses of variance in Table 1. The associations between bisexual gender and transgender status and suicidal intent were statistically significant. Additional post hoc analyses with Dunnett's C revealed that suicide ideations were significantly more prevalent among bisexual females and transgender individuals than among bisexual males. Furthermore, analyses indicated a history of suicide attempts were significantly more common among bisexual females and transgender individuals than among bisexual males.

TABLE 1. Analyses of Variance for Suicidality, Behavioral Problems, and Mental Health Intervention (Proportion of Yes Responses, M and SD) by Bisexual Gender and Transgender Status

| | Bisexual Male | | Bisexual Female | | Transgender | | |
| | N = 1457 | | N = 792 | | N = 73 | | |
Suicidality	M	SD	M	SD	M	SD	F (2,2320)
Ideation	.23	.41	.36	.48	.37	.49	26.484***
Attempt	.07	.26	.17	.38	.23	.43	32.831***
Past Behavioral Problems							
Alcohol	.21	.41	.20	.40	.32	.47	2.492
Drugs	.14	.35	.17	.38	.14	.34	2.020
Sex	.23	.42	.19	.40	.15	.36	3.456*
Treatment History							
Psych Medication	.16	.38	.27	.44	.32	.47	21.136***
Psychotherapy	.22	.42	.36	.48	.53	.50	38.042***
Current Treatment							
Psych Medication	.08	.27	.12	.33	.22	.42	12.177***
Psychotherapy	.05	.21	.09	.28	.18	.39	14.107***

Notes. *P < .05; **P < .01; ***P < .001

Psychiatric Treatment

Analyses also indicated that a significantly greater proportion of transgender individuals and bisexual females than bisexual males reported prior and current psychotherapy as well as prior and current usage of psychiatric medications. Post-hoc analyses using Dunnett's C indicated that transgender individuals and bisexual females were significantly more likely than bisexual males to report that they had been in psychotherapy previously. Transgender individuals and bisexual females were significantly more likely than bisexual males to state that they had previously received treatment with medications for a psychiatric condition. The transgender individuals and bisexual females were significantly more likely than bisexual males to report that they were being treated with medications for a psychiatric condition at the time of the study. Finally, our results indicated that transgender individuals and bisexual females were significantly more likely than bisexual males to be receiving psychotherapy at the time of the study.

Past Behavioral Difficulties

Analyses of variance indicated an association between being a self-identified bisexual female or a transgender individual and self-reported prior difficulties with sex ($p = .032$), but these data were not statistically significant following post hoc analysis using Dunnett's C. Other behavioral difficulties did not differentiate the three groups.

DISCUSSION

The present study is the first to examine differences between bisexuals and transgender individuals. Transgender individuals were found to have higher risks of mental health problems, including suicide ideation and attempts, than bisexual males. However, transgender participants and bisexual females did not differ significantly in their mental health profiles. The findings suggest that sexism and heterosexism have an interactive effect that compounds the social weight of oppression and increases risks for overwhelming sexual minorities' adaptive functioning.

This study complements earlier research (Mathy, 2001, 2002a), which did not address the possibility that the proportion of transgender individuals with mental health difficulties may be significantly greater than bisexual males but not bisexual females. Specifically, this study addressed the previous deficiency by reexamining Mathy's data in relation to transgender and bisexual individuals, to examine possible associations with suicide ideations and attempts, difficulties excessively using alcohol, drugs, and sex, as well as prior and current treatment with psychotherapy and psychiatric medications.

A previous examination of transgender identity and suicidal intent (Mathy, 2002a) revealed a significant relation between transgender identity and suicide ideations and attempts. The study also argued that transgender individuals are subject to both sexism and heterosexism leading to significantly greater amounts of social oppression than heterosexual females and gay males. Mathy's hypothesis logically would extend to bisexual females, as well, a suggestion that has been supported with the analyses present here. Logically, if transgender individuals and bisexual females are subject to both sexism and heterosexism, and bisexual males are subject primarily to heterosexism but not sexism, one would expect to find, as we did, that transgender individuals have higher risks of mental health difficulties than bisexual males but not bisexual females.

A strong relation between bisexual gender and transgender status was revealed by our reexamination. Suicide ideations and suicide attempts were significantly more prevalent among bisexual females and transgender individuals than among bisexual males. A greater proportion of transgender individuals and bisexual females than bisexual males reported (a) prior and current psychotherapy and (b) prior and current use of psychiatric medications. Reexamination of the original data did not yield a significant association between sexual orientation or gender group and either drug or alcohol problems. However, we did see a trend towards an association when dealing with prior difficulties with sexual behaviors.

As suggested by the "GLBT" acronym, sexual minorities are often perceived to be a homogeneous group. These findings once again elucidate the importance of not aggregating these disparate groups, as researchers often have done previously. This study suggests that sexism and heterosexism may have an iterative effect that could, in fact, increase risks for both suicidal intent and mental health conditions among transgender individuals and bisexual females in contemporary North American society. We would argue that greater recognition of the diversity between and within each constituency of the gay, lesbian, bisexual, and transgender groups (GLBT) is at least as great as that between heterosexuals and each of the other sexual minority identities. Put somewhat more directly, researchers and not "GLBT" constituents are the "others," and the attempts to compress all nonheterosexuals into a composite category for comparison to heterosexuals effectively obscures the diversity that rigorous research seeks to reveal.

In sum, it is clear that the suicidal intent and mental health of bisexual females and transsexual individuals cannot be properly addressed within the aggregate group of "GLBT" individuals. Bisexual females and transgender individuals appear to have unique mental health needs and risks that surpass those of gay males and heterosexual females. Their needs and risks may reflect the sequelae of rejection and isolation from the heterosexual community and something akin to an inadvertent second-class status within the "GLBT" community. Further research is needed to test the sociological and psychological dimensions of mental health and resilience among bisexuals. It is important for researchers to study self-identification as well as sexual behavior across the lifespan in order to determine risks of suicide and sexual orientation at different life stages. Theoretically, substantial same-sex as well as other-sex attractions provide bisexuals and transgender individuals with perceived choices in living a heterosexual lifestyle. This apparent choice in lifestyles, despite substantial same-sex and other-sex attractions, may structure a different set of risks and protections that are unique to bisexual identity formation and maintenance at different ages.

The present study had a number of limitations. First, it relied upon retrospective self-report, which may be subject to recall and response biases. Second, the study was cross-sectional, making it impossible to assess any causal relations in the data. For example, it would be important for future studies to determine whether mental health treatment mediated prior difficulties with alcohol or drugs before or after the behavioral difficulties began. Third, the data were collected via the Internet Website of an international news organization. This has advantages and possible disadvantages. One possible disadvantage is the underrepresentation of economically disadvantaged individuals, of whom a disproportionately large number are ethnically diverse. However, this potential deficit can be compensated for by oversampling from economically disadvantaged and ethnically diverse groups. Administration of surveys via computing technology obviates the need for intrusive interviews or expensive paper-and-pencil methods. However, the ultimate reliability of the Internet as a research tool remains unknown. Notwithstanding the rigor with which these data were gathered, further research is needed to rigorously determine whether individuals who answer surveys online differ significantly from those who participate in offline research. Contemporary research suggests that Internet samples gathered with carefully designed methods can yield samples that are just as robust as those obtained by professional polling organizations (Mathy, Schillace, Coleman, & Berquist, 2002). With appropriate methodological controls, research rigor and reliability can be significantly increased, reducing the chances that unreliable participants will be included in one's data (Cooper, Scherer et al., 2001; Mathy et al., 2002). The use of the Internet as a sampling tool is, in any case, far superior to the conventional snowball sampling method often used to obtain samples of sexual minorities. Snowball methods require at least some interaction, increasing the possibility for researcher and participant biases to confound the data. Administration of surveys via the Internet obviates the need for sexual minority participants to have had some connection with GLBT community-based agencies or social or recreational venues that could potentially influence their responses.

·As evidenced by the evolution in random digit dialing over the past half century, the technology used to administer surveys is less important than the rigor with which researchers create new ways to reach a heterogeneous and unbiased sample of participants whose responses cannot influence those of others. Obtaining a truly random sample of bisexuals and transgender individuals is impossible precisely because the stigma and oppression of sexual minorities limits self-disclosure, thereby making the population parameters of nonheterosexuals unknown. The methodology we used to gather the data for the present study obtained a very large, international sample ($N = 40,395$) by seeding the survey in the Website of a professional news organization. Although this is a relatively unbiased source, participants may have been more aware of public events than the general population. Nonetheless, further research is needed to determine whether large, unbiased samples of sexual minorities can be reliably obtained via the methods used in the present study. Thus far, prior research by the author and others engaged in the development of this technology for use as a research tool has suggested the data are valid and reliable (Cooper, Scherer, et al., 2001; Mathy et al., 2002), provided that methodologists employ the same research rigor, with the same attention to creating control and comparison groups, as scientists do when creating various experimental protocols (e.g., randomized control trials), random digit dialing, case-control studies, and other offline research methods.

As the Internet becomes increasingly integrated into the everyday life of North American culture, its use may become an even more valuable tool for conducting research with sexual minorities and members of other hard-to-reach groups who have been traditionally underrepresented. To be sure, many of the studies of sexual orientation and suicidal intent published to date have combined bisexuals with gays and lesbians because they found too few sexual minorities (even in large, population-based samples) to generate sufficient statistical power to conduct hypothesis testing with discrete sexual minority subgroups. Nor has research been published until recently (e.g., Jorm et al. 2002) that suggested there may be a clinically and methodologically important reason for doing so. The present study aimed to make a small but meaningful contribution to the research concerning bisexuals and transgender individuals, using a sampling methodology designed specifically to obtain data from difficult-to-reach and underrepresented populations (Mathy et al., 2002). Although the sampling design is suboptimal relative to nationally representative, random sampling, it has enabled us to empirically substantiate that bisexual females are more similar to transgender individuals than to bisexual males. Like transgender individuals and unlike bisexual males, bisexual females must cope with both heterosexism and sexism. As a possible consequence of the dual effects of heterosexism and sexism, transgender individuals and bisexual females have higher risks of mental health problems, including suicide ideation and attempts, than bisexual males. Future research may improve our understanding of between-group differences among discrete identities included in the "GLBT" acronym as well as those between heterosexuals and sexual minorities.

ACKNOWLEDGMENTS

The authors express gratitude to Susan Cochran, Tony D'Augelli, Vickie Mays, and Michael Maratsos for comments regarding earlier drafts of this paper. Marc Schillace provided helpful research assistance. This work was supported, in part, by an NIMH Supplemental Grant for an Individual with a Disability and an NIA Predoctoral Fellowship to the first author, and a grant from the American Foundation for Addiction Research.

REFERENCES

Cooper, A., Griffin-Shelley, E., Delmonico, D. L., & Mathy, R. M. (2001). Online sexual problems: Assessment and predictive variables. *Sexual Addiction & Compulsivity, 8*(3/4), 267-285.

Cooper, A., Morahan-Martin, J., Mathy, R. M., & Maheu, M. (2002). Toward an increased understanding of user demographics in online sexual activities. *Journal of Sex & Marital Therapy, 28,* 105-129.

Cooper, A., Scherer, C. R., Boies, S. C., & Gordon, B. L. (1999). Sexuality on the Internet: From sexual exploration to pathological expression. *Professional Psychology: Research & Practice, 30*(2), 154-164.

Cooper, A., Scherer, C., & Mathy, R. M. (2001). Overcoming methodological concerns in the investigation of online sexual activities. *CyberPsychology & Behavior, 4*(4), 437-447.

D'Augelli (2002). Mental health problems among lesbian, gay, and bisexual youths ages 14-21. *Clinical Child Psychology and Psychiatry, 7*(3), 433-456.

Desjarlais, R., Eisenberg, L., Good, B., & Kleinman, A. (1995). *World mental health: Problems and priorities in low-income countries.* New York: Oxford University Press.

Diamond, L. M. (1998). Development of sexual orientation among adolescent and young adult women. *Developmental Psychology, 34*(5), 1085-1095.

Diamond, L. M. (2000). Sexual identity, attractions, and behavior among young sexual-minority women over a 2-year period. *Developmental Psychology, 36*(2), 241-250.

Diamond, Lisa M. (2003). Was it a phase? Young women's relinquishment of lesbian/bisexual identities over a 5-year period. *Journal of Personality & Social Psychology, 84*(2), 352-364.

Garber, M. B. (1995). *Vice Versa: Bisexuality and the eroticism of everyday life.* New York: Simon & Schuster.

Grossman, H. G., D'Augelli, A. R., & O'Connell, T. S. (2001). Being lesbian, gay, bisexual, and 60 or older in North America. *Journal of Gay & Lesbian Social Services, 13*(4), 23-40.

Herek, G. M. (1990). Notes on cultural and psychological heterosexism. *Journal of Interpersonal Violence, 5*(3), 316-333.

Hershberger, S. L., Pilkington, N. W., & D'Augelli, A. R. (1997). Predictors of suicide attempts among gay, lesbian, and bisexual youth. *Journal of Adolescent Research, 12,* 477-497.

Jorm, A. F., Korten, A. E., Rodgers, B., Jacomb, P. A., & Christensen, H. (2002). Sexual orientation and mental health: Results from a community survey of young and middle-aged adults. *British Journal of Psychiatry, 180*, 423-427.

Kessler, R. C., Borges, G., & Walters, E. E. (1999). Prevalence of and risk factors for lifetime suicide attempts in the National Comorbidity Survey. *Archives of General Psychiatry, 56*(7), 617-626.

Mathy, R. M. (2001). A nonclinical comparison of transgender identity and sexual orientation: A framework for multicultural competence. *Journal of Psychology & Human Sexuality, 13*(1), 31-54.

Mathy, R. M. (2002a). Transgender identity and suicidality in a nonclinical sample: Sexual orientation, psychiatric history, and compulsive behaviors. *Journal of Psychology & Human Sexuality, 14*(4).

McDaniel, J. S., Purcell, D., & D'Augelli, A. R. (2001). The relationship between sexual orientation and risk for suicide: Research findings and future directions for research and prevention. *Suicide and Life-Threatening Behavior, 31*(Suppl.), 84-105.

Mathy, R. M. (2002b). Suicidality and sexual orientation in five continents: Asia, Australia, Europe, North America, and South America. *International Journal of Sexuality and Gender Studies, 7*(2-3), 215-225.

Mathy, R. M., Schillace, M., Coleman, S. M., & Berquist, B. E. (2002). Methodological rigor with internet samples: New ways to reach underrepresented populations. *CyberPsychology & Behavior, 5*(3), 253-266.

Mościcki, E. K. (1994). Gender differences in completed and attempted suicides. *Annals of Epidemiology, 4*, 152-158.

Muehrer, P. (1995). Suicide and sexual orientation: A critical summary of recent research and directions for future research. *Suicide & Life-Threatening Behavior, 25*(Suppl.), 72-81.

Robin, L., Brener, N. D., Donahue, S. F., Hack, T., Hale, K., & Goodenow, C. (2002). Associations between health risk behaviors and opposite-, same-, and both-sex sexual partners in representative samples of Vermont and Massachusetts high school students. *Archives of Pediatrics & Adolescent Medicine, 156*, 349-355.

Weinberg, M. S., Williams, C. J., & Pryor, D. W. (1994). *Dual attraction: Understanding bisexuality.* New York: Oxford University Press.

Weissman, M. M., Bland, R. C., Canino, G. J., Greenwald, S., Hwu, H.-G., Joyce, P. R., Karam, E. G., Lee, C.-K., Lellouch, J., Lepine, J.-P., Newman, S. C., Rubio-Stiped, M., Wells, J. E., Wickramaratne, P. J., Wittchen, H.-U., & Yeh, E.-K. Prevalence of suicide ideation and suicide attempts in nine countries. *Psychological Medicine, 29*, 9-17.

REAL(IZING) LIVES: PERSONAL AND THEORETICAL B/T IDENTITY FORMATIONS

The Story So Far

Thaniel Chase

http://www.haworthpress.com/web/JB
Digital Object Identifier: 10.1300/J159v03n03_08

[Haworth co-indexing entry note]: "The Story So Far." Chase, Thaniel. Co-published simultaneously in *Journal of Bisexuality* (Harrington Park Press, an imprint of The Haworth Press, Inc.) Vol. 3, No. 3/4, 2003, pp. 111-116; and: *Bisexuality and Transgenderism: InterSEXions of the Others* (ed: Jonathan Alexander, and Karen Yescavage) Harrington Park Press, an imprint of The Haworth Press, Inc., 2003, pp. 111-116. Single or multiple copies of this article are available for a fee from The Haworth Document Delivery Service [1-800-HAWORTH, 9:00 a.m. - 5:00 p.m. (EST). E-mail address: docdelivery@haworthpress.com].

SUMMARY. In "The Story So Far" I discuss my evolving gender and sexual identity as an FTM transsexual pansexual Leatherman. From feeling isolated as a youngster, to moving through various Queer communities, to being a member of the SM community, I explore my maleness and create my own definitions within my changeable nature. *[Article copies available for a fee from The Haworth Document Delivery Service: 1-800-HAWORTH. E-mail address: <docdelivery@haworthpress.com> Website: <http://www.HaworthPress. com> © 2003 by The Haworth Press, Inc. All rights reserved.]*

KEYWORDS. FTM (female-to-male transsexual), Leatherman, queer, SM, sadomasochism, daddy, transsexual

Daddy, boy, man, Leatherman: all aspects of one socially-defined gender and/or sexual orientation, and all concepts that many would say they understood. But these concepts, being born in the human mind and manifested in human behavior, must necessarily be malleable, no matter how desperately some try to pin them down. If ever I doubt that people change, and our ideas manifest in wildly varying ways, despite our conscious plans, I need only consider my own sexuality. I don't see it as *constructed* so much as *unfolding*: full of lurching advances, plateaus, and pauses to catch my breath. I may think I've figured it all out but other elements always seem to reveal themselves. This part of my nature has developed and changed along with the rest of me. (For all I know I'm not done yet.) This long tweaking process has been one of the few constants in my life.

I can't imagine coming to any understanding of my maleness without having learned about my sexuality as an integral part of it. I see my sexuality as a drive and my gender as an expression of it. I don't know who I would be, as a man and an adult, if my sexual nature were different. And I favor field-tested data, not speculation: the raw undeniable facts of whom and how I desire has made me comprehensible to myself in a way theory never could.

I was born female, in 1957, but for many years I had no real sense of my gender. I've heard many FTMs say they always knew they were really boys. Not me. I didn't feel female *or* male. I was just me. My childhood survival as a gender dissident was predicated on my perception of myself as *singular:* apart from everyone, different from other children. I was a bookworm in a working-class town. I was too loud and too physical for the girls, and too kind for the boys. Being an only child made it even easier to feel separate, and to escape. An active imagination helped me escape from the real world into realms where I didn't have to pay the (increasingly high) social price for being just me. In these realms my heroes–and friends–were people like Mr. Spock (the patron saint of all smart misfit kids). I read voraciously. I drew and played pretend-games and told myself stories. I was singular in my stories, too. But people liked me for it there.

However, in the real world, I didn't understand why or how I was supposed to change, because I didn't know what I was doing wrong. (I didn't think I *was* doing anything wrong.) All I knew was that my errors were, apparently, far too grievous to discuss, because nobody ever addressed them directly. When my parents dealt with my nature at all, it was with emotional blackmail, guilt-trips, the implication that I was sick, and thinly veiled threats. So my singularity became isolation, cultivated in various ways by all parties: myself *and* the people around me. I just couldn't accept conformity as the price for community, so I was cut from the herd as much as I withdrew from it. I suffered for it, and from it, but I tried to make a virtue of necessity. Fine, I thought. I don't need you either.

This was a useful delusion for quite a while. Then my teenage libido woke up screaming. My underdeveloped social skills, along with the lesson forced on me along the way–that nobody really wanted to be around me anyway–made my separateness truly painful. Suddenly I needed other people, but since I wasn't quite sure for what, I had no idea how to go about it.

I tried being a lesbian, thinking that perhaps I was that kind of outsider. That seemed to help for a while. I knew something about it had some relevance. But there were hints that I didn't belong there, either. Lesbians usually thought I was "weird." This was in the mid-70s, with Lesbian-feminist politics in full flower. I'd put on overalls, trying to do that mid-70s Amazon drag, but my inner queen would always seep out: a satin shirt here, a strand of rhinestones there . . . Oops. I just didn't get why they had to be so *serious*. I thought it was supposed to be exuberant. I was too much of a disco baby to be so glum. I'd go dancing and hang out with the queens.

When I was a baby Queer in the bars, it was the queens who were the most exciting and vibrant people, and the funniest. In many ways I was raised by the wonderful Old Guard queens I found there in the bars. I loved their strength, flamboyance, and wit. They were the keepers of the tribal lore. They knew a misfit when they saw one, and they made a place for me, in ways the women's community didn't, and perhaps couldn't. They had STYLE–hell, they *were* style. They were the keepers of our history, the best news sources, and the ones who took newcomers in tow and held their hands as they attempted to navigate the 24-7 Technicolor circus, psychodrama, and road show that is Queer Culture. They were also the bravest, most "out" Queers I'd ever seen: no apologies, no regrets. They could face down a hostile crowd with attitude and humor. But if it came to it, they could fight like wild animals. They despised self-pity, and they *never* gave up on the possibility of love. Sharp, silly, some-times savage, but always real, they were my mentors and friends as I struggled to sort out my complicated Queer identity.

Recently, as I revel in being who I am, I've thought a lot about these nellies, with gratitude and affection. I never had an internal sense of "femininity," but I learned about "effemininity" from them. My understanding of style as a pansexual transsexual man comes mostly from them: knowing that I can be as "masculine" or "feminine" as I feel, and knowing that it's ALL drag, and ev-erybody else is making it up as they go along, too.

In a time when so many of these men are dead–for alcohol, heartbreak, and violence took their toll on sissies even before AIDS entered the picture–I keep an ongoing connection with their spirit. Something of their essence lives on, in this strange boy to whom they were so gently kind, many years ago. They won't have passed without a trace while I'm still here.

In the early 80s, I realized I was attracted to men as well as women. I came out as bisexual. I found in men an ability to enjoy sex for its own sake, to de-light in the act without first having to deconstruct it or put it in a historical con-text. It could be fun; or even *just* fun, with no need for ideological underpinning. (If they feel sure you're not going to make fun of them, men will try *anything* in bed.) It was with men–at that point–that I could *play*, experi-ment, and get an idea what my next move might be, because I knew there had to be more for me; somehow, *something* was still missing.

So, around the same time, I added SM to my mix. The rituals, the toys, and the heightened sensations were deeply satisfying to me. And, in the best parts of the SM world, people maintain an openness to new ways to express sex and gender, allowing one both the social space to try new personas, and the prag-matism to adopt whatever works. So I could finally find what worked for me: pansexual, Queer, transsexual, Leatherman. Ironically, the feeling of singular-ity that kept me alive long enough for me to grow into myself probably made it harder for me to figure it all out. I was so used to thinking that I was different from everyone–that what I thought and felt was just me–that I wasn't really looking for any commonality. So it was doubly satisfying to encounter at least some others for whom "identity" did not signify a cast-iron box.

I am a Leather Daddy. In fact, I am several kinds of Daddy: a Leather Daddy, and the Dad of a Queer family, The House of Phoenix. These are vastly different roles with the same name, and neither has much to do with any main-stream father figure. Besides me, our House includes a collection of adults as Mother, Son, Daughter, and, as time passed, an assortment of Cousins, Uncles, and In-Laws. None of these roles has much to do with how any of us experi-enced childhood or parenting.

I'm not impressed, overall, with the role models men are offered, or with the way most lifelong males handle their familial and intimate obligations. In the past, too many men failed to consider such things to be *obligations* at all. Then the feminist resurgence of the early 70s dealt mainstream male culture a blow from which it never recovered. The status quo was shattered. This confusion is uncomfortable, of course. But it affords us a great opportunity: when all bets are off, that's when the greatest strides are made, after all. And so *I* get to decide what kind of man *I* want to be; perhaps even more than most men, because as a trannie I have no "male" social niche, no prefab identity to either accept or rebel against. (All too many people don't even believe FTMs exist.) I get to pick and choose, because if I let someone else decide for me, huge chunks of who I am would be lost.

So where has all this taken me? It would seem that in many ways I remain singular, or at least, separate. There aren't many groups or venues where I don't feel like I'm expected to check large parts of myself at the door. The kind of man I am, and the sexual behaviors I practice, are not welcomed in many venues. Most Queer SM events are arranged according to the participants' genitalia, and I'm pretty indifferent to that sort of thing. I can't guarantee, at any time, that I'll be involved with someone whose equipment will admit us to a gay man's event, and I can no longer attend women's parties. I'm not comfortable at many straight SM events–I feel much more at home in Queer culture, although I have to say that some of the friendliest, least judgmental people I have met have been in straight groups. The people I've encountered who seem to look at me with some of the same sense of possibility I bring to intimacy have been mostly Bisexual men and women. But not living in a big city, access to a thriving Bi or FTM SM scene is limited. So, as has been the case all my life, I have learned to make do with limited amounts of what I want. But at least these days it's not because I don't know what that is.

I wear my leather like I've earned it because I have. I may wear rhinestones and satin scarves too, because I can. I never met a gender I didn't like. I will use any object or orifice available, yours, or mine, in pursuit of happiness, because life's way too fucking short to give in to the pressure to deny and censor. I have far more experience in coming out, breaking taboos, losing friends, and getting blacklisted, than any human needs. And I'm still here.

And the story's still unfolding. Recently, I've been thinking a lot about the Master/slave dynamic, from the bottom as well as the top. So I may be exploring those options next. There are way too many possibilities to pass up!

Social Bodies, Pagan Hearts

Laura Anne Seabrook

http://www.haworthpress.com/web/JB
Digital Object Identifier: 10.1300/J159v03n03_09

[Haworth co-indexing entry note]: "Social Bodies, Pagan Hearts." Seabrook, Laura Anne. Co-published simultaneously in *Journal of Bisexuality* (Harrington Park Press, an imprint of The Haworth Press, Inc.) Vol. 3. No. 3/4, 2003, pp. 117-127; and: *Bisexuality and Transgenderism: InterSEXions of the Others* (ed: Jonathan Alexander, and Karen Yescavage) Harrington Park Press, an imprint of The Haworth Press, Inc., 2003, pp. 117-127. Single or multiple copies of this article are available for a fee from The Haworth Document Delivery Service [1-800-HAWORTH, 9:00 a.m. - 5:00 p.m. (EST). E-mail address: docdelivery@haworthpress.com].

SUMMARY. Are sex, sexuality and gender, real determinants of character, or are they just misconceptions and misdirections? The author suggests that "logocentric" reasoning creates illusionary divisions and perceptions, where false dichotomies are presented as the "natural way of things." Events such as the Sydney Gay and Lesbian Mardi Gras illustrate how the public identities of minorities such as bisexual and transgendered persons may become invisible. Arguments that claim queer and other persons are "born that way" are contested, and other dichotomies suggested. *[Article copies available for a fee from The Haworth Document Delivery Service: 1-800-HAWORTH. E-mail address: <docdelivery@haworthpress. com> Website: <http://www.HaworthPress.com> © 2003 by The Haworth Press, Inc. All rights reserved.]*

KEYWORDS. Sex, sexuality, gender, bisexual, transgendered

Sometimes I think that talking about sexuality and gender is a little like the Sherlock Holmes tale "The Red-headed League." In that story, Holmes' client presents him with a conundrum–he is by trade a pawnbroker but has, by virtue of his red hair, been employed (out of hundreds applying for the position) by the above mentioned league. His duties are to do nominal work (transcribing the *Encyclopedia Britannia*) in another office during the day for a handsome reward. These duties don't conflict with his business, as most of his trade comes in the evening. Then, abruptly the office in which he does these duties is closed, a note left that the league is dissolved and the client is unable to gain any further information. What was happening?

Why, out of hundreds of red headed men was he picked, and why did the employment stop? Holmes resolves this puzzle in his usual effortless way. It transpires that the whole series of events was a scheme to lure the client away from his place of employment, while bank robbers tunnelled into a Bank next door. The "red-headedness" of the client was just a way of making his employment appear arbitrary. The robbers are caught and another mystery is solved; though Holmes' client is still out of a job.

The general culture of western society still promotes and embraces the idea of bipolar sexes (female and male), with "appropriate" genders (girl/woman and boy/man) and a "normal" sexuality of "heterosexual." Variations are allowed, but these are portrayed as "exceptions to the rule," deviations to the mean. I suggest that sexuality and gender is just like the Red-headed league. They are concepts that appear to give those following certain assumptions about them certain benefits, but ultimately they are misconceptions and misdirections.

Such concepts have the most power when they are considered "natural," as much a part of what is and what should be as any other part of the status quo (and hence cannot be disputed). And yet, clearly this is an assumption about the world and how it operates, not by deduction, but by statistical observation. If everyone else you meet considers these to be givens (and especially if they assume they apply to themselves), there's a powerful social pressure exerted on oneself not to consider it any differently. Unless, of course, like myself, you just happen to be an individual who doesn't match that template of expectations.

Being a bisexual transsexual woman forced me to reconsider such ideas. From this personal viewpoint, what matters is not what is "normal" and what isn't, but that the way I present myself, and how I follow my desires, be an honest reflection of who I believe myself to be. And yet, such a perspective is not an obvious one. There are so many traps and dead-ends on the way.

One response is to initially assume that such conditions are unique to the self, implying that one is a "freak" or "aberration" to the norm. This is why it's so important to have some positive representation of both bisexuality and different genders in the media; and why events like the Sydney Mardi Gras march are crucial. Not only do they show the general community that there are sexual and gender variations out there, but also (assuming Bi and Trans participation or representation) demonstrate to the "gay and lesbian/queer community" that there are variations and minorities within itself as well. If you aren't represented, if you don't show up on the night, people assume you don't exist–out of sight is out of mind.

Part of the problem seems to be that of logocentric reasoning. In such a scheme, concepts are presented as comprised of binary opposites: left/right; male/female, capitalist/communist; man/woman; science/myth; hetero-/homosexual. The idea is that such "opposites" define the boundaries of the concept (which in the previous list would be: direction; sex; economics; gender; knowledge; and sexuality). All very well; however, in such schemas one side of the definition is always favored over the other (which one depends upon your view point) and such polarities tend to exclude or marginalize other qualities which don't necessarily follow the proscribed polarization. Thus, intersexed, transgender and bisexual qualities become "problems" for those with a vested interest in maintaining such dichotomies.

Consider the heterosexual/homosexual split for example. The Kinsey scale qualified this, where "zero" was wholly heterosexual, and "six" was wholly homosexual. Bisexuality then, was seen more or less as a "three." But we could easily turn this scale around, where say "mono-sexuality" (as in both homo- and heterosexuality) would be a "zero," and bisexuality a "six." People who fell somewhere between these two extremes would be folk who tended to prefer a set gender, with occasional interests in other genders. From this example it can be seen that such scales are for the most part arbitrary, reliant upon unsaid or unnoticed assumptions.

And then we have yet another dichotomy: either the *GLBTI* or *Queer* community (take your pick). The GLBTI (short for Gay/Lesbian/Bi/Trans/Intersexed) seems to add an initial every so many years. Originally, in Australia, everyone was lumped together as being "Gay." When an impromptu demonstration in a central Sydney street became an annual event, it was originally called the "Sydney *Gay* Mardi Gras." Some years later, after action and protest from lesbians, it became the "Sydney *Gay & Lesbian* Mardi Gras." It may only be an illusion, but after that name change the event seemed to become more exclusive, promoting both Gays and Lesbians while playing down the other "labels" within the community.

The "T" got added, I suspect, primarily because of the drag queens, rather than for other transgendered participants. It's easy to see how both gays and lesbians (including both drag queens and kings) can coalesce into a real community. Such groups have broadly similar agendas in regard to rights and sexual/social prerogatives. A community helps achieve this. It's more difficult to see how people exhibiting such a broad spectrum of transgendered behavior (which might range from persons wearing items of the "other gender's" underwear underneath their street clothes, to full-blown sex-change), might form such broad communities,[1] let alone mix with other "sexualities" in the GBT soup.

In reality such transgender communities, if they truly exist, are fragmentary and divisive at best. Certainly, there are beacons of hope and activity, such as the Gender Centre in Sydney, or lobby groups elsewhere, but such groups are created and maintained for very specific reasons, rather than become all-embracing self-perpetuating umbrella organizations. Trans folk as a whole act more like an interest group (like say, a newsgroup on the Internet) than a community. A community is more than just a group of individuals networking together, but is also a "social space" within which such may interact, explore, and play; where opinions and issues become important and have impact.

Even if the GLT community represents only a portion of gays, and lesbians,[2] it is likely that it represents a much smaller proportion of trans folk. Those individuals that it does include (or rather, include themselves within it) are those that have undergone the process of transcending any internal homophobia, or found the community to be a refuge from the larger community as a whole.

The "B" seemed to be added grudgingly at best. Every year in the Mardi Gras parade there is a Bi contingent, but even at the best of times its participation is played down. One year when I marched with this group (comprised of the members of the Australian Bisexual and Sydney Bisexual Networks), we passed the reviewing stand and were announced as "the gay and lesbian bisexual group"! Sorry, but that just wasn't right.

Perhaps part of the problem here is that it's easy to marginalize transgendered and bisexual participants at such events, and elsewhere. Transgendered folk either "pass," or they don't. If they do pass, then they may be assumed to be monosexuals of their "assumed" gender. If they don't pass, they may be mistaken for drag queens and kings, and still fit a perceived cliché. Likewise, bisexual folk don't (unless they're wearing an appropriate t-shirt or button) have any way (other than their actions) of identifying themselves as such. Hence, both bisexual and transgendered people, unless there is a deliberate attempt to stand out, tend to merge with the crowd–their public identities lost to the assumptions of time and place.

The letter "I" for Intersex, has been added only recently. I suspect this to be a mistake. All the other letters are there because the peoples they label take certain social actions. To be intersexed you just have to be "born that way" (with an incidence of about one in every 1,500 to 2,000 births). It was recently reported[3] that one intersex person (with 47XXY chromosomes) was awarded an Australian passport with an "X" in the sex field. This was in part, recognition that an entry of either "M" of "F" would not be accurate.

Now I realize that there are those who would argue that gays, lesbians, bis, and transgendered folk *are* born that way, but I don't believe this to be the case. At best, we may have been born with a "propensity" or "preference" towards certain types of desires and actions. At best, these are internal pressures to do what we need to do, and become who we are. Countering this are external pressures to conform (and not just to a heterocentric majority, either). What we are left with then is a "path" of development, created by all the choices we've made, or failed to make over the years. As such, it's a *spiritual* path.

For every person who finds an identity of "gay," "lesbian," "bisexual," or "transgendered," there are uncounted others who, while not embracing such labels, may indulge in part or the whole of the activities associated with such labels. Hence we have: "men who have sex with other men" (but maybe that's *all* they do); and males who undergo gender reassignment surgery but not gender transition, just because they wanted a "pussy" (there is at least one such case). But the dichotomies we create to normalize our passions make such people nominally invisible. Either we don't know that such exist, or we don't want to know that they do. And once again, the participation, or lack of participation, of these people in any community is their own decision and part of their *own* spiritual path.

And so we come to the other alternative, that of a "Queer" community. Is it just a synonym for *GLBTI*, or does it imply something else, something more fluid? Certainly, much of queer theory seems to have a post-modern base, implying a "space" that cannot be properly or distinctly defined. In such a space gender, sex, and sexuality might be either irrelevant or perhaps accessories or extras, rather than the main event. Such a queer space, it would seem, would allow for much greater personal expression and development. But if that's the case, why is it so damned unpopular?

The idea of a "queer" community certainly seems much misunderstood. In a recent issue of *Out Now* (March-April 2003), a local magazine produced by the AIDS Council of New South Wales, a reader's letter criticized the advertising of a dance because it was listed as a "Gay and Lesbian Community Event," and such had offended the reader's queer sensibilities. The response was to change the labelling so that future advertising would list it as a "GLBTIQ" event! Perhaps the term "queer" is going the way of "transgender"[4]–a cooked term which ambiguously is not just an umbrella concept, but has also become a subgrouping.

In a way, it's easy to play and explore areas (and even to transgress them) if you know what the boundaries are. But an unfixed zone of play and activity leads to uncertainty and indecision. Being monosexual means that a person can ignore, (for the purposes of sexual and intimate affection) half the people you meet. It gives a sense of boundary within social play. It doesn't matter if one is either hetero- or homosexual, the effect is the same. Being bisexual on the other hand, opens up avenues of uncertainty. Such paths may lead to pleasure and experience, but they are uncertain all the same. It's *easier* to ignore about half the opportunities of intimate contact that come along, hard to admit that one's heart may be more open than one's mind. Perhaps this is why bisexuals are seen by some as being "fence-sitters," in the same way some mothers call childless women "selfish" with children.[5] It's easier to pour scorn on those making an effort, rather than admit that one's own path is more restrictive.

Likewise, fluidity in gender, while practiced by some, also seems to be unpopular. When transgendered expression became pathologized in the 20th century, and "transsexuals" were the result, it was easy to assume that such persons were aberrations of birth, medical misfits who could be "cured" with the right hormones and a good surgeon. This was partly because the "experts" told us so, and partly because this is what a goodly number of transgendered folk (including myself) wanted. Janice Raymond (1979) in *The Transsexual Empire* suggested that she-males (sic) were the creation of the "medical-psychiatric empire." While the application of medical science has helped implement the desires of transgendered persons, it does not *define* them. Transgendered behavior both predates the 20th century, and occurs in non-Western cultures.

The most notable of the ancient transgendered peoples were the Roman *Gallae*, male followers of the goddess *Cybele*, who castrated themselves in public displays and thereafter often lived as women. The general public of the day considered them to be eunuchs, but there is clear evidence to suggest that the Gallae themselves had different ideas. In many ways they were similar to the modern Indian *Hijra*–both performed their own medical procedures (which was also a rite of passage), both lived in self-contained communities, and both terms denote a wide range of sexualities and genders. Thai culture has the *Kathoey*, their own version of transgendered males, as do other cultures.

If transgendered behavior predates modern culture, and is not exclusively a Western Cultural phenomenon, then what can this tell us about the nature of gender itself? Only that it, like sex and sexuality, are constructed (and "arbitrary") rather than givens and constants. The proof is both in the variation and the degree to which each culture considers its own version of these "givens" to be *the* natural way of things.

Sex is a "constructed" quality as much as sexuality and gender are. Rather than absolute, chromosomal outcomes and the body's reaction to such have quite a wide variation. It's only that the results are statistically weighted toward 46XX chromosomes producing what we consider a "female" body, and 46XY to a "male" body. Other variations (such as the 47XXY mentioned above) happen at much lower rates. When they *do* happen, the child is either arbitrarily ascribed a gender, or considered a "problem" (to be "fixed" somehow). Hence the logocentric division of male/female is maintained.

But if all these qualities are essentially "arbitrary" (though hardly random) what then? Doesn't this lead us out of those "rigid areas of doubt and uncertainty" into uncharted waters? I don't think so. Most attempts to do so, or prod others in to doing so, seem to fail. I suspect that the reason they do is that it's hard to provide role models in the great unknown–if you're *following* someone else then you've missed the point. My own response is somewhat different. While I accept that the labels bisexual (or as I prefer "bi-amorous") and "transgendered" describe me accurately, they are *not* the *primary* labels I use to describe myself. Rather, those are "Goth" and "Pagan."

The Gothic subculture grew out of the punk and post-punk music scene in Britain, spreading to America and Australia in the early 1980s. The stereotypical depiction of goths, as always dressing in black and being obsessed by death, is simplistic and inaccurate. In any case, it provides me with a social arena where my efforts are appreciated, and gender play is an accepted given.

Sexuality and gender in the subculture are less important than the forms in which they are presented.

Goth boys in their make-up and skirts can be cute (or not as the case may be), and such play is accepted. Expressions of fetish clothing is par for the course. Who cares if you're straight or gay, provided you're *interesting*?

And just what is interesting in such a subculture? While sex and gender distinctions still exist within this subculture, they are played down and secondary to other considerations. Certainly, there are favored themes and tropes that tend to predominate. There is an extended heritage of Gothic revival which may not be apparent at first inspection. Like other subcultures, the forms are followed not by any central dictate, but by an assumed knowledge of what is "cool" and what is not.

Those definitions are heavily influenced by Gothic and Romantic traditions, certainly, but also by punk rejection of complacency, and appreciation of the darker elements of life. Variety though, is rife. Some Goths only wear black to clubs, others never. It's the attitude that makes one Goth, not the clothes.

And being pagan is also a state of mind, as well as being a religion. My own version of neo-paganism acknowledges that *The Goddess* and *The God* (as in the forces of the feminine and the masculine) exist in all living things. Respecting this means treating expressions of variety and diversity as aspects of The Goddess–to be honored rather than rejected. Not that this is always easy to do–witness the fall from grace of "Lady Tamara," who was the transsexual head of the Wiccan Church in Western Australia (my home State). The event was a media bashing from start to finish.

As well as being a pagan I am also a modern Gallae. My "day of blood" took place in Phuket in 2000 with the addition of prayers and altar, not just the surgeon's skill (and Cybele *was* there for me). For me, it's being part of a spiritual tradition, and validation that the path I'm on is a *spiritual* one. And that's the point, at least for me. I realized long ago that there was no point to gender (or any other) transition if it was merely a shift from one stereotypical gender to another. Rather, the point of the transition was to find myself, even if, I didn't yet know whom that was. Any other outcome was secondary.

Initially, the driving desires were an overwhelming social association with the gender of "woman," and an overwhelming body image of being "female." And even if such things are "constructed" they are still realities in day-to-day existence. They are still things that must be dealt with as if concrete objects, until finally a balance is reached and rather than foreground considerations, they become background facts. And in opening up myself to change, I had to be prepared to go wherever those changes took me, outside my (then) "comfort zone," until a new one was created within which I could play, and express my identity.

That also included sexuality. Recognizing that who one loves is *not* dependent on gender marks me as a bisexual. I can't help it. I follow my heart, and it's a pagan one at that. And all the analysis, sometimes I think, is arbitrary too. It seems "humanist"–a term misused too often and assumed to mean "atheist" (at least by Creationists, if no one else). And yet, if through analysis the cardboard cathedrals of belief we call "sexuality" and "belief" get shattered, what do we replace them with? Myself, I'd like to see as much variation and diversity as possible. Not only because it gives more expression (for me) of the divine, but also because it's more fun. And ultimately that, past issues of reproduction, is what sexuality and gender should be about, don't you think?

NOTES

1. Male transvestites, for example, might form support groups in order to have a safe space to "dress" and trade experiences. Such venues and groups have less appeal to male-female transsexuals (apart from an intermediary stage) since dressing "full-time" is part of the process of transition, and this is done in public.

2. It can never include all gays and lesbians, since there will always be those who while perhaps being gay or lesbian, never identify with such labels or seek involvement with such groups.

3. See *www.thewest.com.au/20030111/news/perth/tw-news-perth-home-sto84205. html* (12 March, 2003). [Article no longer available online–Editors.]

4. "Transgender," coined in the late 1980s, now also means a non-operative transsexual.

5. See "The Selfish Jean" in *Different for Girls* by Joan Smith (1997), in which she finds that some mothers claim childless women too "selfish." Smith's conclusion was that such resentment was based less on emotional attachment and more on patriarchal expectations.

REFERENCES

[*Out Now*'s Editorial Response]. (2003, March-April). *Out Now, 33*, p. 6.

Raymond, J. (1979). *The transsexual empire: the making of the she-male*. Boston: Beacon Press.

Smith, J. (1997). *Different for girls: how culture creates women*. London: Chatto & Windus.

WORKS CONSULTED

Diamond, M. (1984). *Sex watching: looking into the world of sexual behavior*. London: Prion.

Jagose, A. (1996). *Queer theory*. Melbourne: Melbourne University Press.

Money, J. (1988). *Gay, straight and in-between: the sexology of erotic orientation.* Oxford: Oxford University Press.

Queen, C., and L. Schimel. (Eds.) (1997). *Pomosexuals: challenging assumptions about gender and sexuality.* San Francisco: Cleis Press.

Weinberg, M. S. (1994). *Dual attraction: understanding bisexuality.* New York: Oxford University Press.

"There Are Different Points in Your Life Where You Can Go Either Way":

Discussing Transsexuality and Bisexuality with Some Women of CrossPort

Jonathan Alexander

http://www.haworthpress.com/web/JB
Digital Object Identifier: 10.1300/J159v03n03_10

[Haworth co-indexing entry note]: " 'There Are Different Points in Your Life Where You Can Go Either Way': Discussing Transsexuality and Bisexuality with Some Women of CrossPort." Alexander, Jonathan. Co-published simultaneously in *Journal of Bisexuality* (Harrington Park Press, an imprint of The Haworth Press, Inc.) Vol. 3, No. 3/4, 2003, pp. 129-150; and: *Bisexuality and Transgenderism: InterSEXions of the Others* (ed: Jonathan Alexander, and Karen Yescavage) Harrington Park Press, an imprint of The Haworth Press, Inc., 2003, pp. 129-150. Single or multiple copies of this article are available for a fee from The Haworth Document Delivery Service [1-800-HAWORTH, 9:00 a.m. - 5:00 p.m. (EST). E-mail address: docdelivery@haworthpress.com].

SUMMARY. This article, in interview format, presents the ideas of four male-to-female transsexuals, two of whom are married to women who also participate in the discussion. The conversation focuses primarily on the intersections between transsexuality and bisexuality. Other themes discussed include the effect of transitioning (from one gender or sex to another) on an individual's perceived sexual orientation, the impact of that transitioning on the *partner's* or *spouse's* perceived sexual orientation, and the implication of transitioning for gender identity. *[Article copies available for a fee from The Haworth Document Delivery Service: 1-800-HAWORTH. E-mail address: <docdelivery@haworthpress.com> Website: <http://www.HaworthPress.com> © 2003 by The Haworth Press, Inc. All rights reserved.]*

KEYWORDS. Transsexual, bisexual, transgender, MTF, partners of transsexuals

INTRODUCTION

Part of my research into bi/trans intersections has led me to professional, and now even personal engagement with many members of CrossPort, the greater Cincinnati area's transgender support and social group. According to their Website,

> CrossPort's *mission* is to provide social, educational, emotional, and functional support for all facets of the Transgendered community including their partners, families, and friends. We also promote mutual understanding, acceptance, and equality to achieve a more positive and healthy society.

The organization, which has been in existence since 1985, conducts bi-weekly support group meetings for transsexuals and cross-dressers–sometimes together, but usually separately.

I attended my first CrossPort meeting in early 2003, after having met a group from the organization at our local LGBT Youth Summit in the Fall of 2002. The group conducted a stimulating panel about a variety of transgender issues, and it was evident from many in the audience that this was the first real contact they had had with trans-identified individuals. During that panel, presenters, and then a few audience members, characterized themselves as variously transgendered, as transsexual (both pre- and post-op), as cross-dressers, or as transitioning from one to the other, such as moving from identifying as a cross-dresser to being a pre-op transsexual. The same holds true for those attending the bi-weekly CrossPort meetings.

As I began attending meetings, I announced carefully that I was an "outside observer"–one who was working on a book-length project about trans and bi issues, and that I wanted to become more familiar with trans issues in my own home city. After a group vote to determine if everyone was comfortable with my presence at the meetings, the group was very welcoming and friendly, inviting me to attend future meetings and talk openly about my work.

Several members of CrossPort were eager to share their stories and talk about their lives, so we set up a time to conduct a "group interview." I wanted to capture, in as much as I could, the "give and take" of conversation and discussion that makes the CrossPort meetings so stimulating. I know, though, for privacy considerations, I could not record an actual meeting, so a smaller, willing group of us met at the home of Sasha and Martha for a "potluck" dinner and conversation. After meeting and greeting for a while, I took out my tape recorder and we talked for well over 90 minutes. As can be expected, the initial discussion was a bit stiff, with everyone a little "too aware" of the tape recorder, but participants quickly became comfortable, sharing much about their lives, loves, views, and beliefs.

Attending the potluck were two married couples and two single trans women, Cindy (post-op) and Cynthia (pre-op). The married couples included Martha (female) and Sasha (male-to-female pre-op), and Marie (female) and Catherine (who is pre-op but does not identify as transsexual). Our discussion was wide-ranging, stimulating, and at times provocative, but three main themes emerged: the effect of transitioning (from one gender or sex to another[1]) on an individual's perceived sexual orientation, the impact of that transitioning on the *partners'* or *spouses'* perceived sexual orientation, and the implication of transitioning for gender identity. As I reflect on the conversation, it is clear to me that *transitioning* poses substantive challenges to notions of sexual identity, sexual orientation, and even gender identity. Part of the transitioning for many participants–both transsexuals and their partners–involved transitioning from one sexual orientation to another, and the presence or potential for bi-erotic identifications surface again and again as part of that process. In some ways, transitioning itself prompts an intersection with bisexuality. Much further discussion is needed of this complex process.

What's most valuable to me about this discussion is that these are people who are "walking the walk," who are experiencing what it means to be trans, or bi in some cases, on a daily basis. As such, they are intimately engaged with many of the issues the contributors to this book have been discussing in their essays. Moreover, their involvement with CrossPort has provided them a space for intense, ongoing self-reflection about what it means to be transsexual and/or bisexual. They have–and frequently take–the opportunity to debate, often contentiously, bi/trans intersections and other pertinent topics related to trans/bi lives. Our own knowledge about these issues can only gain from paying attention to their reflections. Indeed, by including this dialogue in this collection, we are hoping to capture some of the dynamic, dialogic nature of their debate and reflection, as they "walk the walk" about which many others only theorize.

Note: for purposes of clarity and readability, I have edited the transcript, and I have also highlighted the main points of discussion with subject headings; in the process of highlighting the themes that we discussed, some discussion points have been moved. In no way have I altered the *content* of what was said during the interview, and I asked each participant to review this document before I submitted it for publication. My intention in presenting this discussion is to provide, in as much as possible, the authentic voices of those who are *living* lives in transition, and to capture their thoughts about sexuality, sexual orientation, and possible intersections among bisexual, bi-erotic, and transgendered experiences and perspectives. I wish I'd had the opportunity to interview some female-to-male transsexuals; however, CrossPort is primarily attended by male-to-female transsexuals. I fully acknowledge that more work needs to be done in understanding–and listening to–those undergoing transition–whether male-to-female or female-to-male.

"THE NAME GAME": SOME INITIAL INTRODUCTIONS

I asked everyone initially to introduce themselves, and their individual self-descriptions reveal the diversity of views through which they think about sex, sexuality, and gender identity.

Jonathan: We might just want to get everybody's name and just a brief description of who you are and if you have an identification. If you identify yourself or define yourself in a particular way, it would be good to hear what that is and why, and if you don't that's cool too.

Martha: My name is Martha and I am married to Sasha. We've been married thirty-one years. About a year and a half ago Sasha came to me and told me that she was a transsexual male-to-female. She told me in the fall of the year 2001 probably. She told me about it and we learned a lot about it. Basically the reason that we didn't have a problem with it and still don't is attributed to the fact that Sasha took it very slowly and gave me a lot of hints beforehand. It was at least a couple of years beforehand because she had already known this for about five years prior to telling me. She kind of gave me hints and in the work that we do there was plenty of opportunity for her to show her relationship to women versus men and how she related and how successful she was at relating to women much more so than men. I wasn't surprised and I say this over and over again but I think the biggest and most important thing to us is that Sasha has had enormous emotional problems throughout her life and this was the missing piece. I see it to this day. It was kind of miraculous that she finally discovered who she is and now she can go further with it.

Sasha: I am Sasha, the person of whom my wife just spoke. I am a male-to-female pre-op transsexual. This week there was a catharsis around here and Martha and I agreed, in fact, that I am going to have my reassignment surgery. It wasn't until maybe six years ago that I realized that I need to transition into being a woman. Before then I thought I might be gay or I might be a lot of things but all I was really doing was just pushing it away. At this point and beyond, as Martha said, it was the missing piece to a lot of what was going on with my life.

Cindy: Okay, I'm Cindy. I'm a post-op transsexual and I'm seventy years old. I have been a cross-dresser since I was seven years old. I really repressed it because it just wasn't done. It wasn't until after my wife of thirty years died that I started exploring a little bit. The Internet was where I found out that there were other people like me. I joined CrossPort and I started going to meetings. I figured I was going to be a happy cross-dresser. Then I realized I was more attracted to some of the transsexual members of the group and that's when I ran kicking and screaming to a therapist and after several years of therapy it was pretty obvious that I could either live a lie for the rest of my life or I could transition. Two years ago I started living full-time as Cindy Robertson. I changed my full name legally. It's all down at the courthouse. I had surgery last May. It was less than a year ago. I have been very, very happy. My brother practically shot me when I told him. I said, "I'm getting a bump in the road out of the way so that I can go along and do the things that I want to do as Cindy and go do them."

             I would have to say that my former male self was fairly heterosexual. Now Cindy is a lesbian. I'm attracted to females but it's interesting that that has been changing slightly in the sense that I had long talks with both my therapists and both agreed on the path to take. We discussed sexuality and my answer was laughter. I said, "At my age it's more about friends than anything else. Let it go and we'll go from there." That doesn't mean that I am without sexual feelings. That's not true at all. What I am saying is that I would much rather have friends and go from there. That's where I am right now.

In one sense I've wasted a couple of years and in another sense I've found myself. One of the things I have to tell you is that Charlie [Cindy's pre-op male self] used to stutter. Somebody pointed out to me even before I was full-time [living as a woman] that Charlie used to stutter all the time and Cindy doesn't much. For what it's worth I'll throw that out. I feel that I'm living in my own skin properly now. We'll just let it go at that.

Cynthia: I'm Cindy Jeffries. I've been living as a female, my female self now for over three years. I'm very happy. I am considered pre-op and I will be post-op in a few short months because my surgery is scheduled on the 22nd of September and I'm trying to just live my life now. I'm just going about my normal stuff and doing my business. I'm just living life. I don't know how to describe it. It's more like it's just a normal and natural thing going on. I went through this transition and now all of a sudden everything is the same as it was only now I'm living as a woman and that's what I am. Life has been great and I've never regretted it—not for one second. I know it was right for me. I've lost a lot of friends and family. They don't understand and I don't think they ever will.

I'm still married but we've been separated. I consider myself divorced in the spiritual sense. I just haven't gone through a legal divorce. Yes, Christmas of 1999 my ex left and that was because that was two weeks before I started full-time living. Why she picked that particular day I don't know. I guess she wanted to leave an impression.

Catherine: I guess I'll introduce myself as Catherine. I'm thirty-three and a pre-op transsexual, but I don't consider myself *transsexual*. I consider myself *female*. I've just always thought of myself as female. That is sort of like a label that you have to put on yourself or whatever. To me [transsexuality] always brings to mind the Jerry Springer aspect of people who wear the clothing of the opposite sex. It's not about the clothing to me. It's not about the clothing I'm wearing. Most of the time I'm in jeans and t-shirts and I'm an average looking individual. I'm getting ready to transition on the job shortly, which will be interesting. I consider myself to be pretty realistic about it. I'm also bisexual. I like men and women. I don't identify as transsexual.

Marie: My name is Marie. I've been married for a little over twelve years to Randy who is changing her name to Catherine. We have two children. I don't know, I guess we have been doing Randy's gender thing for seven or eight years now. It's kind of an on again off again kind of thing.

HARDWARE AND SOFTWARE: TRANSITIONING AND SEXUAL ORIENTATION

As the conversation progressed, we turned our attention to the effect of transitioning, of beginning the process of living as another gender, on one's perceived sexual orientation. Our first substantive discussions of bi/trans intersections quickly emerged.

Cindy: I am attracted to females but I also like people. I'm a "people person" so it's been occurring to me that I had better at least think about my men friends, if you will. There ain't nothing going to happen at all but I'm simply more open to the idea that I might be attracted sexually to a man. Again, one of the problems is that at my age [70] it's much more important to have friends than it is to have bed partners.

Jonathan: But are your feelings post-op primarily or did you have these feelings beforehand?

Cindy: They are definitely post-op. They are also post-hormone and I have not been taking hormones for that long. As a matter of fact I want to talk to my endocrinologist about that. At what point should I stop taking them and go into a normal menopause, if you will, since my testosterone producing organs are long gone? He said I probably ought to stay on the dose I am on now for about ten years from the time I started. Having said that I don't know whether it's the hormones or it's simply my realization that I do have female hardware.

Catherine: Or software, as the case may be.

Cindy: As a person who's done some professional computer work I would say I definitely have the hardware. I'm not sure about the software yet. But Dr. Meltzer does excellent operations. I *am* capable. Whether I will ever do it or not is quite another matter.

Part of it is the age. Seriously, I am seventy years old. People say I don't look it. [And she doesn't–JA]

I have a feeling that people who really understand that they are the wrong gender at an early age tend to be more interested in the person of the same biological gender, which means that after they transition they are heterosexual. A lot of the younger ones, from what I've read and talked to, first think that they are homosexual and that they are gay. They are attracted to people of their own gender. They think, gee, that means I'm gay. Then they realize that the feelings towards them are not the same as the people they are meeting. They are not interested, for example, in being a man with another man, or being a woman with another woman. They are interested in *being* a man or *being* a woman. I also think that people my age are more apt to stay with the same orientation that they had.

Jonathan: So, in other words, you were heterosexual.

Cindy: We use loaded words. I would have considered myself heterosexual. I wasn't interested in having relations with another man. I had a bad experience with a cousin of mine when I was a youngster and that may have turned me off. I hadn't thought about that for years. I had buried that very deeply until I was in therapy. I'm still attracted to women. When I look at a *Vogue* magazine I'm interested to know if there is anything in there for me but I also think, "Isn't she gorgeous?"

Jonathan: So this is why you identify as lesbian?

Cindy: Yes. If you take a look at the most recent picture on *Vogue*, which has a very pregnant Brooke Shields in a very skinny dress. I have several different thoughts about that and one of them is how attractive she is. I also wish I could have been pregnant at one time. It's an interesting set of feelings. I think if I had known and faced this issue thirty years ago or even before that then things might have been different. You have to think about thirty or forty years ago the only transsexuals were people like Renee Richards.

Jonathan: How might it have been different if you had tried to transition then?

Cindy: How would it have been different? Well, in the first place, at that time I was married, and one of the things that I was most disappointed with was that I was never able to discuss this with her. We would have come to some sort of resolution; whether it would have been the same kind that Marie and Randy

[Catherine] are coming through or even Martha and Sasha are coming through, I have no idea. We would have worked something out.

On Palm Sunday I'm supposed to talk to a group of teenagers at church who are studying choices and my example is the choice that, once I knew who I was, what were the choices that I had? The choices were to live a lie for the rest of my life, however long or short that might be, or to do something about it. I put it clearly and this has nothing to do with sexual orientation it has to do with gender identity. Those are different things in my opinion. The gender identity is something that I am so much more comfortable with and you have no idea how uncomfortable I was as a youngster; I always knew I was different but I didn't know why.

Jonathan: Catherine, what are your thoughts about changing gender identity and sexual orientation?

Catherine: I was younger and I was interested primarily in women and there was some curiosity towards men but it was very standoffish curiosity. When I started taking hormones that changed. It became really, really way more open and I'm like, "Hey, check it out." I would attribute that primarily to taking hormones. That's when it started, actually.

Jonathan: So, while you don't want to be identified as transsexual, you would identify as bisexual?

Catherine: Right. Bisexual is a fairly generic term. I'm attracted to both men and women. That's a generic term and most bisexual or gay people or lesbian people that I've met are not psychopaths.

Sasha: Yeah, there are interesting things that happen after SRS [sexual-reassignment surgery] to gender identity and bisexuality. Everything that Cindy described has already happened to me prior to my surgery . . .

Jonathan: In terms of what?

Sasha: In terms of my changing feelings of sexuality. I'd like to address what Catherine said as well. Having been in the theater almost all of my life I had millions and millions of bisexual and gay friends. I prided myself that I was always the one that got the girls because I was always the heterosexual actor and director. Oh no, never the bisexual or homosexual stereotype that is prevalent in the theater, which is not true anyway. Imagine my surprise. When I began transitioning, I was shocked and I have been shocked at what I consider almost even metaphysical aspects of what happen to me or deeply, deeply ingrained genetic situations that were dormant in me. For example, when I really knew that I had to be a woman I got on the Internet and I got into a creative funk on the Internet, writing as a woman. My writing became so popular with men and women that I began to get paid for it. I have over 3,000 pages that I have written. I have won awards. I have been paid with lingerie and all kinds of things get sent to me all the time because here is this acerbic–it's like Erma Bombeck on speed. That's the way I write. I don't know where it comes from. My vocabulary, obviously I have an extremely female vocabulary, which I never studied. My male vocabulary doesn't work. People only relate to me in a real sense as a woman. They have never as a man. So with the vocabulary and with the writing style, my moods, and the way I look, etc. etc. I have not studied any of this. I might be a good actor but I've never studied this. I've never studied gender switching and sex switching. I can't tell you that I know exactly why. I decided quite a while ago that I would just go with it. If I stop and start analyzing what the hell is really happening other than the fact that if I can't physically be a woman and work at living as a woman despite my birth gender I would rather die–and all of us feel that way at one time or another anyway. I have learned not to question it all that much and because of that I think I'm all the more natural. You've been out with us several times socially, Jonathan, and I don't see any difference between myself and any other woman in a restaurant. I might compensate on the fashion but that's about all.

Jonathan: And you, as a woman, are happily married to a woman . . .

Sasha: Exactly. Exactly. Bringing it back to that, I was absolutely stunned when I started becoming attracted to men. I am basically still a lesbian. I would say 70 percent or 65 percent. I have kissed a few men, I have held hands, and I have had arms around me. I've had proposals. I've been sent flowers and it just goes on and on and on. Whether or not I'm confusing my attraction with my being paid attention to in all this "white knight syndrome," I am really extremely attracted to men. Time will tell but being monogamous, being married to a genetic woman, I am going to have to train myself to be extremely civil and not do a damn thing about it. I don't think our marriage can take that. I don't think any marriage could take that.

Jonathan: You would locate your attraction to men as pre-transition or once you initiated your transition . . .

Sasha: After. Yes. Absolutely. That was not happening in the weeks
              beforehand. Now I'm very much settling into it and enjoying it.
              I love the attention and I hated being a man but I have found so
              much that I love in men. Now I see from the other side and I
              don't have to do that anymore so I can just enjoy it in other peo-
              ple.

Catherine: I, on the other hand, will do it any chance I get.

              [Laughter . . .]

"YOU ARE A LESBIAN": TRANSITIONING SEXUAL ORIENTATION IN PARTNERS OF TRANSPEOPLE

   While transitioning impacts our participants' perceived understanding of
their own sexual orientations, its impact on *partners* of trans people is less
well documented. I attempted to turn our attention to this subject.

Jonathan: Martha, how do you respond to what Sasha is saying? What is
              your feeling when Sasha says that she might have feelings for
              men?

Martha: Jealousy.

Jonathan: Jealousy?

Martha: Oh yeah. Initially, but it's a lot easier to take now that I really
              understand the mechanics of it, but every step of the way I've
              had different responses in either a shock or a negative way
              through all the little things that made up the transition. We have
              fun with it and we laugh about it. Even the fact, initially, when
              Sasha said, kind of jokingly but very realistically, "You know
              that means I'm a lesbian."

Jonathan: But *you* aren't a lesbian?

Martha: No. She said that about herself. She said, actually, jokingly,
              "*You* are a lesbian." I said, "What! I'm not a lesbian." I totally
              pushed that away until we talked and read and looked at what
              was going on as far as the reality of our relationship and where it
              was going and how I was going to perceive or be perceived in
              public. That's actually the deadening thing initially. That's the
              deadening thing for any female who is in a heterosexual rela-
              tionship. "Oh my God, I'm not a lesbian," you think. Until you
              grasp it and you let it sink in and then all of a sudden you could

care less about what society thinks. Who cares? The important thing is, is this the person I'm going to spend the rest of my life with? Do I accept it? Do I embrace it? Do I love this person? Well, then let them think what they want. Those were the steps that I had to take.

Now, the bisexual issue I totally understand it now even though sometimes it's incredibly confusing. It was incredibly confusing in my mind. But I do understand it. I totally under-stand it. The confusion *she* is going through is not confusion; it's reality that she's going through. That reality means that there may be an attraction to a male. Again, I've kind of gone this route and been on the road. I got to different understandings and different points in our relationship and I'm okay with it, but it's bizarre. It's really hard. Sometimes I'll sit there and say, "You know, I don't want men to be attracted to you. I don't like that. Stay away." That's kind of the feeling because we are mar-ried and we are happily married. There is a reality there. There is a guy at our church who is a gay guy and he's incredibly at-tracted to Sasha and it's so obvious and so sweet. We go into church and he is straining to see what she is wearing that day and I kind of watch that and that kind of helped to be honest with you because it's not that it's innocent.

Jonathan: Does he know that Sasha is transitioning?

Martha: Oh yeah.

Sasha: The church knows.

Martha: Everyone there knows. I watched that and that kind of helped. It's confusing but it's real and it helps to know that she would not act on it. That is very helpful. Fantasy is a good thing.

Jonathan: Let's talk about fantasy. Would you consider dressing as a man in order to satisfy or *try* to satisfy some of Sasha's desires?

Martha: If that was a real requirement I would consider it, since my nick-name by Cynthia is Jethro anyway or Ricky with a "y." Actually, I think Sasha and I pride ourselves on being pretty open sexually and not that we haven't through the years experi-enced all kinds of different things and this was just another thing that we had to get into as far as understanding how we are going to go on our sexual route. But sure, if that was something that was really important to her. There is one other thing too. One of the things that really made it easier for us in a sexual way is that way back when I've always sexually been into the feel of nylons on Sasha so even in our marriage Sasha wearing nylons was sometimes kind of a fun part of what we did.

Jonathan: So would you consider yourself bisexual?

Martha: No.

Jonathan: You identify as a straight woman?

Martha: Oh yeah.

Sasha: Sure and she lives with another woman.

Catherine: A straight woman who loves a woman.

Martha: A woman who loves nylons. No. Absolutely. I'm not at all bisexual. I wouldn't be attracted to anyone else.

Jonathan: Sasha, what is your response to Martha dressing as a man to help you experience sexual intimacy with a man?

Sasha: Well, it might be cute but as far as anything to do with a penis . . . If I were to place my lips around a hunk of quivering latex then I would rather not do anything.

Jonathan: So, no quivering hunk of latex.

Sasha: No quivering hunk of latex would substitute for the real tin tabulating quivering flesh that I would require in my new bio youngish body.

[Laughter . . .]

Jonathan: Marie, how do you feel about everything that's been happening with Catherine? Partners of people who are transitioning often have the most difficult time.

Marie: You just wonder. It's totally not my story. It's not like I don't have a part in it. I'm not saying that. It's not me.

Jonathan: Do you consider yourself a lesbian?

Marie: Am I a lesbian? I wouldn't identify as a lesbian. No. Actually, I was just called or identified as a lesbian yesterday. Although in the grand scheme of things, what other people think of you is garbage. It means so little. We have kids and I've been a soccer mom and have done all the mom things. I guess I felt that I was given this role and you have to fit into that. To be called a lesbian was just absolutely wonderful. It was just so great to me; I mean regardless or whatever, it was so freeing. Finally I feel like I've been recognized as someone who's got my own thing. It was like it was me. It was great.

Sasha: How did you feel after you had been recognized as that? I want Martha to answer it—her first time as a lesbian.

Martha: This was actually last fall or last summer. We went to an Alice Cooper concert in Louisville. I wore my normal tennis shoes and pants. We were in a women's bathroom. I reached over and touched Sasha's cheek and a woman came in and looked at us with total disgust. This is an Alice Cooper concert keep in mind. Granted, I don't look like I belong at an Alice Cooper concert either but she was totally disgusted. That is the first time I had ever experienced that and I was so embarrassed that I turned around and ran. I ran out of the women's bathroom. I was so embarrassed and ashamed. All of a sudden I got out and I thought, you know, she really had balls to do that. I got really pissed off.

That was my first experience of that. All of a sudden it occurred to me that that was what was going to start happening and I had to be prepared for it. So, those are the types of experiences that finally got me to the point where I say, you know, I could care less about humanity. Let them think what they want. If they want to think that I'm a lesbian, then you know, I've been married thirty-one years and they can just deal with it.

Jonathan: Let's follow-up with Marie about that. Marie, Catherine has been very open about her bisexuality. Do you ever see yourself identified as bisexual?

Marie: Yes. I have before.

Jonathan: Was it before or after Catherine's transition?

Marie: Before and after I guess.

Catherine: We've done some pretty kinky stuff.

Jonathan: Do you think that's helped you with accepting Catherine's transition?

Marie: I think so. I think that everyone at a certain time is male and everyone at a certain time is female. If you are going to accept society's standards I don't believe that anyone is 100 percent homosexual or 100 percent heterosexual. There are different points in your life where you can go either way. Is it a given absolute or not? I really don't think that's true.

"WHAT DOES BEING A WOMAN MEAN?": TRANSITIONING AND GENDER IDENTITY

Over the course of the conversation, a more fundamental issue–the vexed nature of *gender* identity, not just sexual orientation–began to emerge. Are male-to-female transsexuals really women? Were they every really men? Such questions intersect directly with questions of sexual orientation identity.

Cindy: It's almost a generational thing because if you were growing up the way I was in New England in the '30s and '40s and even early '50s, then some of these questions would not have come up. It was real simple. A doctor took a look at the baby and said it's a boy or it's a girl or we are going to do something to make it either a boy or a girl.

Jonathan: Most doctors still do that.

Cindy: And there were certain things you did and certain things you didn't do. There wasn't any discussion whatsoever of gays and lesbians. They didn't exist. What I'm getting at is the idea that there were definite standards for boys and girls and these standards were not broken and that was the way I grew up.

Recently, we have had a couple of young people come to our support group meetings. They've found out about the possibility [of being trans]. I don't know what any of them really are, maybe TSs or whatever, or if they are just mixed up kids. That isn't what I'm getting at. The fact is that they can find out that these are possibilities at that age is a big big big enormous difference. The fact that my niece could buck her family and tell them "Yes, I am gay"–and make it stick. It couldn't have happened in my generation the same way. This would not have happened.

Marie: I agree. Catherine and I have a son whose name is Alex. He just turned ten years old. Alex has never seen Catherine. He has never seen him. He has no idea at all.

Catherine: Other than the fact that I look like a girl. A lot of times people comment.

Marie: Other than that his daddy has a rack but other than that, pretty much nothing. It's never been openly discussed with him yet. We were in Penney's shopping about two weeks ago and Alex says to me, "Wouldn't it just be great if I could go to a different school and no one would know I was a boy, and I would go in as a girl and grow my hair and everyone would treat me like a girl?" He has had no exposure to anything. He has never read and never seen literature or nothing.

Cindy: I'm going to be a little bit theoretical if you will and state that those of us that transition will never be totally women. It can't happen.

Cynthia: That's true.

Cindy: It can't happen for several reasons. Some of them are biological but some of them are the length of time that we have been men. I'm probably more so than the others just because I have been a man longer. What I am trying to say is none of us will ever go back and experience the entire bringing up in our society that a genetic female goes through. We can't be reborn that way. It isn't going to happen. This also brings up a philosophical point and again I don't want to belabor the point because some of the others have heard this. But what does it mean to be a man or a woman? We say or I say, that I'm now as close to being a woman as I can get and that's where I want to be. What does that mean? What does being a woman *mean*? Is it totally in the head? Is it totally in the presentation? Is it being brought up? I don't think this is being answered because I think that unfortunately the answers might be upsetting to an awful lot of people. People who choose to stay with their birth gender and people who choose to live differently. I'm certainly living *differently*. I'm probably about as out as anybody. Anybody in the neighborhoods knows. I came out to the guy that runs the local gas station and I had all my neighbors believing. Everybody knows in town that Cindy used to be Charlie.

Jonathan: Do you tell people that you just meet?

Cindy: No.

Jonathan: So you pass as a woman?

Cindy: Yes, and a lot of the activities that I'm involved in it never comes up. A lot of these are mixed groups. Some people know exactly what is going on and have seen my letters that I used when I was transitioning. For example, our adult Christian Ed[ucation] group has a couple of new members and somebody else may have told them but it's not something we discuss.

Sasha: Okay. Cindy brought up a philosophical point and I want to continue that . . . You asked the question what is a man and what is a woman and I want to kind of pose something that I thought about for many years. In fact, I wrote about it in the CrossPort newsletter. Were we ever men? Do we really know how men feel? I really don't think so. I don't think that I was ever a man in any way but the fact that I had physical attributes of a man. The odd thing about myself, about Randy and about Cynthia—some of us do look like genetic mixes. I have a female face and my body is a female type accept for the appendage. To me I am a bit of a hermaphadite anyway. That plus the other things that have happened to me, the automatic writing and the automatic vocabulary. I'm beginning to ask myself a lot of questions about what I really was when I was born. I don't know.

Jonathan: So you wouldn't rule out intersexuality?

Sasha: I would not but if anybody could have hidden that from me it would have been my family. I don't think I'm going to delve into it but I have my own feelings. I know my own hormone levels and they are through the roof on estrogens. Something is in there somewhere.

Jonathan: Do you take hormones?

Sasha: No I don't. This is me without hormones.

Jonathan: What initiated your transition? Did your transitioning begin when you started to cross-dress?

Sasha: It depends on your definition of the transition. I went out myself for about five and a half years before I told Martha anything. I would go to the mall and go shopping. I hid my clothing in the basement. I was doing a lot of studying. I read thousands of pages. I talked to counselors. I was trying to raise myself above my feelings to be just academic enough to make certain of my own accuracy and determining what this is. I knew what it was but I had to have the proof. I had to have it proven by an awful lot of people because I was becoming too emotional about it. The question is Cindy, Cynthia and Catherine and me—were we ever men?

              If the brain is an organ and we were born with the female power of reasoning and basically a female brain, then we are, and I told Martha this and she disagrees. We are a certain type of hermaphrodite if the brain is an organ. (That might be interesting to explore at a later date, Jonathan.)

              All that I can tell you is that I really do wonder looking back now at the literal torment from the day I can remember of trying to fit in with the male persona even as a child. How could I have been a boy? How could I have been a man under those specific conditions?

Catherine: I say that it's up to the individual interpretation. There are not a whole lot of things that you can pick out in the world that are necessarily male or female. There are very nurturing and gentle males and there are very nurturing and gentle females and there are very violent women and very violent men. Not all women like pink and not all men like blue and so everybody is an individual, just like everybody else, as they say. It's kind of like, be yourself in whatever you are. It's my own interpretation of it and I don't know if I fit the stereotypical male role (probably not) or a stereotypical female role (probably not).

Cindy: As a man or a woman?

Catherine: It doesn't matter. You can't pin anybody down into a category and say this is necessarily male or this is necessarily female. It's all up to an individual interpretation and whatever you want to call yourself is fine. That's just my vent.

Jonathan: Will post-op Catherine be bisexual?

Catherine: Yes. Definitely.

SOME LEGACIES OF BISEXUALITY AND TRANSSEXUALITY

To close out our rich discussions, I asked each participant the following question: What do you think that transgenderism in general, transsexuality in particular, and bisexuality can teach the rest of our society about sex and gender?

Martha: I think that what can be taught to the public is that, yes, tolerance and compassion is the number one thing. What this teaches people is that you can walk to a different drummer and you should be allowed to walk to a different drummer. You should be allowed to express yourself the way you need to whether it is gay, lesbian, transgender, intersexed or whatever. It's got to be okay and accepted and frankly appreciated. I've always been for civil rights and as most of you know in this room I have a major problem when civil rights are not respected. I also have a major problem when civil rights are abused. That's what this comes down to to me. We are all human beings and we are all just trying to live in this world. Sometimes a god-awful world and sometimes a wonderful world, and you know in this day and age if we are supposedly intelligent and growing in our intelligence and growing in our appreciation of different bents and for God's sake we better as hell understand it. Use that intelligence to go with tolerance and compassion.

Cynthia: Well I think what's very important and probably the most important is that everybody should be who they are and who they feel they are. Don't let other people determine for you who that person is. Whatever it takes for you to get to the point that you are happy within yourself, then you need to seek it out and search for it. Find out whatever it takes because ultimately you have to find your own happiness. If you can't find your happiness then you are not going to be able to help anybody else around you because you will be totally consumed by guilt, shame, fear, or whatever. For me I know that it [transitioning] was the best thing I ever did in my life. Probably everybody that has done it wishes they would have done it sooner. As far as falling in love, it's my opinion that we all try to put gender in a box and that I don't think that true love has any gender boundaries. Okay.

Cindy: I'm in the process of working up this talk for these kids at church on Sunday. One of the things is diversity. One of the things that we could add is that diversity is okay and that just because a person is different in the sexual area doesn't mean that that person isn't to be valued and listened to. I'm a very great believer in community. One of the things that has changed and it has nothing to do with sex but may have a great deal to do with gender is (I will admit it) that I was pretty much of a loner all of my life. Now that I'm more into my skin, I am much more comfortable working with people. I don't what that has to do with. If I were to tell someone what the most important thing is, it's the ability to judge people for who they really are and not for their appearance, their gender attraction, their plumbing, their looks even, or even their intelligence. Stupid people are people too.

Marie: I think that transgender and bisexual people should actually be respected and admired to a certain degree because I think that it takes a lot of courage to go against what society has handed you for all of your life and to come out and say [that society is] wrong. That is not what I am. *This* is what I am. I really admire that kind of courage and instead of ridiculing and casting those people aside I wish society would see that as being courageous because I believe it is.

Catherine: I just want everybody to leave me the hell alone. I mean, really. I'm who I am and I don't care what they think or say. Just let me be myself . . .

Sasha: If I were to say something to society it would be just simply stop pushing us away. We exist. There is nothing that you are going to do and there is no mandate that can come down from the Pope or your mom or your dad or your doctor or lawyer or anybody else that is going to tell you that there is no such thing as a transsexual because, being one, I can tell you that there is such a thing as a woman who was born looking like a man. I am living proof of that. I would stake my life on the truth of what I am saying because I am not lying to myself. I would not be going through this. I love saying this but this is a hell of a thing to go through to wear pantyhose in public. No, there is more to it than that and I've told a lot of college kids this as well. If you leave me alone and you stop trying to push me away, there are some rewards in this somewhere along the line: because instead of getting a very pathetic, malfunctioning, suicidal man re-entering society, they'll get a strong, sensitive, much more complete human being who can give to society. It's like the old black hymn, "Free at Last, Free at Last, God I'm Free at Last." I feel that way, as I was not able to function as a man. The whole thing was totally repugnant to me. I was the new man of the year for Penn Mutual Life Insurance Company in 1971, or 1972–I forget. What they didn't know was that every time whether I sold a client or I did not sell a client on an appointment I would go home and throw my dinner up. I was almost bulimic. I could not stand it. I could not stand the role that I was put in because I wanted to nurture, I wanted to hold people, I wanted to create and I needed what was gentle in this world. I wanted to bring some beauty into this world. I didn't want to be someone who punched another clock with a hard hat and say, "Okay honey, I'll work a third shift for you babe." No. No. The ability to be myself, which cost society absolutely not a damn thing. I can maybe touch a whole lot of people and as myself can inspire others. I have to laugh at it at this point. We are and there is no way to stop us. We will enter society. You will not be able to tell the difference, or if the doctor or the lawyer you are seeing or the pilot who is flying your plane might have been born another gender. That's what we are after and that's all we are asking for and it really doesn't harm a soul.

    As far as bisexuality, that will float as it floats. This should be a time of completion. The end of a very hard road. I hate to see that, once people like us reach that point in which we are transitioning now and physically we will become a good likeness of who we thought we were born—I would hate to see that further complicated by the garbage that society just loves to hand people who don't function on their block. Frankly, God help us all. I wish us all well. We are going to need it.

NOTE

1. At this point, I feel compelled to say "sex *or* gender," noting how transsexuality seems to disturb the constructed difference between the two, with "sex" being a biological reality and "gender" the social constructions and normalizations surrounding a fixed biological reality. Given those definitions, some transsexuals who feel they are female, even though they may be born male, seek sexual-reassignment surgery not simply to comply to a perceived set of social norms clustering around the female gender, but because they feel they are actually *female*. Note how one interviewee, Catherine, maintains that she is *not* transsexual; she is *female*. This seems to me an issue of *sex*, not just gender; the transsexual, in some cases, radically recasts his/her body, at the biological level, to be another sex. Nonetheless, gender norms surrounding the sexes are certainly appreciated and "performed" by many transsexuals, so there is ultimately, with regard to transsexuality, no easy distinction between sex and gender. A separate essay, though, will have to take this discussion up in more detail.

Looking Toward the InterSEXions:

Examining Bisexual and Transgender Identity Formation from a Dialectical Theoretical Perspective

Michaela D.E. Meyer

http://www.haworthpress.com/web/JB
Digital Object Identifier: 10.1300/J159v03n03_11

[Haworth co-indexing entry note]: "Looking Toward the InterSEXions: Examining Bisexual and
Transgender Identity Formation from a Dialectical Theoretical Perspective." Meyer, Michaela D. E. Co-pub-
lished simultaneously in *Journal of Bisexuality* (Harrington Park Press, an imprint of The Haworth Press, Inc.)
Vol. 3, No. 3/4, 2003, pp. 151-170; and: *Bisexuality and Transgenderism: InterSEXions of the Others* (ed:
Jonathan Alexander, and Karen Yescavage) Harrington Park Press, an imprint of The Haworth Press, Inc., 2003,
pp. 151-170. Single or multiple copies of this article are available for a fee from The Haworth Document Delivery
Service [1-800-HAWORTH, 9:00 a.m. - 5:00 p.m. (EST). E-mail address: docdelivery@haworthpress.com].

SUMMARY. This paper theorizes how bisexual and transgendered identities are socially constructed through relationships. Traditional models of sexual identity formation have concentrated on the development of gay and lesbian identities, but these models do not adequately explain identity formation for bisexual and transgendered individuals. Furthermore, these models tend to privilege psychological explanations of identity formation. Bisexual and transgendered individuals are caught between the heterosexual and gay/lesbian communities, and thus the ongoing, dynamic process of identity formation for these individuals differs from traditional models of sexual identity formation. Utilizing research on dialectical theory, this essay applies relational dialectical approaches to the formulation of sexual identity "other" than heterosexual or lesbian/gay. Narrative data from published testimonies of bisexual and transgendered individuals highlight the potential applications of this theoretical approach. *[Article copies available for a fee from The Haworth Document Delivery Service: 1-800-HAWORTH. E-mail address: <docdelivery@ haworthpress.com> Website: <http://www.HaworthPress.com> © 2003 by The Haworth Press, Inc. All rights reserved.]*

KEYWORDS. Identity, sexuality, bisexual, transgender, narrative, dialectics

"Out on the sidewalk I'm anybody's guess at queer. In the queer community some lesbians have me pegged as a traitor to all that's female, while gay guys act like I have an infectious disease. I'm taking shit from all directions."

"I can relate," Gordon commiserated in his gravelly voice, "because I've caught a lot of the same stuff for being bisexual. I'm either a fence-sitter or stuck in a phase, according to all sorts of people. It never dawned on me that transgenders would experience the same sort of thing bi's do. You know, a lot of people don't come out 'til they go to college . . . maybe they're trying so hard to be proud of being gay, lesbian, and straight that they can't accept anyone who doesn't seem to be at one end of the scale or the other." (Rogers, 2000)

In the narrative passage above, the author, a female-to-male (FTM) transgendered individual, speaks about his experience with identity expression in the lesbian, gay, bisexual, and transgender (LGBT) community on his campus. His bisexual friend agrees, and attempts to theorize these difficulties. This passage links the experiences of bisexual and transgendered individuals and illustrates how these individuals struggle with the expression of sexual identity. Each individual mentions difficulty being accepted by the lesbian/gay community, and each makes reference to relationships with individuals in that community. In other words, relationships are central to the formation of sexual identity formation, despite a psychological theoretical bias present in most student development literature. Further, the acceptance, or nonacceptance, of the community itself influences the formation of identity.

Sexual identity formation is central to understanding the challenges of LGBT individuals. Yet, models of sexual identity formation frequently focus solely on gay and lesbian identity development, and assume they can be applied to all queer individuals. Some researchers have noted that bisexual and transgender identity formation may not fit these models, but alternative models rarely delve into theoretical underpinnings of identity formation (Evans, Forney, & Guido-Dibrito, 1998). Moreover, these models tend to privilege psychological explanations of identity development, concentrating on awareness of difference and individual action. In order to truly understand bisexual and transgender identity, we must reconceptualize sexual identity formation as a social process and product.

This essay seeks to theorize bisexual and transgendered identity from a dialectical framework. Bisexual and transgender identities are dialectical constructions that rest largely on tensions and interplays between "both/and"-ness of bisexuality and transgender. Bisexuals are "both" heterosexual and homosexual, transgendered individuals are "both" male and female, and both groups adopt discursive patterns and actions of both the heterosexual and lesbian/gay communities. While scholarly research tends to define bisexual identity in terms of a heterosexual/homosexual dichotomy, and transgender identity as a male/female dichotomy, identity for these individuals is a far more dynamic process that includes a constant, day-to-day adaptation of identity defining the sexual self. In other words, bisexual and transgendered individuals are displaced from heterosexual and lesbian/gay communities, to the point that their identities become *debatable* by the social system. When a social system is based on an assumed sexual identity, it displaces those who do not fit into the assumption, particularly when those assumptions occur along binary systems (Calhoun, 2000). Because bisexual and transgender identities do not "fit" into binary constructs of sexual identity, these identities are continually challenged by heterosexual and gay/lesbian communities. Thus, there is a fluidity and flux associated with these identities, making it difficult for bisexual and transgendered individuals to claim these as constant identities. Reconceptualizing identity as a dialectical process rather than a series of fixed endpoints or changes throughout one's life allows for the incorporation of a dynamic approach to identity construction–one that resonates with bisexual and transgendered experience.

To find the intersections of bisexual and transgender experience in sexual identity formation, this essay outlines some of the existing problems with sexual identity research, applies a relational dialectical perspective to identity formation, and provides narrative data of bisexual and transgendered individuals struggling with identity formation. Presenting the experiences of bisexual and transgendered individuals together is not meant to disconfirm or minimize the unique differences presented in bisexual and transgender narratives. Instead, some common themes emerge that provide ways of understanding intersections and applications of the relational dialectic perspective to identity formation for bisexual and transgendered individuals.

PROBLEMS IN THEORETICAL RESEARCH ABOUT BISEXUAL AND TRANSGENDER IDENTITY FORMATION

Despite ample evidence supporting the existence of bisexual and transgendered individuals, theoretical work attempting to explain identity formation of these individuals has been a surprisingly absent factor in sexuality research (MacDonald, 1981; Paul, 1985) and in identity development literature (Evans, Forney, & Guido-Dibrito, 1998). Three factors have contributed to truncated theorizing about bisexual and transgender identity. First, sexuality research was originally, and still is to an extent, conducted in a dichotomous fashion. With the introduction of scaler models to evaluate sexual preference in the late 1940s and early 1950s, sexuality researchers claimed to incorporate a broader view of human sexuality than simple polar models. In Western traditions, bisexual and transgender behavior was labeled as homosexuality. Scaler models evaluated sexual behavior as a continuum with homosexuality and heterosexuality as endpoints. Though bisexuality was the mid-point of scaler models, it was seen as a transition phase through which one would eventually reach one endpoint or the other (e.g., Kinsey, 1948; 1953; Shively & DeCecco, 1977). This theoretical mindset led to popular viewpoints that "one drop of homosexuality indicates latent homosexuality in a straight," a standpoint similar to the theoretical approach applied to race in the 1960s when the dominant white majority claimed that "one drop of black blood makes you black" (Hutchins & Kaahumanu, 1991). Under these medically theorized models, any individual engaging in acts that could be deemed *not* heterosexual was labeled a homosexual individual.

While bisexuality was often theoretically conceptualized as "an intermediate stage between heterosexuality and homosexuality" (Rust, 1997), transgender identity was frequently theorized as a psychopathological conflict between gender identity and biological sex (Stryker, 1997). Models sought to explain transgender identity as a psychological conflict, one in which the individual was "transplanted" or "accidentally" born into the wrong sex (Bullough & Bullough, 1993; Feinberg, 1992). In essence, the underlying assumptions of each were the same: bisexual and transgender individuals are "confused" about their sexual identities. This assumption produced a lack of concrete definitions for bisexual and transgender identity, thus generating a second challenge to the conduct of research on bisexual and transgender identity.

As a result of the medical discourse surrounding sexuality, embracing bisexual identity was "considered to be an evasion of stigma and a denial of one's real self" (Ponse, 1978). This viewpoint was socially reinforced through popular culture. Throughout the 20th century, examples of the fascination with bisexuality as an "experimental" or "transition" phase exist. One of the most salient historical examples are the widely popular "pulps" of the 1950s and 1960s which often told stories involving "unnatural love," "sinful strangers," and "women who dare to live that outcast world of twilight love" (Faderman, 1992). In recent years, bisexuality has gained marginal acceptance as a transition phase, or a process of experimentation, but those who profess their bisexuality past this point of tolerance are seen as promiscuous swingers or sexual predators. In the end, these attitudes hinder the ability to define bisexuality as a valid social identity.

These same problems occur in theorizing about transgender identity. Just as bisexuality is seen as a transition phase, transgendered individuals are often seen as in "transition" to their "appropriate" gender (Califa, 1997). Discussions of transgender identity often center on the question of whether or not it is acceptable to "pass" in society (Allen, 1996; Feinburg, 1993). Passing in one sense is conceptualized as repressive for the transgender individual who must hide her/his true identity, yet others see passing as liberating. Only now are theorists distinguishing between transgender identity and transvestitism, demonstrating that much theoretical confusion still exists in defining "transgender" (Hausman, 2001).

Conversely, the heterosexual majority finds defining gay and lesbian identities simpler–an individual who is not straight is gay. As Dinno (1997) notes, "Our culture has a very strong sense of the gay or lesbian person. These are part of our cultural iconography or typology of persons. Whether or not they are presented in detail or as positive or negative, they are available for the developing youth to grasp and manipulate" (p. 205). Often bisexual and transgendered identities are defined in relation to gay/lesbian identities rather than being defined as unique sexual identities. In essence, "bisexual" and "transgendered" can mean so many things, and thus becomes problematic for the general public to understand. Further, these identities present a challenge to researchers struggling to provide definitions for phenomena that seem to have polysemous definitions.

A third set of issues emerges when factoring in the political climate in which sexuality research is conducted. First, there is an issue of heterosexual bias in sexuality research. This bias can deter researchers from the topic of bisexuality or transgender because of bi-/trans-phobia. Researchers seeking to study bisexual or transgender issues (and even gay or lesbian issues to an extent) must balance their desire to study these topics due to the risk of their scholarship "labeling" them as one of these sexual or gender minorities. The difficulties conducting this research do not stop at the psychological level of the researcher and/or institution. Social and economic pressures on sexual identity, particularly in America, have become increasingly visible in marginalizing individuals of any identity other than heterosexual, with bisexual and transgender identities being particularly suspicious. Thus, researchers face substantial challenges in finding "out" bisexual or transgender individuals willing to participate in research experiments when scholarly research has frequently been used to further marginalize or discriminate against them by disconfirming their identity choices. Issues of trust and secrecy make it difficult for researchers to access the population they wish to study, particularly when there is no consistent definition of bisexual or transgender identity. Not only are the operational definitions of bisexuality and transgender constantly changing, but variations in cultural contexts also serve to challenge the construction of these constructs, which are predominantly Western in orientation.

These three challenges contribute to a general lack of serious academic theorizing of bisexual and transgender identity formation, and consequently, the available literature for educative purposes is scarce. Bisexual and transgender individuals questioning sexual identity have little educational literature to work from, making it difficult if not impossible to formulate identity. Society's malaise with these sexual subject positions makes accounts of bisexual and transgender individuals difficult to locate in print form, and near impossible to locate in media programming. The systematic erasure of bisexuality and transgenderism in media has been coupled with a more progressive approach to gay and lesbian lifestyles, presenting a further challenge to those wishing to find voice on these issues.

BISEXUAL AND TRANSGENDER IDENTITY FORMATION AS DIALECTICAL PROCESS

The dialectical viewpoint has been used to construct argument, analyze debate, examine social tensions, and applied to relational maintenance, however, dialectics as a theoretical framework for identity construction has yet to be explored. While identity formation has not been explored from a dialectical perspective, some research has used dialectical theory to theoretically situate queer issues. Dindia (1998) examines experiences of gay and lesbian individuals in the coming-out process by using a dialectical approach to highlight the management of disclosures about sexuality. She claims, "disclosing private and risky information about self is a dialectical phenomenon in which all the assumptions of the dialectical perspective apply" (p. 105). The process of "coming out" is ongoing and problematic in many instances, and many individuals report experiences of continually managing the coming-out process depending on which other individuals are involved. This work reframed dialectics within the language of the LGBT community, however, it appropriates dialectics only in terms of self-disclosure, not in terms of sexual identity construction. Scholars have noted that sexuality appears to be a fluid concept, in that many individuals self-identifying as gay, lesbian or bisexual at one point may adapt that label as life progresses (Huston & Schwartz, 1996; Wood, 2000; 2001). Despite these observations, the study of sexuality and relationships continues to operate from a predominantly heterosexual framework.

Leslie Baxter and Barbara Montgomery (1996) synthesize traditional views of dialectics and apply them specifically to the context of interpersonal relationships, which provides a framework for examining bisexual identity construction. They claim *relational dialectics* is "a belief that social life is a dynamic knot of contradictions, a ceaseless interplay between contrary or opposing tendencies" (p. 3). This view expanded traditional stage models of interpersonal communication that assume a relationship begins, progresses to intimacy and then potentially dissolves (e.g., Knapp, 1978; Taylor & Altman, 1987, see also Lannutti & Cameron, 2002). The theoretical framework of the linear, dichotomous models of interpersonal relationship formation is strikingly similar to the scaler models used to evaluate sexual identity.

Unlike scaler models that work toward a fixed endpoint, relational dialectics views relationships as a never-ending process of co-creation. This same theoretical framework can be adapted to explain the process of bisexual and transgender identity formation precisely because the process is on-going, dynamic, and highly personalized. Baxter and Montgomery (1996) and Montgomery and Baxter (1998) explain that relational dialectics theory incorporates four elements present in any given interpersonal relationship: contradiction, change, praxis and totality. Contradiction "emphasizes how parties manage the simultaneous exigence for both disclosure and privacy in their relationships and, especially, how the 'both/and'-ness of disclosure and privacy is patterned through their interplay across the temporal course of the relationship" (Baxter & Montgomery, 1996). In other words, relationships are built on the notion that individuals involved in them want both privacy and openness in the relationship, and the contradiction between the two determines how the relationship is managed. This same principle can be applied to the formation of a sexual identity other than heterosexual–an individual struggles to maintain the privacy or secrecy of one's sexual differences, while at the same time longs to be open and honest with those s/he cares for about her/his sexual orientation. As a result, individuals questioning and exploring their sexual or gender identity must constantly manage this tension in formulating that identity. This is especially true for bisexual and transgendered individuals who find themselves having to come out to *both* the heterosexual and the gay/lesbian (nonaccepting) communities.

Change is traditionally conceptualized as events that happen which alter the course of a linear path. In a dialectical perspective, change is seen as a spiral rather than a punctuated series of events. The spiral allows "recurrence but recognizes that phenomena never repeat in identical form; a spiral thus combines elements of cyclical change (recurrence) and linear change (the absence of identical repetition)" (Baxter & Montgomery, 1996, p. 13). Applying this to interpersonal relationships, cyclical change can be seen in reoccurring arguments some couples experience. The subject matter of the argument may be the same, but the argument never replicates itself entirely. Instead, the same issues are explored in different ways through dialogue and eventually results in different arguments. A similar experience can be applied to the formulation of bisexual and transgender identity.

Bisexual and transgender individuals must frequently adapt to changes in identity formation. For bisexual individuals, this tension manifests based on their choice of partner. Identity struggles occur any time an individual parts with a significant other, and when one finds a new significant other, some redefinitions of identity are inevitable. However, bisexual individuals must mediate their identity based on the sex of their significant other. For example, a bisexual woman dating a woman might attempt to redefine her identity to mirror a lesbian identity, but later if she begins to date a man, she may redefine her identity to reflect more heterosexual components. The results can be socially problematic. For example, if the woman was involved in a women-only support group with her previous partner, she may no longer be allowed to attend with her male partner. In effect, the overhaul of identity formation based on changes in dating partners causes a large tension for many bisexual individuals. Furthermore, in cases of polyamorous relationships, individuals involved face not only the challenges of sexuality, but also of attempting to alter a traditional monogamous social framework. For transgendered individuals, similar situations can occur that effect change in given relationships. Issues of sexuality also come into play with the transgendered individual's choice of partner, but is mediated through gender choices rather than sex choices (though both could occur simultaneously for the transgendered individual).

The other two theoretical factors deal with the relational context in which the dialectical situations occur. Praxis is the idea that individuals are simultaneously actors and objects of their own actions. Praxis means that individuals have the ability to make communicative choices based on past experiences that will drive future interactions. From a dialectical perspective, communication is used as a symbolic resource from which meanings are produced and reproduced within any given relationship. The communicative choices made by participants in the relationship will alter the dialectical tensions the participants may face in the future. For example, individuals who perceive a relationship having too much autonomy and not enough interdependence may move "from naively optimistic efforts to gloss over or ignore the tension, to efforts that emphasize increased interdependence and decreased autonomy, to fatalistic efforts to accept the inevitability of their situation, to efforts to redefine what they mean by togetherness and separation" (Baxter & Montgomery, 1996, p. 14). Whether the participants move through all of these phases or fixate on one particular way to solve the tension, the relationship is futuristically defined by the communicative choices of the individual participants.

Similarly, bisexual identity formation is driven by futuristic communicative choices, primarily with respect to the "option" of both genders as sexual partners. In many instances, past experience serves as a way to mediate future identity formation from relationships (e.g., "the last time I dated a lesbian, she was suspicious that I was bisexual and would leave her for a man, thus if I date another lesbian we'll have to fight about the same issue"). These past experiences keep the formation of identity within a futuristic framework that is constantly redefined based on prior experiences and the future option of various gendered partners. While transgendered individuals can also experience this tension in gender of partner, futuristic choices lie predominantly in gender performance. For example, how can FTM transgendered individuals define themselves with respect to the more formalized "butch" lesbian identity, and how do they differ? The communicative choices in the performance of gender in these situations are often based on identity claims from the individuals involved, and without defining multiple gender identities scholars "will fail to change existing gender hierarchies" (Halberstam, 1998). Thus, the potential for multiple spaces and multiple voices predicts a futuristic track for communicating about sexual and gender identity.

Totality is a similar concept to praxis, but is differently synthesized. Totality assumes that phenomena can only be understood in relation to other phenomena. Dialectical tensions occur because of interaction with others, and thus, individuals in relationships jointly own tensions created by the relationship. Totality deals with three specific issues of context: where contradictions are located, interdependencies among contradictions and conceptualization of contradictions. First, the tensions are specific in their contexts. They can occur within a relationship (internal) or it could be caused by factors outside of a relationship (external), thus altering the location from which the tension begins and is mediated. The particular context of the interaction also relies on the interdependence of contextual variables in terms of what type of relationship is being studied, at what time that relationship occurs, issues of race, class or other mitigating factors of context must be taken into account when examining relational dialectics. Issues of location and interdependency challenge the researchers to conceptualize the contradiction in a complex way that accounts for all of these variables simultaneously. Totality in bisexual and transgender identity formation can manifest in many ways. Often bisexual and transgendered individuals must balance their gender and/or sexual identity with other marginalizing factors that contribute to identity formation such as race, class, ethnicity, and education status. Also, tensions on identity formation for bisexual and transgendered individuals come from both internal (within the LGBT community) and external (within the heterosexual community) sources.

THEORETICAL ISSUES IN PRACTICE: NARRATIVE EXAMPLES OF DIALECTICAL COPING

The dichotomy surrounding sexuality emerges because of societal pressure to identify with one of the ends of Kinsey's spectrum and leads to a narrowing of sexual identity for all individuals (Tucker, 1995, p. 40). Using dialectical theory to explain theoretical issues behind the formulation of bisexual and transgender identity provides a theoretical framework from which narratives of bisexual and transgendered individuals can be more fully understood. Sexuality and gender are dialectical constructions that develop when individuals define themselves in terms of dichotomies (heterosexual/homosexual, and/or, male/female) that do not allow space for framing these identities outside polar endpoints. For bisexual individuals, narrative data focuses on *sexual practice*, while narrative data from transgendered individuals focuses on *gender performance*.

In narrative accounts, bisexuals note that their identity often evolves from relationships: if the individual dates someone of the same gender, they are "homosexual" and if they date someone of the opposite gender, they are "heterosexual" regardless of prior experiences. As one bisexual noted, "my gay and straight friends . . . seemed to share the same criteria: 'How many men and how many women have you slept with?' as if being sexual with a certain number of men and a certain number of women makes me a 'true' bisexual" (Leyva, 1991). For this individual, defining bisexuality was a constant struggle between what straight friends and gay friends thought of him based on assumed numerical formulas. Similarly, bisexual women in long-term relationships with men often struggle with their socially constructed image as heterosexual, while other bisexual women in relationships with other women find they must mediate the socially constructed image of themselves as lesbian (Hutchins & Kaahumanu, 1991).

The dichotomy surrounding gender also manifests in narratives of transgender experience. One transsexual commented that since our language to discuss the dichotomy of gender is limited, "it becomes easy to assume that gay and lesbian images and resources are the same as the issues and resources of the transgendered . . . transsexualism, not to mention any of the other transgender conceptions, are hidden and almost nonexistent" (Dinno, 1997). In other words, it appears there are more opportunities within language to discuss the dichotomy of sexuality, but this language has not been developed for discussing the dichotomy of gender. In fact, feminist scholars have been criticized by scholars of transgendered issues for failing to take seriously the language barrier present to discussing the gender dichotomy (Hausman, 2001). As a result, transgendered experience frequently manifests as a dialectical process of managing relational tensions without adequate communicative resources.

Narrative data identifies that the most significant tension for bisexual and transgendered individuals is mediating criticism not only from the straight community, but also from the gay/lesbian community. The constant struggle to define identity in opposition to the heterosexual/homosexual dichotomy produces an on-going dialectical process of identity formation for bisexual and transgendered individuals. Narratives of bisexual experience reveal the dilemma of formulating identity when neither community validates bisexual identity. For example, one bisexual described her experience saying, "Bisexuals huddle nervously in the middle, like kids listening to their parents (the gays and the straights) fight. We protest—we're basically all the same, sex is really just sex, doesn't much matter with whom—a little utopian choir in a war zone" (Queen, 1991). In other words, this individual's understanding of the relationship between sexuality and identity rests in a "utopian" vision where sexual dichotomies are nonexistent. Her explanation of the reception of this view by the heterosexual and the lesbian/gay community shows the disconfirmation of bisexual identity in both groups.

Within the heterosexual community, the resounding understanding of bisexuality is that it is "trendy" and a process of "experimentation" that will eventually lead an individual back to the heterosexual fold. When the straight community does not respond with curiosity, it often responds to bisexual identity with disconfirming anger. One woman noted that the question she was asked most often by her straight friends was, "Why do you spend so much time with gay people if you're not a lesbian?" (Suzanne, 1991). In another account, the author explained the attacks of the straight community on his bisexual friend who was dating a woman, "she has been told, 'that must make you a lesbian, since you have sex with a woman and not with a man.' Her response is that she is still attracted to both men and women. She just happens to be monogamous with a woman for now" (Bryant, 1991). This response is threatening to the heterosexual order, primarily because it leaves open the possibility of "swinging" to another sexual orientation, a practice that creates wariness for the heterosexual community. The bisexual individual becomes difficult to label, and thus becomes problematic for heterosexual society.

Similarly, bisexual individuals encounter problems coming out as bisexual in the lesbian/gay community. Historically, several bisexual and transgendered individuals helped define the gay and lesbian rights movement, but in order to do so, definitions were made that excluded the unique experiences of these individuals (Adam, 1995). Consequently, advocacy in gay and lesbian groups tends to center opposition to "straight" culture. Queer social support groups often do not endorse bisexuality, and frame bisexuality as a kind of limbo where an individual has yet to identify as gay, lesbian or straight. One individual writes about her experience with bisexuality by saying, "I took a gay studies class [in college] and got a little support for bisexuality, and a lot of support for getting past it—'a phase' I was going through" (Queen, 1991). Instead of finding support for a bisexual identity in a queer space, the individual found that bisexuality was treated as "a phase," something to work through on the way to determining a heterosexual or lesbian or gay identity. Bisexual individuals caught in the crossfire between heterosexuality and homosexuality rarely have the opportunity to discuss bisexual issues. Another individual explained her experience by quoting a diversity panel of gay and lesbian students she encountered in college. The lesbian speaking for the community responded to a question on bisexuality by saying,

> Of course, there are a lot of people who are bi in theory . . . people who think being bisexual is "neat" and politically correct. Some even show

up to events, but when it comes to getting political, all of sudden they disappear. They just come to sleep with our women, but as soon as they get the chance, they run back to the protecting arms of heterosexuality. (G. Rodriguez, 2000)

As this narrative shows, the lesbian/gay community often views bisexual individuals as not "committed" to the cause, and this becomes a central dialectical tension in the formation of bisexual identity.

The problem becomes increasingly complex when the heterosexual and lesbian/gay community simultaneously frame the stereotypical "swinger" bisexual image as "true" bisexuality. The resounding platform of the gay rights movement has been a push for the acceptance of gay marriages, implying a commitment to practicing monogamy. Bisexuality is frequently viewed as a threat to such an agenda, since bisexuality is often equated with polygamy, whether or not that is true in practice. One bisexual argues,

A lot of people think they may not be bisexual, because they have a preference for one gender over the other. They have been told that if they can just work through this phase they're going through they will be okay as heterosexuals or as homosexuals. I have never understood why people think that monosexuality is a more natural condition than bisexuality. (Bryant, 1991)

In other words, the focus of the gay and lesbian movement on marriage as an end goal frequently displaces and disconfirms bisexual identity because it threatens the dominance of relational monogamy. Thus, the only way for bisexuals to contribute to the movement is to think of bisexual identity as a "phase" through which one must progress in order to "prove oneself" to the cause. As a result, even within the gay and lesbian community, bisexuality is a relatively invisible concept in terms of support systems and conceptualizations of identity. More often than not, bisexuals must align themselves with support groups based on their current relationships and manage the tension accordingly depending on the sex of their partner (Fox, 1991).

Narrative experiences of transgendered individuals often reflect a similar quandary. Transgendered individuals report finding a similar lack of support from both the heterosexual and the lesbian/gay community. As one transgendered individual described it, "When you say you're gay, it's pretty clear what you mean. Most people, however, have never even heard the word transgendered, nor have they met someone who identifies as such. My coming out was a continual challenge" (Fried, 2000). Transgendered individuals also face similar dialectical tensions in identity formation. One young transsexual commented that time and time again, members of the heterosexual community disconfirmed her identity choices:

> "You're not really queer." By whose definition? The lack of a language to deal with these issues does not help. Nor does the fact that so much is couched in sexist and heterosexist terminology. "Oh it's a sexual thing right?" "But Alexis, you're so male!" (Dinno, 1997)

The problem here comes from a lack of language to adequately define the transgender experience for the heterosexual majority. Further, the disconfirmation of gender identity in this passage illustrates how the heterosexual community may understand the dichotomy of sexuality more so than the dichotomy of gender. The response to the individual's disclosure of identity is countered with "You're not really queer," implying that sexuality makes one queer, not gender. A similar problem with inadequate language was explained by a transgendered individual,

> I never thought I was confused about my gender until I realized gender was confused with me. Cut my hair, and suddenly it's "Sir! Sir!" And I can't tell you how many children have come up to me and asked, "Are you a boy or a girl?" One kid even argued with me. "I'm a girl!" I said, and pulled a gender trump card, illustrating my breasts [but] there was no convincing him. I simply lacked proper identification. And ever since that happened, I've realized it is rather confusing, "Are you a boy or a girl?" I mean, who gets to decide, you or me? (Lusero, 2000)

In this passage, the understanding of gender as a dichotomous binary is displayed. The individual even notes that she did not consider herself transgender until she realized "gender was confused with me." The lack of adequate language to explain transgendered identities becomes problematic for the straight community, which has far less terminology to explain gender phenomenon than language to explain sexuality.

However, transgendered individuals report extremely similar experiences within the gay/lesbian community as bisexual individuals do. Transgendered individuals also feel the gay/lesbian community discourages their participation in the queer movement. One individual illustrated the extreme resistance she feels within the lesbian/gay community,

> The pressure to conform or "shut up" continues to alienate us to this day. We are not heard in the larger LGBT movement unless we play the part of passive victims, unless we look and act exactly like they do–proudly

adorned with rainbow flags, working in co-opted nonprofits, lobbying for mere "tolerance," for more laws. (M. K. Rodriguez, 2000)

In other words, similar to experiences reported by bisexual individuals, transgender individuals do not fit the "mold" in terms of the gay and lesbian movement's agenda. Transgendered individuals also report backlash and anger by the larger LGBT community for "complicating" issues within the movement further. A male-to-female (MTF) individual noted that, "In spite of its pro-diversity stance, the campus lesbian and gay community didn't welcome me with open arms. At the queer meetings my questions and comments were viewed as tedious and annoying" (Gray, 2000). One student in this transgendered individual's gay and lesbian support group commented, "I disagree with him completely. I don't have anything in common with transsexuals. If they want to form their own community, that's fine, but I don't care to have anything to do with them" (Gray, 2000). In essence, the student's response disconfirmed the transgendered individual's identity first by addressing the individual as "him" and then further discrediting her place in the queer community by suggesting that transsexuals "form their own community." Narrative reports like this are common in published accounts of transgender experience.

FINDING THE INTERSEXIONS

Throughout this essay, I have situated the problems in identity formation research for bisexual and transgendered individuals with narrative accounts of bisexual and transgendered experience. The adaptation of dialectical theory to identity formation provides a useful framework for examining the experiences of both groups. Narratives of transgender experiences echo the same kinds of dialectical tensions expressed in narratives of bisexuality and vice versa. Utilizing a dialectical framework to discuss bisexual or transgender identities allows for multiple options in future sexuality research. Dialectical approaches to identity construction can incorporate more fully the ideas of totality and praxis than traditional approaches to dialectical studies. While identity research usually accounts for contradiction and change, totality and praxis are undertheorized dimensions that could be expanded by focusing on dialectics as a means of identity formation. It would allow us to account for the marginality experienced by bisexual and transgendered individuals on a daily basis. It further allows us to theorize more practically about the "messiness" of human existence–that identity is both *social process* and *social product*.

The narrative data presented here display how the tensions of contradiction, change, and totality occur for both bisexual and transgendered individuals when forming identity. In fact, the narratives reveal strikingly similar struggles for both bisexual and transgendered individuals in dealing with both heterosexual and lesbian/gay communities. Praxis is where the narratives seem to differ. The idea of futuristic experiences and communicative choices vary based on the focus: sexuality or gender. Furthermore, narratives of transgendered experience often highlight the problem of insufficient language to describe their gender preferences. In essence, these stories could be interpreted to mean that the gender dichotomy is more pervasive than the sexuality dichotomy. Many individuals noted that the general public understands fundamental differences between "gay" and "straight," while narratives of transgender experience show how problematic the terms "boy" and "girl" become when situated within contemporary language. Examinations of how praxis informs identity choices and communicative action could provide a starting point for examining the experiences of bisexual and transgendered individuals as unique.

To do so, it is imperative that we protect the option for new methodologies, discussions, and explorations in academic forums such as this. Only by exploring that which constitutes difference will we ever achieve an understanding of unity. Part of doing so requires opening a space within academic writing for discussion of bisexuality and transgendered issues. Further, how can bisexual and transgendered individuals support each other in creating space for their discursive voices? I am not proposing that we drop the increased focus on lesbian/gay research in our profession, in fact, I whole-heartedly support these efforts. However, we must understand that research on gays and lesbians does *not* equate to research on all types of sexuality, and the results of this research are not immediately transferable to bisexual and transgendered experiences. Rather, we can learn a good deal by studying the similarities of the bisexual and transgendered experiences together.

My intention is *not* to disconfirm or minimize the unique differences presented in bisexual and transgender narratives. However, the LGBT community frequently emphasizes difference at the expense of finding commonalities that link us all together. The narratives presented here, such as those from bisexual and transgendered individuals reflecting on LGBT student organizations, illustrate the desire of some LGBT members to separate and define specific differences of individuals within the community. These definitions are useful for explaining the LGBT community to outsiders, but staunchly adhering to difference prevents the community from uniting against larger common oppressions for all queer individuals. Future research could focus on how identity defines and redefines community building practices within different LGBT groups. Does the presence of a bisexual or transgendered person fundamentally change a community's understanding of what it means to be "queer"? The answer may lie in our ever-present struggle for identity, and the dialectical nature of human interaction.

REFERENCES

Adam, B. D. (1995). *The rise of a gay and lesbian movement.* New York: Twayne Publishers.

Allen, J. J. (1996). *The man in the red velvet dress: Inside the world of cross-dressing.* New York: Carol Publishing Group.

Baxter, L. A., & Montgomery, B. M. (1996). *Relating: Dialogues & dialectics.* New York: The Guilford Press.

Bryant, W. (1991). Love, friendship and sex. In L. Hutchins & L. Kaahumanu (Eds.), *Bi any other name: Bisexual people speak out* (pp. 69-73). New York: Alyson Books.

Bullough, V. L., & Bullough, B. (1993). *Cross dressing, sex, and gender* (pp. 204-225). Philadelphia: University of Pennsylvania Press.

Calhoun, C. (2000). *Feminism, the family, and the politics of the closet: Lesbian and gay displacement.* New York: Oxford University Press.

Califa, P. (1997). *Sex changes: The politics of transgenderism.* San Francisco: Cleis Press.

Dindia, K. (1998). "Going into and coming out of the closet": The dialectics of stigma disclosure. In B. M. Montgomery & L. A. Baxter (Eds.), *Dialectical approaches to studying personal relationships* (pp. 83-108). Mahwah, NJ: Lawrence Erlbaum Associates, Inc.

Dinno, A. B. (1997). From the perspective of a young transsexual. In G. E. Israel & D. E. Tarver II (Eds.), *Transgender care: Recommended guidelines, practical information, and personal accounts* (pp. 203-207). Philadelphia: Temple University Press.

Evans, N. J., Forney, D. S., & Guido-DiBrito, F. (1998). *Student development in college: Theory, research and practice.* San Francisco: Jossey-Bass Publishers.

Faderman, L. (1992). *Odd girls and twilight lovers: A history of lesbian life in twentieth-century America.* New York: Penguin Group.

Feinberg, L. (1993). *Stone butch blues.* Ithaca, NY: Firebrand Books.

Feinberg, L. (1992). *Transgender liberation: A movement whose time has come.* New York: World View Forum.

Fox, A. (1991). Development of a bisexual identity: Understanding the process. In L. Hutchins & L. Kaahumanu (Eds.), *Bi any other name: Bisexual people speak out* (pp. 29-36). New York: Alyson Books.

Fried, I. (2000). It's a long journey. In K. Howard & A. Stevens (Eds.), *Out & about campus: Personal accounts by lesbian, gay, bisexual, & transgendered college students* (pp. 244-255). Los Angeles: Alyson Publications.

Garber, M. (2000). *Bisexuality and the eroticism of everyday life.* New York: Routledge.

Gray, A. T. (2000). Wearing the dress. In K. Howard & A. Stevens (Eds.), *Out & about campus: Personal accounts by lesbian, gay, bisexual, & transgendered college students* (pp. 83-91). Los Angeles: Alyson Publications.

Halberstam, J. (1998). F2M: The making of female masculinity. In J. Rivkin & M. Ryan (Eds.), *Literary theory: An anthology* (pp. 759-768). Malden, MA: Blackwell Publishers.

Hausman, B. L. (2001). Recent transgender theory. *Feminist Studies, 27,* 465-491.

Huston, M., & Schwartz, P. (1996). Gendered dynamics in gay and lesbian relationships. In J. T. Wood (Ed.), *Gendered relationships: A reader* (pp. 89-121). Mountain View, CA: Mayfield.

Hutchins, L., & Kaahumanu, L. (Eds.). (1991). *Bi any other name: Bisexual people speak out.* New York: Alyson Books.

Kinsey, A. C. (1948). *Sexual behavior in the human male.* Philadelphia: W.B. Saunders Company.

Kinsey, A. C. (1953). *Sexual behavior in the human female.* Philadelphia: W.B. Saunders Company.

Knapp, M. L. (1978). *Social intercourse: From greeting to goodbye.* Boston: Allyn and Bacon.

Lannutti, P. J., & Cameron, K. A. (2002). Beyond the breakup: Heterosexual and homosexual post-dissolutional relationships. *Communication Quarterly, 50,* 153-170.

Leyva, O. (1991). Que es un bisexual? In L. Hutchins & L. Kaahumanu (Eds.), *Bi any other name: Bisexual people speak out* (pp. 201-202). New York: Alyson Books.

Lusero, L. (2000). Excerpts from *Impossible Body.* In A. Sonnie (Ed.), *Revolutionary voices* (pp. 219-236). New York: Alyson Books.

MacDonald, A. P., Jr. (1981). Bisexuality: Some comments on research and theory. *Journal of Homosexuality, 6,* 21-35.

Montgomery, B. M., & Baxter, L. A. (Eds.). (1998). *Dialectical approaches to studying personal relationships.* Mahwah, NJ: Lawrence Erlbaum Associates, Inc.

Paul, J. P. (1985). Bisexuality: Reassessing our paradigms of sexuality. In F. Klein & T. Wolf (Eds.), *Two lives to lead: Bisexuality in men and women.* New York: Harrington Park Press.

Ponse, B. (1978). *Identities in the lesbian world: The social construction of self.* Westport, CT: Greenwood Press.

Queen, C. A. (1991). The queer in me. In L. Hutchins & L. Kaahumanu (Eds.), *Bi any other name: Bisexual people speak out* (pp. 17-21). New York: Alyson Books.

Rodriguez, G. (2000). Creating familia. In K. Howard & A. Stevens (Eds.), *Out & about campus: Personal accounts by lesbian, gay, bisexual, & transgendered college students* (pp. 200-211). Los Angeles: Alyson Publications.

Rodriguez, M. K. (2000). We are the once we have been waiting for. In A. Sonnie (Ed.), *Revolutionary voices* (pp. 219-236). New York: Alyson Books.

Rogers, J. (2000). Getting real at ISU: A campus tradition. In K. Howard & A. Stevens (Eds.), *Out & about campus: Personal accounts by lesbian, gay, bisexual, & transgendered college students* (pp. 12-18). Los Angeles: Alyson Publications.

Rust, P. (1997). "Coming out" in the age of social constructionism: Sexual identity formation among lesbian and bisexual women. In E. D. Rothblum (Ed.), *Classics in lesbian studies* (pp. 25-54). New York: Harrington Park Press.

Shivley, M. G., & DeCecco, J. P. (1977). Components of sexual identity. *Journal of Homosexuality, 17,* 481-497.

Stryker, S. (1997). Over and out in academe: Transgender studies come of age. In G. E. Israel & D. E. Tarver II (Eds.), *Transgender care: Recommended guidelines, practical information, and personal accounts* (pp. 241-244). Philadelphia: Temple University Press.

Suzanne (1991). I have always been one. In L. Hutchins & L. Kaahumanu (Eds.), *Bi any other name: Bisexual people speak out* (pp. 198-200). New York: Alyson Books.

Taylor, D. A., & Altman, I. (1987). Communication in interpersonal relationships: Social penetration processes. In M. E. Roloff & G. R. Miller (Eds.), *Interpersonal processes: New directions in communication research* (pp. 257-277). Newbury Park, CA: Sage.

Tucker, N. (Ed.). (1995). *Bisexual politics: Theories, queries and visions.* New York: Harrington Park Press.

Walter, L. (2000). Teamwork. In K. Howard & A. Stevens (Eds.), *Out & about campus: Personal accounts by lesbian, gay, bisexual, & transgendered college students* (pp. 234-243). Los Angeles: Alyson Publications.

Wood, J. T. (2000). Gender and personal relationships. In C. Hendrick & S. S. Hendrick (Eds.), *Close relationships: A sourcebook* (pp. 300-313). Thousand Oaks, CA: Sage.

Wood, J. T. (2001). *Gendered lives: Communication, gender and culture* (4th ed.). Belmont, CA: Wadsworth.

REEL LIVES: B/T POP CULTURAL ICONS

Trans/positioning the (Drag?) King of Comedy: Bisexuality and Queer Jewish Space in the Works of Sandra Bernhard

Milla Rosenberg

[Haworth co-indexing entry note]: "Trans/positioning the (Drag?) King of Comedy: Bisexuality and Queer Jewish Space in the Works of Sandra Bernhard." Rosenberg. Milla. Co-published simultaneously in *Journal of Bisexuality* (Harrington Park Press. an imprint of The Haworth Press. Inc.) Vol. 3. No. 3/4. 2003. pp. 171-179: and: *Bisexuality and Transgenderism: InterSEXions of the Others* (ed: Jonathan Alexander, and Karen Yescavage) Harrington Park Press, an imprint of The Haworth Press. Inc.. 2003. pp. 171-179. Single or multiple copies of this article are available for a fee from The Haworth Document Delivery Service [1-800-HAWORTH. 9:00 a.m. - 5:00 p.m. (EST). E-mail address: docdelivery@haworthpress.com].

SUMMARY. Within both the heterosexist culture of the West and main-stream lesbian and gay culture, transgender people and expression have been historically marginalized. Yet, bisexuality has offered a critical space for exploring transgender issues. This essay explores the intersection of bisexual and transgender expression in the works of performer and writer Sandra Bernhard. I contend that Bernhard extends a "dysphoric" critique of dominant religious and gender norms in America and has continually as-serted a bisexuality over and against the media's attempts to categorize her as "definitively" lesbian. *[Article copies available for a fee from The Haworth Document Delivery Service: 1-800-HAWORTH. E-mail address: <docdelivery@ haworthpress.com> Website: <http://www.HaworthPress.com> © 2003 by The Haworth Press, Inc. All rights reserved.]*

KEYWORDS. Bisexuality, transgender, media representations, queer, performance, Jewish comedians

Few artists have shown the performative range that Sandra Bernhard has. Through song, stand-up comedy, films, and books, Bernhard's work has tra-versed an array of significant issues: cross-racial desire, the excesses of patrio-tism, violence against women, and, most recently, single motherhood, to name just a few. Unfortunately, academic critics have largely overlooked her sub-stantive critiques of America, defining Bernhard as a kind of "problematic," boundary figure; some have deemed her work racist and a modern form of blackface, a claim that this essay will explore in greater depth. Finally, lesbian scholars have consistently referred to her work as exploring "lesbian desire" and have even, erroneously, identified her as a lesbian.

In this essay, I re/claim Sandra as the beautiful Jewish, bisexual woman that she is; in doing so, I explore how Bernhard's films and writings express bisex-ual desires; these desires often intersect and extend a "dysphoric" critique of dominant Christian norms. Bernhard performs maleness in ways that both ex-tend a feminist sensibility *and* call into question the category of "woman." Thus, I consider the ways in which her works launch a critique of the differ-ences that gender makes.

First, let's set the record queer: as early as 1988, Sandra Bernhard was an out and proud bi-woman. In her first book, *Confessions of a Pretty Lady*, she writes of a crush on her third-grade teacher and a few passages later, discusses how she explored her first boyfriend's body. Later, after her move to L.A., a young college woman flirts with her and initiates a relationship with Sandra. In *Love Love and Love* (1993), she writes of a brief relationship with a young woman whom she meets at an airport. The woman is "with" a wealthy man who is controlling and abusive.

Over and against Bernhard's bisexuality, lesbian critics have read the film version of her stage play *Without You I'm Nothing* as a kind of paradigm of cross-racial desire for a black woman. Cultural studies scholar Elspeth Probyn (1993), in her otherwise eloquent book *Sexing the Self*, introduces Bernhard this way:

> For those unfamiliar with Sandra Bernhard, she can be most simply de-scribed as a performance artist/stand-up comic who achieved notoriety with Madonna as they teased us with the idea that they were lovers. In actual fact, while Madonna has never come out, Sandra repeatedly does so in various *ways that don't quite conform to the dictates of gay and les-bian pride: as a bi-sexual, as involved with a man, as sleeping with dif-ferent women, etc.* (p. 151, emphasis added)

In this "simple" description, Probyn's decision to hyphenate Bernhard's "bi-sexuality" seems biphobic, as it positions bisexuality as either/or. While Probyn is aware of the "dictates" of late 1980s gay and lesbian culture (recall that 1987 was the first year that bisexuals organized a contingent and secured inclusion in the March for Lesbian and Gay Rights),[1] she will refer to her rela-tionship with "Roxanne," the black woman at the center of the film, as "les-bian desire." Listen to how she renders Bernhard's scenes with a black male lover:

> The rhythm this creates syncopates our excitement with Sandra's (and our) excitement which breaks upon a overhead shot of Sandra (on the bottom) fucking with a black man. While this scene obviously stalls the lesbo-eroticism that has been mounting, it also teases us with the knowl-edge that there is more, that the brother is a temporary substitution for the ever evasive sister. (p. 156)

The notion that Sandra's desire for a male can only be a prelude to her longing for Roxanne is a reverse, homo-sexist reading of the bisexual erotic.[2]

In order to understand Bernhard's performative style, some context is cru-cial. After six years of slugging it out on the comedy club circuit, in shows from Los Angeles to Toronto, her success took off in the early 1980s, when she gained a role in Martin Scorsese's *The King of Comedy* (Brunt, 1982). Beating out nearly a thousand other actresses, she landed the character of "Marsha," an obsessed fan of Johnny Carson-esque comedian "Jerry Lang-ford." In doing so, Bernhard began to carve a space as the fan on the margins of celebrity.³ As she developed her own stage act, she had a hit one-woman Broadway show, *Without You I'm Nothing*, in 1987. She has been compared to Andy Kaufman in her persistence in challenging middle-class audience sensibilities. In a subtle, perceptive reading, Philip Auslander writes, "Like Kaufman, Sandra Bernhard interacts confrontationally with her audience and seeks to destabilize her relationship to the spectator and to eschew easy classification or placement in a particular performance genre" (p. 155). But while Kaufman sometimes overstepped the bounds of audience propriety, Bernhard typically stays in the performative mode and signals any shift in monologue or persona.

What is central to Bernhard's performance is her inhabiting of several roles. In the stage performance of *Without You I'm Nothing*, she sings songs that address the rock culture of which she was a part . . . she had close ties with Madonna, but she also spent time with Stevie Nicks, and later, Courtney Love. Thus, she is ". . . pop music fan, pop music performer, satirist, and appropriator" (Auslander, 156). In one monologue, she recounts her meeting with Nicks and the intimate moments they share. What she does best is inhabit and critique both the positionality of the adoring fan and the desire for celebrity. As the ultimate insider/outsider to the entertainment world, her performative lexicon is drawn from Hollywood, independent cinema, and LGBT subcultures. Toward the end of a long monologue that subtly critiques Barbara Streisand's move from Broadway to Hollywood, she says longingly: "We miss you Barbara. Come back to the 5 and Dime Barbara Streisand, Barbara Streisand." Here, she cleverly name-checks one of the few films of the 1980s that included a sensitive portrayal of a transsexual, Robert Altman's *Come Back to the 5 & Dime, Jimmy Dean, Jimmy Dean* (1982), a movie that is also about the celebrity worship of (queer icon) Jimmy Dean.

FROM DRAG KING TO TRANS-PERFORMANCE

It must be noted that drag has emerged, not wholly, but at least partly, in the space of the theater. Traced skillfully by Laurence Senelick, drag as a performative mode has served to challenge dominant social relations, invert hierarchies, and satirize political authority. The act of gender transgression makes visible the vulnerability of the body.

Drag depends on vestmentary transgression, and Bernhard has occasionally appeared in male drag, smoking a cigarette on the back cover of *Love Love Love*. But what happens when an artist "performs" maleness in offering up the personal, in the form of memoir, for public display? Is the performer transgender? In Bernhard's work, she adopts masculine codes at moments when a new relationship seems possible.

In *Confessions*, Bernhard observed that many fans ask how she spends her nights. She shares her response to the question, "Is it glamorous, Sandra?" (p. 82). Her answer is a satirical critique of the rituals of feminine beauty:

> Yes, in a way it really is. I begin with some freshening up in my bath, where I steam, scrub, buff, pluck, dig out ingrown hairs from a recent bikini wax. There in the bathroom, I stimulate follicles to grow and stare at tiny cracks and crevices, which need constant probing and scraping. (p. 82)

Her feminist voice comes through here; her deadpan tone amplifies the power of her words; a similar voice emerges in *WYIN* during a piece that parodies a young upwardly-mobile woman's first day on the job.

The deconstruction of beauty rituals is but one strategy of Bernhard's queer feminist expression. She also refigures her gender identity in innovative ways. Bernhard writes of a trip to New York and her realization that she is lonely. Her friends become aware of it and prod her to date. In an imagined scenario, a close girlfriend calls her and wants to fix her up with Isaac Bashevis Singer, whom Bernhard had met once before at a book signing.[4] She is interested, saying "He's fabulous and I really picked up on a great vibe from him" (1988, p. 91). The girl tells Bernhard to get ready, as he will pick her up tonight.

Singer arrives late, apologizing. Depicted as a domineering figure, Singer takes over the scene, criticizing her appearance: "He hated what I was wearing and rushed me over to Comme des Garçons to buy me a man-tailored suit. He said he liked his woman butch. Who was I to argue? Dinner was incredible . . ." (p. 92). Of course, Bernhard has created a kind of queer fantasia, subtly appropriating Singer's character Yentl, the woman who passed as a boy to gain entrance to Yeshiva, or rabbinical school, an Orthodox space that has historically excluded women.

I read in Bernhard's work the concept of *pluralogue*–that is, the presentation (or juggling, as it were) of several personas to narrate a story or situation. The storyteller who does this adds a multidimensionality to their performance and can recreate entire conversations quite effectively. Bernhard's skill is a "dysphoric" one–she does not use male drag in her stand-up; rather, she is able to channel maleness in a way that is wholly dependent on voice, a key site of transformation for trans-folk. In a memorable pluralogue in *WYIN*, she performs several characters of the "all-American family," the "ultra-WASP-ish" brother and sister "Chip" and "Babe." She sets the scene at Christmastime, with Chip in Babe's room. Here, she transgenders the narrative, gender-switching from herself to Chip, as he harmonizes (in a deep voice): "O Tannenbaum/O Tannenbaum."

RE-POSITIONINGS

Despite Bernhard's deployment of trans and drag codes, the media has tended to misread her work, erasing these signs as either evidence of her troubled relation to "gay culture" or as a way of contesting her sexual orientation. Yet, Bernhard has voiced her own desires *for* trans-people and asserted a continual resistance to the press's attempt to categorize her sexuality.

In a 1988 feature in *Rolling Stone*, writer Bill Zehme recounted this exchange during Bernhard's appearance on *The Robin Byrd Show*, a provocative New York cable-access program hosted by a stripper:

> Male caller: Sandra, what's a guy gotta do to get a date with you? I'm serious.
>
> Sandra: Get a sex change!
>
> Female caller: What's a *girl* gotta do to get a date with you?
>
> Sandra: Get a sex change! (p. 80; 118)

While playful and ironic, Bernhard here complicates bisexuality as she makes visible transsexuality. The following year, in *WYIN*, Bernhard employed drag queens as her background singers. Her willingness to be critically queer continues into the public sphere. When asked about her appearance on Letterman with Madonna and the (supposed) implication that she is a lesbian, she shot back, "I've never implied that," she says, her voice now edgy. "I've implied that *I'm open to different aspects of my personality that embraces many genders–as many as there may be*" (Emphasis added; Walters, 1990). Thus, Bernhard shows an early openness to trans-folk and to gender variance that is linked to her sexuality. It also co-extends a politically engaged, queer sensibility that she has maintained rather consistently. Challenging the assimilationist model of centrist gay politics, she recently told an audience at PrideFest in Tamba Bay: "Be happy you're unique . . . Stop looking for straight America to embrace you. We're all freaks" (Vivinetto, 2001). The crowd went wild.

TRANS/GENDERING BI-DESIRE

Counterpoising the flurry of mid-90s mainstream attention toward bisexuality, Martha Pramaggiore (1996) asks: ". . . do bisexual epistemologies go further than trendiness, *charting* the politics of sexualities in Western culture, *redistricting and redistributing desire, and creating new cartographies for our cultural erotics*" (italics mine; Pramaggiore and Hall, p. 2). Pramaggiore articulates an important issue for bisexual people in a globalized culture–given that we face inacceptance, our love is mobile–we find partners across states, at chance moments, in the ephemera of a society in hyper-speed. For Bernhard the traveling performer, this is even more pronounced. In *May I Kiss You*, she writes of a story she hopes "no one has told you yet" (p. 35); that open secret is the time she fell in love with a topless dancer from Texas. "When I first met Lisa, I was a young boy, open raw like a dog-licked wound, kind of scabby and oozing because that's how I felt–unsure, teetering on life's rickety ladder" (p. 33). Her coupling of boyhood with illness is not just a "lesbian convention" of the appropriation of gender inversion; rather, it is a specifically Jewish queer mode of gendered resistance.

Bernhard encounters the woman just as she is pondering travel, of finding a "romantic ocean liner" to go East, out of America. "I was walking past Studio 54 around back and she just came up to me, exclaiming, 'I've never met anybody like you before; you're so beautiful you could be a boy or a girl. Would you mind if I hug you?'" (p. 36). Bernhard lets her because she too was lonely, and "it was a cold night."

For me, Bernhard is empowering because she makes visible and celebrates bisexual peoples' position vis-à-vis gay and lesbian culture; as a Jew, her gutsy critiques often extend across the religious divide, making visible a "Christian America" that too often leaves Jews and other religious minorities out of the picture. What is most remarkable is that she has articulated this bountiful bisexuality in ways that *include*, if only subtly, transgender expression.

NOTES

1. See "Political activism: A brief history," in Hutchins and Kaahumanu, eds. *Bi Any Other Name: Bisexual People Speak Out*. Boston: Alyson, 1991, 364

2. See also Walton (1994), which does attempt to read ". . . the challenge that she presents to a certain formulation of lesbian (feminist) identity . . ." But Walton, even after citing Bernhard's own coming out as bisexual, focuses fixatedly on her "preference" (i.e., does she like women *more* than men?), a scientized quantification of her sexuality.

3. The film is intriguing on several levels, as Bernhard's performance thematizes her exclusion–her "crazed," largely eroticized obsession with Langford is contrasted with "Rupert Pupkin," whose fanship is more "appropriate" and ordered (he has a life-size picture of Langford in his basement, an autograph book, and a faux-stage set up to practice to his comedy routines). Pupkin is depicted as ethnically Jewish, and the film turns

on his quest to gain Langford's patronage and break into the mainstream comedy business. Thus, the film made visible the degree of privilege that male comedians held vis-à-vis women comedians in and through *Jewishness*. Yet "Marsha," garbed in a crested private-school uniform, is assimilated into a vague, "American" identity–while she does speak a few Yiddishisms to Rupert during the famous kidnapping scene, her Jewishness is largely made illegible.

4. Singer himself is married: "In America he met and married German-born Alma, who helped support him by working as a salesclerk at Lord & Taylor. Here he wrote articles and stories for the *Forward*, though little more of note until after the premature death of his successful brother in 1944" (*Conversations*, p. 236).

REFERENCES

Auslander, P. (1994). *Presence and Resistance: Postmodernism and Cultural Politics in Contemporary American Performance*. Ann Arbor: University of Michigan Press.

Bernhard, S. *Confessions of a Pretty Lady*. (1988). New York: Harper & Row.

Bernhard, S. *Love, Love, and Love*. (1993). New York: HarperCollins.

Bernhard, S. *May I Kiss You on the Lips, Ms. Sandra*. (1998). New York: William Morrow.

Bernhard, S. *Without You I'm Nothing* (Enigma Records 7-73369-1, 1989).

Bernhard, S. *Without You I'm Nothing* (dir. John Boskovich, 1990).

Brunt, S. (1982, August 28). Bernhard 'in love' with Jerry Lewis. *The Globe and Mail*, p. E1.

Farrell, G. (Ed.). (1992). *Isaac Bashevis Singer: Conversations*. Jackson: University Press of Mississippi.

The King of Comedy (dir. Martin Scorsese, 1982).

Pellegrini, A. (1997) "Whiteface performances: 'Race,' gender, and Jewish bodies." In Daniel and Jonathan Boyarin (Eds.), *Jews and Other Differences: The New Jewish Cultural Studies* (pp. 108-149). Minneapolis: University of Minnesota Press.

Pellegrini, A. (1996). "Sandra's Whiteface. You Make Me Feel (Mighty Real)." *Performance Anxieties: Staging Race, Staging Psychoanalysis*. New York: Routledge.

Pramaggiore, M. & Hall, D. (1996). *Representing Bisexualities: Subjects and Cultures of Fluid Desire*. New York: NYU Press.

Probyn, E. (1993). *Sexing the Self: Gendered Positions in Cultural Studies*. New York: Routledge.

Senelick, L. (2000). *The Changing Room: Sex, Drag and Theater*. London: Routledge.

Vivinetto, G. (2001, July 9). 'Mama' Bernhard lays down the laughs. *St. Petersburg Times*, p. 2B.

Walters, B. (1990, June 19). Danger is her business. Sandra Bernhard takes her confrontational humor seriously. *San Francisco Examiner*, p. B1.

Walton, J. (1994). "Sandra Bernhard: Lesbian postmodern or modern postlesbian?" In Laura Doan (Ed.), *The Lesbian Postmodern* (pp. 245-261). New York: Columbia UP.

Zehme, B. (1988, November 3). Who's afraid of Sandra Bernhard? *Rolling Stone*, 538, 76, 79-80, 118-119.

Butch–Femme Interrupted:
Angelina Jolie, Bisexuality
and the New Butch Femme

Cristina Stasia

http://www.haworthpress.com/web/JB
Digital Object Identifier: 10.1300/J159v03n03_13

[Haworth co-indexing entry note]: "Butch-Femme Interrupted: Angelina Jolie, Bisexuality and the New Butch Femme." Stasia, Cristina. Co-published simultaneously in *Journal of Bisexuality* (Harrington Park Press, an imprint of The Haworth Press, Inc.) Vol. 3, No. 3/4, 2003, pp. 181-201; and: *Bisexuality and Transgenderism: InterSEXions of the Others* (ed: Jonathan Alexander, and Karen Yescavage) Harrington Park Press, an imprint of The Haworth Press, Inc., 2003, pp. 181-201. Single or multiple copies of this article are available for a fee from The Haworth Document Delivery Service [1-800-HAWORTH, 9:00 a.m. - 5:00 p.m. (EST). E-mail address: docdelivery@haworthpress.com].

SUMMARY. "Butch-Femme Interrupted: Angelina Jolie, Bisexuality and the New Butch Femme" argues that butch-femme has undergone a transformation and has collapsed from exclusively a relation of two stable, defined identities into a single identity: the butch femme. Angelina Jolie's star text and films are material evidence of this new butch femme subjectivity, and the sexual implications of this emerging identity, which is both an empowering visibility for bisexuality and a move into queer sexuality. Through a detailed analysis of Jolie's startext and her films *Foxfire* (1996) and *Gone in 60 Seconds* (2000), I analyze the appearance and sexuality of the butch femme. I conclude by considering the implications of this identity as the butch femme gains cultural currency. *[Article copies available for a fee from The Haworth Document Delivery Service: 1-800-HAWORTH. E-mail address: <docdelivery@haworthpress.com> Website: <http://www.HaworthPress.com> © 2003 by The Haworth Press, Inc. All rights reserved.]*

KEYWORDS. Bisexuality, butch, femme, film, Jolie, sexuality

"She's a female James Dean for our time," Amy Pascal, chairwoman of Columbia Pictures, christens Angelina Jolie. This is an apt way to characterize the icon of what I will argue is the new butch femme. Bisexual,[2] tough and grrrly, Jolie and her films are cultural evidence of the translation of butch-femme into butch femme. One site where evidence of a continually shifting understanding of the relation of femininity/masculinity and sexuality manifests in our post-*Gender Trouble* culture is in the renewed interest in butch-femme. Films have always mirrored cultural understandings of butch-femme, from the demonized representation of the butch-femme relationship in *The Killing of Sister George* (1968) to the simmering, political, butch-femme relationship in *Thelma and Louise* (1991). Until recently, butch-femme has been portrayed in film as a relationship between two clearly defined identities–one butch, one femme. Today, however, I would argue that butch-femme has undergone a transformation, influenced by *Gender Trouble*, queer activism/queer theory and third-wave feminism, and has collapsed from exclusively a relation of two stable, defined identities into a single identity: the butch femme. Nowhere is this transformation more obvious than in the popularity and success of Jolie. Jolie's films and star text are material evidence of this new butch femme subjectivity, and the sexual implications of this emerging identity, which is both an empowering visibility for bisexuality and a step into queer sexuality. To analyze both the aesthetics and actions of butch femme as manifest in Jolie, I will first examine her star text to establish the importance of the persona she brings to her roles. I will then move into a detailed analysis of the films *Foxfire* (1996) and *Gone in 60 Seconds* (2000) to illustrate the appearance and sexuality of the butch femme. Lastly, I want to consider what the butch femme promises as she gains cultural currency.

In order to successfully interrogate this new identity, it is necessary first to briefly consider the historical understanding of butch-femme in the late 1980s/early 1990s. The primary influence in the resurgence of academic interest in butch-femme in the early 1990s was the publication in 1990 of Judith Butler's *Gender Trouble*. This historical moment of gender theorizing hinged on a very specific positioning of butch-femme as a *relationship* of identities. The most obvious indication of this is the "Index" to *Gender Trouble*. In the index, there is no listing for "butch" or "femme"; instead, only "butch-femme identities" is listed. The identities are constituted as interdependent. This mirrors the popular academic and cultural understanding of butch-femme at this time. Butches and femmes could not exist separately, nor could they be articulated without reference to each other (the butch is the butch because the femme is not and vice versa).

Butler's (2000) primary engagement with this particular, historical understanding of butch-femme is to argue that

> the "presence" of so-called heterosexual conventions within homosexual contexts as well as the proliferation of specifically gay discourses of sexual difference, as in the case of "butch" and "femme" as historical identities . . . [and] the repetition of heterosexual constructs within sexual cultures both gay and straight may well be the inevitable site of denaturalization and mobilization of gender categories. (p. 41)

Butch-femme identities and relationships, with their employment of masculinity and femininity (in actions, dress and discourse) as signifiers of *desire* and not gender, expose how masculinity and femininity are floating signifiers which can be employed by any/every gender and sexual orientation. As Butler (2000) explains, butch identity is not "a simple assimilation of lesbianism back into terms of heterosexuality . . . that masculinity, if that it can be called, is always brought into relief against a culturally intelligible 'female body'" (p. 156). Butch-femme is thus employed to reveal the constructedness of heterosexuality and gender and, as Butler (2000) writes, shows that "gay is to straight *not* as copy is to original, but, rather, as copy is to copy" (p. 41).

Butch-femme, regardless of its status as oppressive copy or liberating theoretical model, has been comprehended as a relationship of identities since the origin of these roles–whether one locates this origin in the 18th century or the working-class bars of the 1940s/50s.[3] This conception of butch-femme relies on an understanding of butch and femme as two stable, clearly defined identities with a strict sexuality attached to them. The sexual orientation that is inseparable from this understanding of butch-femme is lesbian. Butch-femme is obviously not open to heterosexual women, and, I would argue, it is barely open to bisexual women–the bifemme is immediately coded as a lesbian femme when she engages in a butch-femme relationship since, historically, butch-femme has always been read as a relationship between lesbian, not bisexual/queer, women.

The inseparable, lesbian butch-femme dyad is the understanding that was still dominant in the late 1980s and early 1990s cinema. The film *Black Widow* (1986) dramatically stages this understanding. In *Black Widow*, lesbianism is made visible not by sexual activity, but by a butch-femme relationship between the two protagonists. The first shots of the female protagonists clearly establish that Catharine (Theresa Russell) is the femme and that Debra Winger's character Alex (note the masculine name) is the butch. The film opens with a shot of Catharine applying eyeliner in a designer black dress and high-heels. This is juxtaposed with an image of Alex rushing through a busy downtown street in mismatched, frumpy clothing (wearing pants/leggings under her skirt and a man's blazer), with messy hair and arms full of paperwork.

Butch-femme is readable in more than surface aesthetics in the film. Terry Brown (1994) writes that "strong-willed, active, [and] direct goes by the name of 'butch' in the lesbian vernacular" (p. 233). Alex, as the determined investigator who fights with her boss and leaves her job to track her suspect, and then directly pursues and gets involved with Catharine, is certainly butch–despite the more "passing" marks of long hair and the ability to wear a dress (although not well) and attract men. Alex is also continually featured in androgynous clothing and engaged in "butch" activity–playing poker with the guys, packing a gun, and tracking a killer. Alternately, the flirty, seductive Catharine, with immaculately decorated apartments and fashionista desires, is the consummate femme.

Cherry Smyth (1995) argues that "the narrative's attempt to impose difference between the two women unwittingly suggests a butch-femme dynamic" (p. 129). I disagree that this is unwittingly suggested; the difference is too clearly policed and established, and too much of the narrative depends on this dynamic, for it to be accidental. However, the lesbianism that is readable in this film is dependent on the coding of butch-femme as two stable identities. The first lesbian moments in the film take place with Alex gazing at Catherine, and then pursuing her. In the intimate picnic scene, Catherine shortens Alex's pseudonym Jessica to the more butch appropriate "Jessie." If Alex and Catherine were both femmes, the lesbianism would be much less recognizable–it would appear more like female-bonding/friendship than a lesbian relationship so important that Catherine tells Alex that of all the relationships in her life she will "always remember this one."

Though lesbianism is readable in *Black Widow*, it is dependent on a butch-femme relationship. Butch-femme functions as *codes of desire*. Catherine's and Alex's desire for each other is readable, and established, because their identities (the femme, the butch) signal their desire for the opposite. Lesbianism is not readable through the individual, but rather depends on the butch-femme relationship between Catherine and Alex for legibility. Thus, a lesbian reading is dependent on a butch-femme reading. This is not true, however, for reading queer desire in film today, particularly in Jolie's films. The queer reading is not dependent on reading butch-femme, but it is dependent on the emergence of a new identity: the butch femme.

This new identity is most strikingly signaled by Jolie. Jolie's success is inseparable from the sociopolitical climate of the late 1990s/early 2000s. There are three main phenomena that I see as contributing to Jolie's success as an icon of the new butch femme. The first, which I have already discussed, is the renewed interest in butch-femme and queer sexuality that attended the publication of *Gender Trouble*. The second phenomenon is femme theory. Third-wave feminist inspired femme theory and identity-pride resulted in an increased recognition and acceptance of femmes in the feminist and queer communities. Second-wave feminism, with necessary and admirable purpose, was vocal about its anti-traditional femininity stance. While femmes have *never* bought into traditional femininity, Laura Harris and Elizabeth Crocker (1997) explain that in second-wave feminism's "(mis)recognition of femme, feminism denied femme its radical and critical nature" (p. 3). Today, after the work of second-wave feminism which provided women with the option not to be feminine, *femme*-ininity can be reclaimed and celebrated as a conscious, political identity/practice. Femmes do not simply and unthinkingly practice femininity; rather, they choose what are traditionally classified as "feminine" dress and behaviors because they prefer them. They do not dress provocatively or flirt to fulfill heteropatriarchal beauty standards or to titillate men–these sisters really are doing it for themselves. Today, femme is increasingly recognized in critical and radical terms, and to be read as lesbian/bisexual/queer by the "queer community" one no longer needs to trade in her kitten heels for Doc Martens.

The queer movement is a phenomena that is inseparable from third-wave femme-inism, and one which I locate as the third influence contributing to this new idea of butch femme. Harris and Crocker (1997) write, "the agitation of femmes within feminism was central to the formation of a sex-radical position out of which the queer movement grew" (p. 4). Femmes insisted on being recognized as vital parts of the feminist and queer movements, and this insistence translated into queer politics that demonstrated the fissure between gender and sexual orientation which Butler discussed–no longer were people who refused femininity recognized as the only ones who refused heterosexuality. The responses to Butler's *Gender Trouble* also contributed to this–gender and identity had been destabilized in that text, and queer theory was "born." This is also where I see the birth of the career/persona of the new butch femme as epitomized by Jolie. Judith Halberstam (1994) writes about the queer identities that emerged at this time in lesbian zines and elsewhere–identities that featured "queer butches [and] aggressive femmes" (p. 212). Jolie is the icon of a combination of the queer butch and aggressive femme and her star text and films are the material presence of the shift in understanding of butch/femme.

It is critical to examine Jolie's star text before analyzing her films because her films draw heavily on this persona to charge the characters she plays with a bisexual, butch femme subjectivity–not the least of which is that her tattoos are as visible as her breasts in all her films since *Gia* (1998). Jolie signifies the new butch femme in two primary ways. The first is through her appearance. Dress has always been a principal signifier of butch or femme identity. Danae Clark (1993) writes that, "because identities are always provisional, lesbians must also constantly assert themselves. They must replace liberal discourse with camp discourse, make themselves visible, foreground their political agendas and their politicized subjectivities" (p. 199). Jolie's butch femme subjectivity is definitely evident in her appearance. She combines long hair with tattoos and leather pants with sheer tops and high heels. Arlene Stein (1989) explains that, in today's queer culture(s), "you can dress as a femme one day and a butch the next. You can wear a crew-cut along with a skirt. Wearing high heels during the day does not mean you're a femme at night, passive in bed, or closeted on the job" (p. 38). Jolie embodies this. For the Academy Awards in 2000, Jolie dressed gothic in a long black dress with long black hair. In 2001, she arrived in a sleek, white tuxedo with her hair pulled back. In an interview Jolie did for *Time* magazine, the interviewer detailed the appearance of Jolie: "wearing black leather and high-heeled boots, [she] walks across her Beverly Hills hotel room holding a serrated knife in her hand" (Ressner, 2000, p. 72). Butcher one day, femme-ier the next, butch femme always, Jolie is a new identity, and in postmodern fashion, this new identity is a borrowing/blending of two previous ones–the baby butch and the sexually-assertive high femme.

But is Jolie a butch femme or a femme butch? I have chosen to call her, and the style/identity/sexuality she is the postergrrrl of, butch femme because I am privileging Jolie's body and physical appearance over her style/dress. Jolie has long hair, manicured nails, and a classic, pin-up figure–which she emphasizes with tight clothing and midriff-baring tops. Jolie's butchness manifests

more in her actions and style of clothing (which she wears as tightly and provocatively as any high femme does) than in her physicality. Her body is not
butch, she does not, as some butches do, bind her breasts or hide her curves under baggy clothing. Her body is almost excessively feminine–from her
beestung lips to her extremely curvy body. Her passion for motorcycles,
leather, tattoos and knives, however, is butch. Thus, I see Jolie not as the
femme butch, which I see as a more androgynous body clothed in femmey
clothing and with femme traits (such as the femme pause as she waits to have
the door opened for her instead of the butch femme pause to flick a cigarette
before straddling her bike), but as the toughgrrrl femme who manifests a fashion style and no-nonsense attitude that can be read as butch.

Although the butch femme combines the attitude of the no-nonsense butch
with the style of the flirty femme, I do not necessarily see butch femme as a
transgendered identity. Butch femme is not identification with another gender,
especially not to the extent that one identifies as or lives as another gender.
However, like transgenderism, butch femme signals a new way of thinking
about gender, one that has its roots in postmodern gender theories and an understanding of gender as pastiche instead of biology. The butch femme fits under the transgender umbrella only insofar as she plays with traditional gender
definitions and explodes the number of gender categories, although she is not
uncomfortable with identifying as a woman, nor does she identify as a man or
FTM. She does, however, push the boundaries of the popular imagination in
terms of what feminine is, and can create discomfort in others with her combination of butch tough talk and femme appearance.

It is critical to remember that butch and femme are not substitutes for man
and woman, *they are categories of desire.* Femme has recently been freed
from being solely a lesbian identity, but until the late 1990s, femme (and
butch) still read as lesbian. The butch and femme desire each other, and their
style and clothing indicate that desire, but they still desire each other as
women–the femme does not want a man anymore than the butch wants a
woman trapped in traditional femininity. There is a mutual awareness of playing with gender norms, and a desire to attract a partner, through dress/style,
that is similarly aware.

The importance of the butch femme as manifest in Jolie is not just in the
collapsing of two clearly defined desire categories (butch and femme) but in
the sexual implications of this collapse. The traditional butch and femme roles
clearly signified lesbian desire, but the new butch femme does not. I will argue, through an analysis of Jolie's films *Foxfire* and *Gone in 60 Seconds*, that
this desire is bisexual. I classify the sexuality of this new butch femme as bisexual, and not queer, although I qualify this by emphasizing that this bisexuality is an important step towards the appearance and acceptance of queer

sexuality. I will elaborate on this later. Also, I would add that, with Jolie as the most visible icon of this new butch femme, we cannot read the butch femme as queer for two reasons. The first is that Jolie clearly identifies as bisexual, and thus the star text that impacts her films is bisexuality. Secondly, she is received as bisexual and not queer by her audience, and her films capitalize on her bisexuality for charged sexuality in her films. I want to emphasize that because Jolie is so open about her bisexuality, it is inevitably transferred into her films–her roles are infused with her identity, since it is an aggressive and political (in its disruption of normative categories and values) one.

In regards to Jolie's persona, it is important to acknowledge that Jolie talks openly, shamelessly and proudly about being bisexual (Ressner, 2000, p. 72). In an interview with *Elle* magazine, she is quoted as saying: "Honestly, I like everything. Boyish girls, girlish boys . . ." and "I am always on top. It's really unfortunate. I am begging for the man that can put me on the bottom. Or the woman. Anybody that can take me down."[4] In an interview with *Jane* magazine, Angelina declares: "I am the person most likely to sleep with my female fans."

Jolie's characters in films are incredibly similar to her persona, and thus I find it limiting (and impossible) to analyze her films without considering her star text. Furthermore, Jolie is insistent on how her characters amplify her actual self: "Acting is not pretending or lying. It's finding a side of yourself that's like the character and ignoring your other sides" (Ressner, 2000, p. 72). Jolie consistently portrays the strong and assertive bisexual butch femme in her films, whether she is ultimately partnered with a woman or a man. To make my argument that the new bisexual butch femme is made material in Jolie's films, I have chosen to read *Foxfire* and *Gone in 60 Seconds*. In each film, bisexuality is intimated by the script. Also, together these films work to show the bisexuality of Jolie's filmography. In *Foxfire*, Jolie is partnered with a woman and in *Gone in 60 Seconds*, her partner is a man. The gender of her partners changes, but Jolie as butch femme, and the accompanying bisexual implications of this, do not.

In *Foxfire*, Legs (Jolie) wears the requisite butch wardrobe. Lily Burana, Roxxie and Linnea Due (1994) detail butch fashion musts: "Levi's 501 jeans, white tee-shirt . . . black leather boots, . . . black leather jacket" (p. 25). Legs wears only these articles in *Foxfire*, with the addition of the other butch must-have, the ribbed tank top. The first shot of a shaggy-haired Legs shows her in black leather boots, black jeans, and a leather jacket kicking her switch-blade through a school security gate while a guard yells "Young man, young man! Stop when I'm talking to you!" The butch here passes–from behind. However, when Legs turns around, her feminine features and curvy, femme body, emphasized by the kid-sized butch clothes, disturb a reading of Legs as solely butch.

The degree of Legs' butchness is further problematized by her juxtaposition with other characters in the film. This also underscores that the butch femme plays with both butch and femme identities and, as a postmodern hero, can alter her butchness or femmeness by not only switching her shoes, but also her friends. *Foxfire* is a film filled with archetypes–the dyke (Goldie), the rebel (Legs), the nerd (Rita), the bored suburban girl (Maddy), the slut (Violet). These characters serve an obvious narrative function, but I would also argue that they serve the function of positioning Legs as the butch femme. Goldie, the shaved head, androgynously dressed, tattooed dyke is there to make Legs look less butch and, therefore, less (at least stereotypically) lesbian. Legs' pouty lips, curvy body and tight clothes are brought into sharp relief to Goldie's more obvious butch aesthetic when they are framed together, and this emphasizes Legs-as-femme–and therefore renders her less easily identifiable as lesbian.

When Legs is juxtaposed with the hyper-feminine, overly made-up Violet, however, the butchness of Legs is accentuated, and thus her lesbianism is more easily readable. Legs may wear tight, sexy clothing, but it is hardly the feminine, revealing clothing that Violet wears. Alexander Doty (2000) writes "this butch, femme and femmey butch (or butchy femme) triad is repeated in a number of pop cultural texts . . . the star of these kinds of texts always seems to be the character positioned between butch and femme" (p. 75). This negates any sort of reading of Legs as solely butch or femme; instead, she is the butch femme. Unlike butch-femme identities which exist as an inseparable unit, Legs is the butch femme independent of whether she is next to Goldie or Violet–as the opening shot makes clear, however, the juxtaposition of her amongst these characters highlights her skillful mixing of butchness and femme-ininity.

Triads are often (and unfortunately) associated with bisexuality. In *Foxfire*, Legs is not only positioned as the mixture of butch and femme, but her sexuality is equally ambiguous. In the film, it is easy to read Legs as lesbian. The most amusing instance of this is her statement "I vault without poles." However, while I see the validity of such a reading, I would argue that one can also read the somewhat ambiguous presentation of Legs' sexuality as not only sublimated lesbianism, but as a clear articulation of bisexual desire. The most obvious (this movie is nothing if not obvious) metaphor of Legs' sexuality is the bridge.

Legs and Maddy (her girlfriend in all but name) begin and end their relationship on a bridge. The first scene on the bridge, where Legs teases Maddy for asking her name "the morning after" they have spent the night together, has Legs standing in the middle of the bridge. The bridge is a symbol of both the space between, and journey between, heterosexuality and homosexuality. I read the bridge imagery as bisexual because it is clearly a place of temporal movement between two stable locations. I am *not* suggesting that bisexuality is a transitory phase, only that it is not only made possible, but clearly dependent, on lesbianism and heterosexuality–two orientations which are clearly more fixed/recognizable and thus can be interpreted as more stable.

Bisexuality is a sexual orientation that "combines" lesbianism and heterosexuality. When I refer to bisexuality as a third term, I locate the third term as the midpoint of a binary opposition–the term that literally *comes between and combines* the binary opposition. A binary is not three dimensional, it is a linear model composed of polar opposites. If the binary opposition had no midpoint, it would collapse–the midpoint, the third term, functions to define the polar opposites. This third term has a deconstructive function but it is not a transcendent ontological category. In other words, bisexuality functions to clean up lesbianism and heterosexuality–bisexuality lets us know that gay and straight can only ever involve sexual activity with same and opposite sex people, respectively, but never with both, thus fixing the limits of these terms (jut as lesbian and hetorsexual fix the limits of bisexual).

Unlike queer sexuality, which privileges gender and sexual fluidity and is, I would argue, an alternative to the homosexual/heterosexual binary, bisexuality is a third term necessary to the same dual sex/gender system that forces people to define according to man/woman, straight/gay. It is literally the bridge between gay and straight. The third term is a combination of the other two–it depends on their polarity for existence–just like the butch femme depends on the existence of the butch and the femme, or the bridge depends on two fixed, stable structures for its ability to join these structures and provide a space separate from them. While bisexuality is not an acceptance of either/or, it is an acceptance of both/and. I am not positioning queer as a utopic space that completely undermines the sex/gender system, but it is an identity that allows for a fluidity of *gender* and well as of sexuality that bisexuality does not.

To return to the film, which itself returns to bridge imagery a number of times, bisexual desire is also the "unspoken" desire in the film. One example of what I see as bisexual desire in the film is the exchange between Maddy and Legs:

Maddy: If I told you that I loved you would you take it the wrong way?

Legs: What do you mean by wrong?

Maddy: It's just that–I'm not–and you're–

Legs: I'll take it however you want me to, Maddy.

Maddy cannot explain what she, or Legs, is. This can be read as sublimated lesbian desire and the efforts of the film not to distance a heterosexual audience. However, I read Maddy's inability to finish this sentence as an indication that there are simply no words with which to finish it. Legs is the butch femme, the bisexual, and thus, unidentifiable in heteronarrative–and to a mainstream film audience who are more likely to be familiar with lesbianism, or at least the implication of lesbianism (especially after *Fried Green Tomatoes* and *Thelma and Louise*), than bisexuality. Maddy cannot identify Legs' identity/orientation because that identity/orientation is in the process of gaining cultural recognition through the bisexual, butch femme actor who is playing Legs.

The bisexuality of Jolie's character Sway in *Gone in 60 Seconds* is undeniable. Note how the ambivalent, goes-both-ways name emphasizes Sway's bisexuality just as the name Legs emphasized Legs' femme-inine body. *Gone in 60 Seconds* capitalizes on the bisexual, butch femme star text that has accumulated around Jolie in the four years between *Foxfire* and *Gone in 60 Seconds*. Jolie is, again, the butch-femme. But this time, she is with a man and her bisexuality is repeatedly made prominent. I would argue that this is not only because it is more comfortable for heterosexual audiences to accept bisexuality when same-sex activity is not actively portrayed (and when the actor portraying the bisexual is no longer a wild bad girl but an Oscar winner),[5] but also because queer politics/identities have gained attention between 1996 and 2000 and thus Jolie can be read as bisexual without needing to be partnered or sexually involved with a woman.

In *Gone in 60 Seconds*, Sway is more femme than *Foxfire*'s Legs. I maintain that this is precisely because she can be. Jolie's bisexuality is public knowledge and she does not need to be explicitly styled as a butch in order for the audience to infer same-sex desire–her star text is now too prevalent not to impact how the audience interprets her characters. Sway has long hair and polished nails in addition to her curvy body. However, she is consistently kept from being read as heterosexually feminine. The first shot of Sway is the iconic image of the butch femme. Sway is underneath a car, and only her legs are visible.[6] When she slides out, she is clothed in a brown mechanic's jumpsuit, but she is wearing a tight t-shirt underneath. She is also wearing rings and has long, styled blond hair and perfectly (clear) polished nails. She is both mechanic and sex symbol. The next shot of her is at her other job as a bartender where she is in a tank top and tight orange pants–revealing, femme-inine clothing. Sway as a butch femme and not a femme butch is especially obvious when she teases Memphis (played by the perpetually sensitive Nicholas Cage) by offering to "strip down and shine the hood" of a car out back. In this comment, she combines her identity as butch outlaw/car thief with the flirty looks and skillful flirting of a femme–while dressed in femme clothes that reveal a very femme body.

Sway's butchness is most obvious in her profession (as a mechanic), criminal activity and motorbike. Her femmeness is most easily readable in her hair, body, clothing size (she obviously finds it more economical to buy kids' clothing) and flirting. There are numerous iconic shots of the butch femme in this film. The scene where she meets the male car thieves at the pier on a motorbike is one of them. When she stops her bike and takes off her helmet, her long, blond hair tumbles down as she tells them she will help them steal the cars. A striking scene of the butch femme in this film is when she and Memphis steal a "girl car." Sway finds lipstick in the car.

Sway: It had to be a girl car.

Memphis: A girl car? What kind of girl drives a [names car]?

Sway: I'll show you.

(Sway puts on red lipstick)

Memphis: Lipstick?

Sway: Matches the car. (girly giggle)

Memphis: What's next? Blush, mascara?

Sway: Next time . . . next time I'll pull out the leather, high heels and pink underwear for you. (giggles again)

Here, Sway blends car theft and flirting and lipstick and leather to provide yet another iconic moment of the butch femme.

Sway's confident sexuality is unmistakable in this film. It is evident from her first "strip down and shine the hood" comment in the bar to her actions in the BBQ scene where she licks Toby's fingers and then handles and licks a knife as the men say approvingly "sexy, sexy." This is also another allusion to Jolie's star text–Jolie has a passion for knives and blade play.[7] Sway's sexuality is not only confident, but, in true butch femme fashion, it is also bisexual. This bisexuality is never explicitly acted out–her only sexual contact is with Memphis–but it is aggressively present.

Interestingly, there is an absence of any other central women characters. The only other sexualized woman in the film, the woman with no lines who has sex with a man in front of a window while Memphis and Sway watch, is an interesting contrast to Sway. She is seen in all the accoutrements of traditional femininity and engaged in heterosexual sex. The contrast between this woman and Sway is similar to the juxtaposition between Violet and Legs in *Foxfire* and, I would argue, it is also employed to remind the audience that, despite the lipstick and giggling, Sway is not a traditionally feminine (and therefore heterosexual) woman. In contrast with this woman, Sway looks quite butch, and, alternately, her femme-ininity is asserted. Unlike the unpoliticized, stereotypical femininity of the woman behind the window, who is engaged in a stereotypical heterosexual love scene with a stereotypical male, Sway's femme-ininity is brought into sharp relief as a conscious choice—one she alternately accents and mutes with make-up, clothing and tone and, with the help of her tattoos and strut, is never to be mistaken for traditional femininity.

Sway's bisexuality is as obvious as her tattoos in this film. Like *Foxfire*, this film is not concerned with subtlety. Although Sway does not flirt with any women, this is most likely because she is never in the same scene as any other women (with the exception of an older, fellow car thief's wife). I read this as a deliberate effort to eroticize the butch femme while not threatening the predominantly male, heterosexual, scopophilic audience of this film (she is there for their pleasure after all). Sway's desire for other women is attractive as long as it is done for male pleasure and not her own. Sway does, however, flirt with the cars.

In *Gone in 60 Seconds*, cars are always referred to by feminine pronouns (she/her) and they are even more explicitly gendered by the female names they are given by the thieves. In an early scene, Sway strides into a garage, clad in a long coat, tight tank top and leather boots, to steal cars with three other car thieves. She looks the cars up and down with a suggestive "Hello ladies." She then focuses on a red sports car and purrs "Always was a sucker for a redhead." She proceeds to hotwire the car (which involves opening the hood of the car), wink at the camera and drive the car away. Later in the film, after Memphis and Sway safely deliver two cars to the awaiting ship, she informs a colleague that the cars are stowed with a sexual metaphor: "Alright, two ladies home safe. He's tucking in Vanessa and Bernadine just took me for a ride." It is also important to note that in the majority of scenes where she steals cars with Memphis, she is the one driving the car. Clearly, she knows how to handle a woman.

She also knows how to handle a man. This is most obvious in the scene where Sway and Memphis make out in the car. This is a critical scene for reading both Sway's bisexuality and the disruption that bisexuality causes. Before they make out, Sway tells Memphis that she is upset that he left her behind when he moved away, and Memphis responds that he asked her to go with him. Sway tells him "I wasn't ready," and Memphis points out, "You're straight now." This is obviously intended to signify Sway's reform from outlaw into productive member of society, and thus her ability to move away from what is literally the scene of her crimes. It is, however, also readable as a moment of reformed sexual outlawry. It definitely seems that her return to outlawry, with her sexual, suggestive comments to the "ladies" (cars) signals active same-sex desire—perhaps her reform from crime had also reformed her from sexual deviancy. I would further argue that Sway's return to being a law-abiding, productive member of society (after this final boost) can be read as Sway's readiness to commit to a relationship that will be perceived as heterosexual (since she will be involved with a man, she will be read as heterosexual—the classic bind of the bisexual woman whose sexual orientation is too often determined by her partner's gender). Her reform from outlawry is concomitant with a return to (at least perceived) heterosexuality.

Immediately preceding this, while Sway and Memphis are waiting to steal a car, their theft is interrupted by a heterosexual sex scene. Outlawry, boundary breaking and transgression are interrupted by socially approved, status quo sex. This is important for two reasons. The first is that this works to assert the historical alignment of civil/political outlawry with sexual outlawry—the heterosexual couple is in their home while the bisexual couple is waiting in the driveway of this home to steal the heterosexual couple's car. More importantly, however, it functions to differentiate the relationship between Sway and Memphis from the heterosexual couples' relationship. Sway and Memphis are in a car, a mode of transportation, while the heterosexual couple is in a house—here we can read bisexuality as both transition and mobility, while heterosexuality is marked as stable. The bisexual couple succeeds in stealing the car as the couple engages in intercourse. Bisexuality is thus marked as deviant, while heterosexuality is law-abiding—and literally threatened by bisexuality. It is when the heterosexual couple moves into the bedroom, the place of procreation and the reproduction of social order, that the bisexual couple successfully steals their car.[8]

The alliance of sexual outlawry and civil/political outlawry is made even more obvious when Memphis tells Sway that "having sex while stealing cars" is better than either of those activities in isolation. Sway answers, "That's a good line . . . doesn't work on a lot of girls though," and slinks closer to him. It does not work on a lot of girls because this phenomena of the bisexual butch femme is a new one and the number of (visible at least) outlaws is still growing. This combination of civil/political outlawry is not open to "most girls" because most girls are straight, law-abiding, ones—or at least perceived that way. But the line does work on Sway who moves even closer to Memphis.

While they are making out, Sway keeps an eye on the heterosexual couple and, when she sees them move into the bedroom, she pushes Memphis away and says, "Oh it's time to work." The heterosexual couple is shown having intercourse while Sway and Memphis steal the car. I read this as a very bisexual moment. In the heteronarrative that is this film, bisexuality is representable only through allusion (to cars and to Jolie's star text) and a bisexual act (for a bisexual woman with a seemingly heterosexual man is still a bisexual act) is unrepresentable. Sway and Memphis cannot complete having sex because bisexual sex is unrepresentable in heteronarrative. Thus, the heterosexual couple, the only couple that can be portrayed having sex, does it for them–in a house, with perfect bodies, clothes and make-up. The film ends with the car thieves returning to their law-abiding lives, but Jolie and Memphis drive away in a stolen car–a suggestion that bisexuality and fluid sexuality are still present, even in the perceived-as-heterosexual relationship.

Bisexuality is never completely contained by the films–Jolie's star text and the ambiguity of her characters refuses this. Despite Jolie's recent roles in films that have an almost exclusively heterosexual focus (*Pushing Tin, Playing God, The Bone Collector, Original Sin, Tomb Raider, Life or Something Like It*), her fans still clearly receive her as bisexual, and she has a fan base of both women and men–many of whom deem her their primary scopophilic passion. Jolie's audience not only accepts but also anticipates Jolie's characters to be charged with bisexual energy. She is listed as one of the top ten bachelor picks for women on one Website.[9] She is clearly the object of both her female and male fans' desire. A webmaster of a fansite for Jolie even had to promise his readers that he is not Jolie and plead "please stop sending me your sexual fantasies–this is directed at you too ladies!"[10] Her status as what I term a *bicon* is indisputable.

The acceptance of this butch femme and her bisexuality signifies an important shift in our culture. Obviously, it indicates an increasing acceptance of bisexuality and strong, capable women. More importantly, however, I see the adoration of Jolie as a sign that the work that *Gender Trouble* and feminist/queer activism began is evolving. If butch-femme, in Butler's terms, denaturalizes heterosexuality and gender roles, then the butch femme further jeopardizes traditional gender codings and compulsory heterosexuality by infusing her identity and sexuality with an ambiguity. This ambiguity is dangerous–if we can no longer determine the gender of someone's partner from their dress/identity then compulsory heterosexuality and social order is not so easily reproduced/maintained.

This new butch femme is gaining popularity. Ressner (2000) writes that "Hollywood is growing addicted to [Jolie's] controversy" (p. 72). The disruption that Jolie is causing has earned her a diverse group of fans and increased star billing in blockbusters. Jolie and the new butch femme do not, however, signal a sudden disregard for normative gender and sexuality categories. Jolie's star texts and the characters she plays are clearly bisexual; and, as I discussed above, just as she/they blend butch and femme, so do they blend heterosexuality and lesbianism.

Bisexuality does, however, allow for sexual fluidity that can give it the appearance of being hypersexual. Colleen Lamos writes that, "butch-femme and related practices have resexualized lesbianism" (p. 94). I would extend her argument and suggest that the new butch femme that Jolie manifests has challenged lesbianism and sexualized bisexuality. Jolie's butch femme is always sexual–whether a mysterious runaway, a mental patient, a car thief or a tomb raider. This is problematic because it reinforces the stereotype of the hypersexual bisexual. However, it also provides a model of (bi)sexuality that complicates normative definitions of what sexy is and encourages toughness and aggressiveness instead of meekness and passivity. This new butch femme identity has also opened up a space for queer sexuality to emerge. Lamos (1994) argues that "the eroticism of butch-femme . . . lies not in the so-called attraction of opposites, as though butch-femme were an ersatz version of heterosexual romance, but in its sexual *de*authorization of gender" (p. 97). With the butch-femme, the eroticism lies in the ambiguity and possibilities. We must, remember, however, that although gender is deauthorized, it is not deconstructed. Jolie's bisexual star text and film characters are clearly into women and men, not just "people."

There is something queer astir, but it is still a phantasm in regards to filmic representation. It has yet to manifest in an icon or mainstream movie character. The queer potential that this new acceptance of bisexuality promises is best exemplified in a scene from *Gone in 60 Seconds*. In a comment reminiscent of the one *Foxfire*'s Legs made about vaulting "without poles," Sway says the problem with sex while stealing cars is "how do you get over the shifter?" She utters this phrase while straddling the shifter and aggressively grabbing it. She adds: "because it gets in the way." I think this is a queer moment in a bisexual film–one that signals the evolution from butch femme bisexuality to queerness. The shifter gets in the way of sex in cars the way that the conflation of sex and gender gets in the way of sexuality. Bisexuality signals a step away from anatomy as determinant of desire, but it still privileges the idea of two genders. Gender/sex is not irrelevant, it is just not used to rule someone out. Bisexuality is, however, one step closer to queer, and getting over that shifter (the conflation of sex/gender/and insistence on a stable identity).

Just as Sister George gave way to Louise, so Legs and Sway will eventually give way to a character that does not blend butch/femme and lesbianism/heterosexuality, but, instead, just is and does not have a rigid sexuality attached to her/him/it. Jolie and her films have granted the butch femme cultural currency but the femme is still invisible–her femme-ininity must still be modified by piercings, tattoos, boots and a motorbike for her to be read as bisexual/lesbian–and to be accepted as such in the pomodyke community (Rugg, 1997, p. 186). The butch femme indexes a queer sexuality, but the femme is still waiting for this reading.

The disruption that the butch femme causes to straight-forward understandings of desire and identity signals the advent of queerness–and its eventual representation in mainstream cinema. Jolie and the characters she plays are never strictly femme. It seems that it remains necessary for there to be some disruption of what is still too easily mistaken as femininity instead of femme-ininity for same-sex desire to be read. This disruption is butchness. Will the butch femme eventually be able to be just femme and be read as queer? Is this the next translation that we can anticipate as queer politics and theory impact popular culture? Jolie's star text and films seem to hint at this possibility. You can just hear the straight men moaning "you mean now I have to worry about the pretty girls too?"

The recognition and ever increasing cultural currency of the butch femme are a threat. The characters Jolie portrays in her films introduce a new threat to heteropatriarchy's control of women–a butch femme whose desire is not only for the clearly butch or the clearly femme, but for her own kind as well. In *Foxfire*, Legs' interest is the very softly butch (burgeoning butch femme?) Maddy. In *Gone in 60 Seconds*, Sway is with a man but flirts with sleek, expensive, beautiful cars. Outside her films, Jolie has stated "I always play women I would date" (*Talk*). She must certainly have a thing for butch femmes. This attraction "to one's own kind" is threatening because it further destabilizes normative gender/sexuality categories. Butch-femme was still a binary that was premised on a clear attraction to an opposite, but bisexual butch femme attraction can include attraction to "same" instead of the opposite. Thus, I would argue that this is almost more homo (as in same) sexual than butch-femme, and definitely more queer. In keeping with butch-femme taxonomies, dress still signifies desire. But this time it is desire not just for opposites, but also for the same.[11]

Jolie and the bisexual butch femme's danger is precisely an increasing deauthorizing of gender and the privileging of a more fluid desire. Another danger is her power. One femme woman explains that "butches take charge of certain things, but it's the femmes who run the show" (Roxxie, 1994, p. 94). The butch femme does both; thus the ability to manipulate and subjugate this toughgrrrl is complicated. In *Foxfire*, Legs was a catalyst for the girls who had been "longing to break free and simply needed a shove to do so" (Shary, 2000,

p. 60). Her danger is not only her large audience of both female and male scopophilics, but the potential desire for scopophilic transubstantiation as the bisexual butch femme gains cultural currency. At the end of *Foxfire*, Maddy climbs to the top of the bridge that she was too scared to climb before she spent time with Legs. The danger is that, as Jolie gains in popularity and people are acclimated to bisexuality, we might follow in Maddy's footsteps—and perhaps want to climb even higher. Wow! You can see queer from up here!

NOTES

1. I would like to thank Dr. Steven Cohan for his guidance and support with this article and my graduate career.

2. I define bisexuality as an attraction to both females and males. I recognize that there are numerous forms of bisexuality—with some bisexuals defining their desire as directly related to the sex of their partner and others claiming sex makes no difference to them. I want to emphasize that bisexuality does not equal queer, and that my critiques of bisexuality are theoretical and not a critique of bisexuality as a sexual identity or as a site for activism.

3. See Lillian Faderman's *Surpassing the Love of Men: Romantic Friendship and Love Between Women from the Renaissance to the Present* for a history of butch-femme.

4. This quote can be read as indicating queerness—Jolie's desire is not for a woman or man but rather for a person who is strong enough to take her down. She is looking for her equal, regardless of gender(s). However, she still frames her desire in terms of a woman or man, most likely because language does not permit a way to frame it otherwise (as *Foxfire* demonstrates).

5. Jolie won a best supporting actress Oscar for her role as the sociopathic mental patient Lisa in *Girl, Interrupted* (1999). Notably, Lisa kisses her best friend, Susanna (Winona Ryder), when they escape from the hospital.

6. I cannot resist citing a passage from a Website that provides "*Gone in 60 Seconds*: The Abridged Script." In this parody, Angelina is given one of two pieces of dialogue that perfectly sum up her role:

ANGELINA JOLIE'S LIPS

I'm hot. My hair is dirty. I'm edgy.
Have sex with me in the back of a
stolen car. I like to be on top.

Not only is this evidence of her star text translating into how the audience receives the film, but it sums up Sway as the sexually assertive butch femme.

7. Jolie's penchant for blade play is well documented (see Ressner or any fansite).

8. I would also suggest that they are robbing the couple not only of their literal means of mobility but also their metaphoric bisexuality. This is a warning about what happens to bisexuals in relationships—they are read as straight if with opposite-sex partners and lesbian/gay if with same-sex partners. Once in a relationship, bisexuality literally disappears.

9. Dumbass and the Fag. "The Top 100 Most Eligible Bachelors." *Dumbass and the Fag.*
10. Sprague, Evan. "Index/Start-up Page." *Raging Bull's Angelina Jolie Page.*
11. In *Gia*, Gia (Jolie) has an affair with a very femme, previously straight woman. In *Girl, Interrupted*, Jolie's character Lisa and the baby butch femme Susanna (Winona Ryder) kiss. I think it is interesting to note the increasing inseparability of bisexuality and butch femme. Jolie's costar in *Girl, Interrupted*, Winona Ryder also adopted a butch femme style in the film–although an infantile one compared to Jolie. Interestingly, in a recent episode of *Friends*, Ryder kissed another woman. Rumors about her sexuality have also surfaced.

REFERENCES

Brown, Terry. (1994). "The Butch-Femme Fatale." In Laura Doan (Ed.), *The Lesbian Postmodern* (pp. 99-135). New York: Columbia Press.

Burana, Lily. (1994). "A Random Sampling of Butches: Eight Questions Asked of Ten Butch Women." In Burana, Lily, Roxxie, and Linnea Due (Eds.), *Dagger: On Butch Women* (pp. 24-8). Pittsburgh: Cleis Press.

Butler, Judith. (2000). *Gender Trouble: Feminism and the Subversion of Identity.* 10th Anniversary ed. New York: Routledge.

Clark, Danae. (1993). "Commodity Lesbianism." In Henry Abelove, Michele Aina Barale, David M. Halperin (Eds.), *The Lesbian and Gay Studies Reader* (pp. 186-201). New York: Routledge.

Doty, Alexander. (2000). *Flaming Classics: Queering the Film Canon.* New York: Routledge.

Dumbass and the Fag. (3 May 2001). "The Top 100 Most Eligible Bachelors." *Dumbass and the Fag.* <http://www.dumbassandthefag.com/features/10men.html>.

Faderman, Lillian. (1981). *Surpassing the Love of Men: Romantic Friendship and Love Between Women from the Renaissance to the Present.* New York: William Morrow and Company.

Foxfire. (1996). Dir. Annette Haywood-Carter. Angelina Jolie, Heddy Burress, Jenny Shimizu. Rysher Entertainment.

Gone in 60 Seconds. (2000). Dir. Dominic Sena. Nicholas Cage, Angelina Jolie. Buena Vista Pictures.

Halberstam, Judith. (1994). "F2M: The Making of Female Masculinity." In Laura Doan (Ed.), *The Lesbian Postmodern* (pp. 210-228). New York: Columbia Press.

Harris, Laura and Elizabeth Brocker. (1997). "An Introduction to Sustaining Femme Gender." In Laura Harris and Elizabeth Brocker (Eds.), *Femme: Feminists, Lesbians and Bad Girls* (pp. 1-12). New York: Routledge.

Lamos, Colleen. (1994). "The Postmodern Lesbian Position: *On Our Backs.*" In Laura Doan (Ed.), *The Lesbian Postermodern* (pp. 85-103). New York: Columbia Press.

Ressner, Jeffrey. (24 Jan 2000). "Rebel Without a Pause." *Time*, 72.

Roxie. (1994). "Who Says There's Only Two Genders?" In Burana, Lily, Roxxie, and Linnea Due (Eds.), *Dagger: On Butch Women* (pp. 93-5). Pittsburgh: Cleis Press.

Rugg, Rebecca Ann. (1997). "How Does She Look?" In Laura Harris and Elizabeth Brocker (Eds.), *Femme: Feminists, Lesbians and Bad Girls* (pp. 175-89). New York: Routledge.

Shary, Timothy. (2000). "Angry Young Women: The Emergence of the 'Toughgirl' Image in American Teen Films." *Post Script–Essays in Film and The Humanities* 19(2), 49-61.

Smyth, Cherry. (1995). "The Transgressive Sexual Subject." In Paul Burston and Colin Richardson (Eds.), *A Queer Romance: Lesbians, Gay Men and Popular Culture* (pp. 123-146). New York: Routledge.

Sprague, Evan. (3 May 2001). "Index/Start-up Page." *Raging Bull's Angelina Jolie Page*. <http://members.nbci.com/_XOOM/ragingactors/jolie/jolie1.html>.

Stein, Arlene. (1989). "All Dressed Up, But No Place to Go? Style Wars and the New Lesbianism." *OUT/LOOK* 1(4), 37-48.

WESTERN INTERSECTIONS, EASTERN APPROXIMATIONS

Living More "Like Oneself": Transgender Identities and Sexualities in Japan

Mark McLelland

Digital Object Identifier: 10.1300/J159v03n03_14

[Haworth co-indexing entry note]: "Living More 'Like Oneself': Transgender Identities and Sexualities in Japan." McLelland, Mark. Co-published simultaneously in *Journal of Bisexuality* (Harrington Park Press, an imprint of The Haworth Press, Inc.) Vol. 3, No. 3/4, 2003, pp. 203-230; and: *Bisexuality and Transgenderism: InterSEXions of the Others* (ed: Jonathan Alexander, and Karen Yescavage) Harrington Park Press, an imprint of The Haworth Press, Inc., 2003, pp. 203-230. Single or multiple copies of this article are available for a fee from The Haworth Document Delivery Service [1-800-HAWORTH, 9:00 a.m. - 5:00 p.m. (EST). E-mail address: docdelivery@haworthpress.com].

SUMMARY. This paper looks at the development of transgender identities in twentieth-century Japan, from their "professional" antecedents in the kabuki theater, through post-war paradigms based in the entertainment world, to recent notions of "amateur" transgenderism and crossdressing. It is argued that early paradigms of transgenderism centered on occupational categories and that, despite modern understandings that associate transgender performance with homosexuality, the traditional bisexual potential of the transgender body was never completely occluded. In recent years transgender individuals have emerged who, distancing themselves from the entertainment world, have sought to interrogate mainstream notions of "normal" sexual and gender identities–arguing instead for a "gender free" society in which gender expression and sexual orientation are not tied to biological sex. *[Article copies available for a fee from The Haworth Document Delivery Service: 1-800-HAWORTH. E-mail address: <docdelivery@haworthpress.com> Website: <http://www.HaworthPress.com>* © *2004 by The Haworth Press, Inc. All rights reserved.]*

KEYWORDS. Japan, transgender, bisexuality, homosexuality, crossdressing, identity

EARLY-MODERN TRANSGENDER PARADIGMS IN JAPAN

Japanese society has long been familiar with the notion of gender malleability, originally via the Buddhist concept of *henshin* or "change form" in which deities could appear in either male or female manifestations according to the needs of their followers (Robertson, 1998, p. 85; McLelland, 2000, p. 79), as well as Daoist notions of yin and yang which posited a shifting balance between female and male energies in each individual (Mishima, 1978, p. 117). However, probably the most conspicuous Japanese transgender image, for foreign observers at least, has been the *onnagata* or female-role player in the all-male kabuki theater. After Yoshizawa Ayame (1673-1729) developed a sophisticated philosophy of female-role acting it became standard for *onnagata* to live as women both on and off stage (Laderriere, 1984, p. 236).[1] Yet, despite living in the female gender, it was normal practice for *onnagata* to marry women and father sons who could inherit their stage name and continue the family lineage–Yoshizawa himself had three sons who each became *onnagata*. However, only the most successful *onnagata* performed on the stage–a much larger category of transgendered males were the *kagema*–apprentice actors who also served as prostitutes. Many boys who took up this trade did so out of necessity, some being sold by their parents (Leupp, 1995, p.134). Based in *kagemajaya* or *kagema* "tea shops," they served as prostitutes for both men and women, including wealthy widows and female attendants from the Shogun's harem (Watanabe and Iwata, 1989, p.104).

During Japan's feudal period (1600-1867) when kabuki was the most conspicuous and popular of dramatic arts, there was no necessary connection made between gender performance and sexual preference because men, samurai in particular, were able to engage in both same- and opposite-sex affairs. Described as *nanshoku*, or "male eroticism," elite men were able to pursue male youths who had not yet undergone their coming-of-age ceremonies, as well as trangendered males of all ages from the lower classes who worked as actors and prostitutes (Leupp, 1995). The latter group, *onnagata* included, were understood to have become transgendered for professional purposes– that is, to earn a living–and while they would offer sexual services to other men (and women)–their transgender performance said nothing about their sexual preference. At this time *nanshoku* (eroticism between men) and *joshoku* (eroticism between men and women) were not seen as mutually incompatible, *onnagata* or *kagema* were not yet, in Foucault's terms, distinct "species" (1990, p. 42), but rather occupational categories, albeit stigmatized ones.

However, the Meiji period (1868-1912), during which Japan was opened to Western influence, coincided with the development of European sexological discourse. From this time on, discussions of "perverse desires" (*hentai seiyoku*) began to circulate in popular magazines which advocated the improvement of public morals in pursuit of "civilization and enlightenment"–a popular slogan of the period. The previous discourse of *nanshoku* and the transgender practices associated with male prostitution were portrayed as feudal, incompatible with "civilized morality," and something that ought to be eradicated.

During this time, Japan developed a significant publications industry devoted to the discussion of sexuality–in the 1920s there were at least six journals with the word "sex" (*sei*) in the title. However, due to censorship, writers needed to ensure that they endorsed only "wholesome" sexual acts and gender identities that reflected the eugenic policies of the nations' leaders. Journals specializing in sexual knowledge, as well as articles and advice pages contributed to newspapers and magazines by a newly emerging class of sexual "experts," could discuss "perverse sexuality" but only to the extent that they diagnosed it as a problem and recommended its cure. One side-effect of this process was that notions that in scientific language might be too difficult for the common reader were recast into the form of confession and "expert" re-

sponses in advice columns (Fruhstuck, 2000), resulting in the widespread pop-
ularization of sexological "knowledge." However, Japan's descent into
militarism in the early 1930s saw the temporary suspension of publications of
a sexual and frivolous nature as sex and gender roles became increasingly polarized, with women being cast as mothers whose purpose was to breed sons
for the emperor and men being seen as fighting machines, part of the national
body (Low, 2003).

Yet, as might be expected, the wide dispersal of new paradigms of sexual
knowledge did not result in the instantaneous "reform" of institutions that had
long been associated with transgender practice. Despite attempts early in the
Meiji period to redefine kabuki as an elite art form (Takahashi, 1995), it remained connected with male prostitution until well into the twentieth century.
In an essay in 1931, the art critic Andō Kōsei commented on how *kagema*
could still be found "everywhere" in Tokyo:

> By the pond in Hibiya Park. At the benches behind the Kannondô [a tem-
> ple and famous sight-seeing spot] in Asakusa. But those in Ginza [the
> site of the newest and largest kabuki theater] are [particularly] special. In
> the Ginza the majority are *onnagata* connected to kabuki. (cited in
> Furukawa, 1994, p.106)

Despite the fact that by this time, transgenderism was very closely aligned in
the public imagination with homosexual practice, there were still echoes of the
earlier paradigm in which transgender *performance* was understood to have no
necessary bearing on sexual *practice*. Indeed, since there was no indigenous
tradition of women appearing on stage, women's roles in many of Japan's
early films, from 1909 to 1919, were played by male actors trained as
onnagata (Mitsuhashi, 2001, p. 5).

In the movies of the 20s and 30s when female actresses were finally playing
women's roles, there was a boom in popularity of "the effeminate male star"
(Roden, 1990, p. 48). Known as *nimaîme*, a term deriving from kabuki and signifying a second or subsidiary star, these male actors appeared rather soft and
flimsy when paired with the newly emergent woman actors on screen. Some,
like Hasegawa Kazuo (1908-1984), had received their early training as kabuki
onnagata and, indeed, Hasegawa played the role of an *onnagata* in the extremely popular movie *Yukinojo henge* (An actor's revenge), which was originally filmed in 1935 and remade in 1962 with Hasegawa playing the lead in
both versions. The story basically concerns Hasegawa's attempt to exact revenge on the theater owner and his cronies who defrauded his father and
caused his suicide. He does this through seducing and then betraying one of
the Shogun's concubines which he does *while dressed as a woman*. The plot is

only plausible to the extent the audience understands that transgender performance is not *in itself* incompatible with heterosexual interests and moreover, that a transgendered man could be considered a suitable love interest for women,[2] as is still the case today with the boys in Japan's cross-dressing "image bands" (McLelland, 2000, pp. 75-6).[3]

THE POSTWAR PERIOD: 1945-1960

Although transgender expression in early modern Japan has been extensively described (Watanabe and Iwata, 1989; Leupp, 1995; Robertson, 1998; Pflugfelder, 1999), more recent Japanese transgender experience has received less attention. Since I am not aware of any English accounts of the historical development of diverse transgender practices in post-war Japan, I shall confine myself to a fairly linear description of the main terms through which transgender practices have been understood. Until recently, all transgender practices and identities have been developed in relation to the entertainment world, through what can be termed an "exhibition model," which stresses exterior performance over interior identity or desire (McLelland, 2000, pp. 44-7).

After Japan's defeat, a new kind of sexual culture emerged very rapidly. Street prostitutes sprung up everywhere "like bamboo shoots after the rain" and there was a boom in the pedaling of amateur pornography (Shimokawa, 1995, p. 172). The Occupation Forces were more interested in monitoring political than sexual content, Rubin commenting that the Civil Censorship Detachment "had no concern with material that was obscene or pornographic, providing that material was not detrimental to Occupation objectives" (1988, p. 170). Hence, it was possible for new kinds of sex-related publications to emerge in Japan which were considerably more frank than pre-war magazines, or than any publications that existed in English at this time. The immediate post-war years saw the development of a *kasutori* (low-grade, pulp) culture which Dower describes as "a commercial world dominated by sexually oriented entertainments and a veritable cascade of pulp literature" (2000, p. 148). Japanese writers were now free to dispense with the "wholesome" preoccupations of earlier literature and instead explore more "decadent" themes (Rubin, 1985, pp. 72-3), including a whole genre of "carnal literature" (*nikutai bungaku*) in which the physicality of the body was emphasized over more spiritual concerns. Developing out of earlier, fly-by-night publications, from the early 1950s, a range of more high-brow magazines appeared that allowed readers to indulge their interest in "perverse desires" (*hentai seiyoku*). The popularity of these magazines—by the mid-50s there were at least five similar titles in circulation—was discussed by writers and readers alike who put it down to the sense of "release" (*kaihô*) from hegemonic gender and sexual norms experienced at the war's end. As Rubin mentions, "the Japanese were sick to death of being preached at constantly to be good, frugal, hardworking, and self-sacrificing" and were consequently attracted to "a decadence that was simply the antithesis of prewar wholesomeness" (1985, p. 80).[4]

The "perverse" or "mania" magazines, as they were termed, had an extremely wide range of interests and, purporting to offer true accounts, drew upon anecdotes from Japan's feudal past as well as stories from European and Asian societies, often relying on anthropological reports.[5] Significantly, these early magazines did not segregate the material into hetero- or homosexual-themed issues, as became increasingly common in the 1970s, but presented a wide range of "perverse desires." The most long lived was *Kitan kurabu* (Strange-talk club) published between 1950 and 1975 which, albeit mainly focusing on SM, included discussions and illustrations of a range of "queer" (*katayaburi*) topics, including homosexuality and male and female cross-dressing.

The "experts" who wrote for the perverse magazines of the 1950s were different from those writing in the pre-war sexological publications in that few claimed any kind of medical or psychiatric training. Referred to as *sensei* (teacher), most writers were more literary in bent, and their authority derived from their extensive reading about both Japanese and foreign *fūzoku* or "sexual customs" which included sexological and psychoanalytic works but also anthropological, historical and literary treatises. While a familiar repertoire of theories from sexology and psychoanalysis such as "inversion," "arrested development," "fetishism," "narcissism" and "penis envy" were rehearsed in these articles, more affirmative theories deriving from writers such as Gide, D.H. Lawrence and Genet were also discussed as were the findings of the Kinsey report into American male sexual behavior. One magazine, *Ningen tankyū* (Human research), acknowledged on its cover that it offered articles on "sexual science" for "cultured persons" (*bunkajin*) and many writers referred to themselves and their readers as members of the "intelligentsia" (*interi*) among whom interest in sexual perversity was held to be particularly keen.[6]

The breadth of reference in these magazines and the fact that readers often wrote letters and contributed longer descriptive pieces about their own "perverse desires"[7] meant that pathologizing medical, criminal and psychoanalytic theories did not establish such a firm hold on popular discourse about transgenderism and homosexuality in Japan as was the case in Anglophone, particularly American popular writings, at this time, and consequently, there was no equivalent in Japan to the 1950s American discourse about the "homo-sexual menace" described by D'Emilio (1992). Indeed, many writers asked for increased understanding and tolerance of a wide range of sexual behaviors, in-cluding homosexuality (Honshi, 1954, p. 98). The coalition between religious fundamentalism and conservative politics that made open discussion of "sex variants" all but impossible in English-language cultures did not eventuate in Japan and, since Japan lacked the various "sodomy" laws that were used in most Western societies to target homosexuals and cross-dressers, criminal dis-course was also largely absent in these discussions.[8]

According to reports in these magazines, the most visible transgender cate-gory to appear immediately after the war was the *danshō* or cross-dressing male prostitute who plied his trade beneath the trees in Tokyo's Ueno Park. Several reasons are given for an apparent "boom" in male prostitution, the main one being that many men had been introduced to homosexual sex and de-veloped a liking for it while serving in the army. It was also noted that some decommissioned men, having lost contact with their families while away at war and living in a state of social confusion, were turning to prostitution to sur-vive. However, unlike the previous paradigm of transvestite prostitution asso-ciated with the kabuki theater, contemporary *danshō* were considered to have a predilection for passive anal sex which, although they may have become ac-customed to it while in the army, was part of their psycho-physical makeup.

The terms most commonly used to describe them were "urning" (*ūruningu*), a sexological term that had been devised by German sexologist and homosex-ual, Karl Ulrichs (1825-95), to designate a "female soul in a male body" and "effeminatio" (*effeminachio*) which also stressed their effeminate nature. Their male customers, on the other hand, were understood to be different sexual "types," referred to as "*pede*" or "*pederasuto*" (from pederast) which, in the 1950s Japanese context, was used to signify a man interested in transgendered as well as younger men. Urning were considered to have woman-like bodies, small genitalia, an "innate" (*sententeki*) desire for passive anal sex and a predisposition toward narcissism which led them to turn to pros-titution as a way of fulfilling their desires as well as earning a living. They chose to practice as *transgendered* prostitutes because their constitution meant that they were already woman-like. Pede, however, were thought to have "acquired" (*kōtenteki*) homosexual interests, either during the war, or through disappointment in previous relations with biological women and were considered to be the "active" partners in sex.[9]

However, despite the strong association between male prostitution and ef-feminacy, there were some male prostitutes who failed to conform to this sys-tem by dressing in "smart male clothes"; referred to as *dondengaishi* or "reversibles," they were considered able to go either way (Miyazono, 1953, p. 79). Indeed, one source (Kogure, 1952, p. 30) refers to *danshō* known as *donten* (a contraction of *dondengaishi*) who "become partners for both men and women" (*otoko mo onna mo onajiyōni aite suru*).

The frequent insistence on the *danshō's "passive" sexual nature was also confused by reports that some were heterosexually married, just as many kabuki onnagata* had been (Honshi, 1954, p. 93),[10] suggesting that the earlier bisexual pattern of male prostitution had survived into the post-war era. Indeed, one account reputedly written by a *danshō* mentions that he was approached by a middle-aged female customer precisely because he resembled an *onnagata* whom she had been attracted to in her youth. He reported that her lovemaking that night was "absolutely passionate" (Hirano 1947, p. 146). The neat division between the "passive" prostitutes and their "active" clients was also clouded by the acknowledgement that some male clients wished to be penetrated. Writers tried to maintain the integrity of the classificatory system by suggesting that these clients suffered from "penis envy" (*fuarus naido*), whereas the *danshō* who offered this service had both large penises and a strong exhibitionist streak (Honshi, 1954, p. 95).

While in the decade immediately following the end of the war, *danshō* was the most conspicuous transgender category, from the mid 1950s, the perverse magazines began to interest themselves in a new form of transgender expression: the "gay boy" whose place of work was not the streets but the bars. The early 50s had seen the development of a new style of "gay bars" (*gei bā*) where transgendered male hostesses known as "gay boys" (*gei bōi*) served drinks and provided conversation for customers, often making themselves available for after-hours assignations. Unlike the *danshō*, *gei bōi* did not completely cross-dress, instead preferring to wear make-up and a few items of (Western) women's clothing (Tomida, 1958, pp. 181-4) although the "mama-san" who ran the establishments were still liable to style themselves as *onnagata;* indeed, some had been *onnagata* in their youth (XYZ, 1955, p. 76).

The term *gei* (gay) had entered Japanese via homosexual cliques within the Occupation Forces among whom it was a common self-referent, whereas *bōi*, used to refer to a waiter or barman, dates back to the café culture of the Taishō period (1912-1926). By the late 50s *gei*, especially as part of the compound *gei bōi*, was frequently used in the Japanese media to describe effeminate homosexual men, and featured as the title of Tomida's book, *Gei*, where he described *gei bōi* as "more feminine (*joseiteki*) than today's boyish young women" (1958, p. 181). In some discussions, like the *danshō*, the gay boy was considered to have a "passive" predisposition toward feminine behavior which resulted in both the desire to cross-dress and to participate in sexual in-

teraction with gender-normative men (Honshi, 1954, pp. 96-7), and yet in testimonies by some self-identified gay boys, some claimed to be married to
women (Tomida, 1958, 67, 181) suggesting that transgender performance in
certain milieu was still seen as an occupation. That *gei bōi* was understood, at
least in part as an occupational category, was reinforced by the fact that *gei*
(written in the *katakana* syllables used to transcribe foreign loanwords) is a
homonym of *gei* (written with the character for "artistic accomplishment"–as
in geisha). Gay boys were sometimes spoken of as *gei wo uri*, that is "selling
gei." In this phrase *gei* designates not sexual orientation but a kind of artistic
performance.

The fact that unlike *danshō*, gay boys were not primarily prostitutes but
worked in the bars taking care of and providing entertainment for guests–not
unlike female hostesses in some regular bars–enabled them to develop skills
as performers. One aspect of this performance was heightened transgendered
behavior, a trend that accelerated in the next decade. In 1961, for instance,
Fūzoku kitan described the "flourishing" business for "geisha boys" at
high-class restaurants in Tokyo who, dressing as *onnagata*, performed for an
elite clientele.[11]

1960s–THE BLUE BOY BOOM

Another term used to describe transgendered males which became widely
popular for a time in the 1960s was "blue boy" (*burū bōi*). Although first used
to refer to transgender performers from French nightclub Le Carrousel de
Paris, it later came to refer to all male-to-female transgenders, especially those
who had undergone surgical procedures.[12] Le Carrousel first performed in Tokyo in 1963 at the Golden Akasaka nightclub and such was their critical success that they were invited back in 1964 and 1965. The troupe's most famous
members had undergone sex-change surgery in Casablanca and much was
made of them in the Japanese media. In 1964, for instance, the scandal magazine *Hyaku man nin no yoru* ran an article entitled "the man-made beauties
from Paris" (*Pari kara yatte kita jinkōbijin*) which led to a spate of articles
about sex-change operations.

The arrival of the Carrousel performers was not the first time that Japanese
media had interested themselves in the phenomenon of "sex change"
(*seitenkan*) since there had been several high-profile performers who had undergone male-to-female reassignment surgery in the 1950s. Japan's first operation, on cabaret singer Nagai Akiko, took place in 1951, one year *before* the
case of Christine Jorgensen brought international attention to the procedure.

However, the phenomenal success of the Carrousel performers in Tokyo has been likened to the arrival of the black ships[13] for Japan's gay world (Mitsuhashi, 2001). Some *gei bōi,* who were already conspicuous for their effeminate mannerisms, were encouraged to go further in developing a transgendered appearance. Mitsuhashi suggests that many were encouraged to further transgender themselves, even to the extent of undergoing surgical procedures, for primarily economic reasons. As she comments "for the purposes of entertainment, the value of male nudity was basically nil. Accordingly, if men changed sex to female, their value would be raised," all the more so since such performers were relatively scarce (2001, p. 7). "Formerly male-female performers" became an item in many cabarets and traveling revues, engaging in erotic dancing and stripping as well as singing chanson in their husky voices.

As mentioned, during the 1950s and early 1960s in Japan, there had been a number of castration and sex-change operations performed on male entertainers. In 1960 Ginza Rose, who had begun her career as a show dancer for the Occupation Forces, received a sex-change operation so that she could (unofficially) get married and in 1962, the singer Carrousel Maki had her testicles removed as the first stage in her transition to womanhood which was finally completed in Morocco in 1973. However, in 1965, in what became known as the "Blue Boy Trial" (*burū bōi saiban*), a doctor was investigated for removing the male sex organs of three men who were later investigated on prostitution charges. In 1969, a ruling was passed down that since he had interfered with otherwise healthy sex organs he was in violation of Clause 28 of the Eugenic Protection Law which forbade any unnecessary procedure that would result in sterilization. From this time on, the category of blue boy gradually faded from public view and sex-change operations were not resumed in Japan until 1998 when strict, new ethical guidelines for the procedure were enacted (Ishida, 2002).

THE 1980s–THE NEWHALF BOOM

Once the blue boy boom passed, *gei bōi* remained the most prominent term for describing transgendered men working in the entertainment industry until the early 1980s. At this time two new Japanese-English neologisms appeared: "newhalf" (*nyūhāfu*) and "Mr. Lady" (Mr. *redi*) which designated entertainers who had gone beyond the wearing of women's clothes, make-up and hairstyles and had developed breasts through the use of hormones or implants. Creation of the term newhalf dates back to 1981 and is attributed to Betty, the mama of the Osaka show pub Betty's Mayonnaise who said of herself "I'm half man and woman" (*otoko to onna no hāfu*). "Half" or *hāfu* in Japanese is a term used to refer to individuals of mixed race, usually Japanese and Caucasian. The "new half" was therefore another indeterminate figure, not of mixed race but of mixed gender.

This term might not have gained such wide currency had it not been picked up by the media but, on 14 April 1981, *Suppōtsu Nippon* ran an article entitled "Gay singer named Betty is called a newhalf." However, it was the massive media attention given to "Roppongi girl" Matsubara Rumiko in May of that year that ensured the new term became widespread. Matsubara, while hiding her biological status as a man, had won a beauty promotion staged by businesses in Roppongi (a popular Tokyo nightlife area), becoming the cover girl for a poster campaign promoting the area's clubs and bars. Once her transgender status was revealed, she was quickly elevated to idol status–posing semi-nude in *Heibon panchi* on 8 June 1981, releasing an album of songs entitled *Newhalf* in September 1981 and acting in the movie *Kura no naka* (In the storehouse; Toei, 1981, dir Yokomizu Seishi).

Newhalf is a complex category that covers a range of sexual identities and practices but not lifestyles. Like the other transgender categories discussed, newhalf is primarily used to designate transgendered men who live and work in the sex and entertainment world and is best understood as an occupational category (McLelland, 2002, 2003a; Lunsing, 2002). Komatsu's collection of newhalf life stories *Nyūhāfu ga kimeta "watshi" rashii ikikata* (On deciding to be a newhalf and living like "myself") features seven individuals who are all to some extent involved in the sex-trade or bar world. However, they display a range of transgender attributes–some having developed breasts through the use of hormones and some through implants. Newhalf also differ regarding their attitudes towards their male genitalia, some having undergone castration only, others having had complete sex-change operations and yet others declaring a sense of identification with their penises. Cherry, for instance, says "I love my well-shaped penis" (2000, p.126) which she is happy to use for penetrative purposes with her clients while rejecting the notion that she might use it to penetrate her boyfriend. A brief look at the online personals page on *Newhalf Net*[14] shows that newhalf and their admirers are interested in a range of sexual interactions including "lesbian relationships" (*rezu na kankei*).[15] Newhalf are therefore an example of what Valentine has termed "disruptive bodies" since they destabilize the "coherence between gender, sexual practices, and somatic makeup" that characterizes medical discussion about transsexualism (1997, p. 215).

TRANSGENDER AND SEXUAL "IDENTITIES" IN JAPAN

So far, the transgender identities discussed have all been developed in relation to the sex and entertainment world which in Japanese is described as the *mizu shōbai* or "water trade" and as such can be seen as a continuation of the *onnagata* model rather than a radical departure from it. Like the *onnagata*, the categories of *danshō*, gay boy, blue boy and newhalf are as much occupational designations as they are expressions of personal identity. Individuals who work in the *mizu shōbai* often comment on how they came to take "this path" (*kono michi*) or found their place in "this world" (*kono sekai*) as if discussing a career choice. In other words, these terms are all *professional* designations and the term *puro* (pro) is widely used in Japanese to describe men who express themselves through forms of gendered behavior normally associated with women in order to earn a living.

The fact that Japan has had an unbroken tradition since the Edo period (1600-1867) of social spaces in which transgendered men could pursue their careers relatively unhindered and that homosexual acts, except for a brief period at the end of the nineteenth century, have never been criminalized (McLelland, 2000, pp. 37-41), has enabled the development of very visible transgender identities centered around commercial activities. To a certain extent, this has worked against essentializing discourses of "sexual identity," since performing as a woman or engaging in certain sexual acts can be understood as a necessary part of the job (McLelland, 2000, pp. 44-7; 2003a, p. 60).

Certainly, discourses prevalent in the 1950s and 1960s which drew upon sexological and psychoanalytic models in order to explain transgender behavior established a strong connection between transgenderism and same-sex desire. Yet, as discussed, the literature did not offer a coherent picture as to whether these predispositions were innate or acquired or whether they could or should be cured. Indeed, when compared with discourses in English surrounding homosexual and transgender phenomena, Japanese sources seem remarkably *uninterested* in searching for causes or designating cures so long as the site for the performance of these identities is the entertainment world. I have therefore avoided discussing the transgender categories outlined so far in terms of what Pflugfelder calls "the currently canonical trinity of 'homosexuality,' 'heterosexuality,' and 'bisexuality'" (1999, p. 5) since the location for the performance of transgender identity has, until recently, been the entertainment world, hardly a sphere where one expects to find the expression of "deeply rooted personal identit[ies] based on the biological sex of the preferred sexual object" (Pflugfelder, 1999, p. 6)–either in Japan or the West.

In the remaining part of this paper, I want to look at a recent development which also undoes the connection between transgender practices and specific forms of "sexual identity" and which challenges the frequent connection made between transgenders and the sex and entertainment world–the rise of an "amateur" transgender movement.

NOT ABOUT SEX:
THE RISE OF THE "AMATEUR"
TRANSGENDER MOVEMENT

Despite the sustained media attention given to "professional" transgenders who have worked in the entertainment world as companions, hostesses, entertainers and sex workers, there is another group of transgendered men whose existence has largely been overlooked both by media in Japan and by researchers–the "amateur cross-dressers" (*amachua josō*).

I have yet to come across information indicating whether there were clubs or loose associations of men who met together to express their interest in cross-dressing and other transgender practices before the war, but such organizations rapidly emerged in the early 1950s and have proliferated greatly in recent years due to the spread of the Internet. While "professional" transgender practice has been inexorably associated with sex, particularly homosexuality, because of its location in the sex and entertainment world, many of those expressing interest in part-time or amateur cross-dressing, are insistent that their transgender practice is *not* about sex.

We know about the existence of early cross-dressing associations from small-scale *minikomi* (a pun on "mass communications"–the term refers to privately printed and circulated newsletters) that have survived from the 1950s (Mitsuhashi, 1998). These included *Engeki hyōron* (Theatrical Review) associated with the *Engeki Kenkyūkai* (Theatrical Society) that was supposedly concerned with cross-dressing in the theater but mainly included articles by members detailing their own experiences with cross-dressing, often including photos. Later, the *Fuki Kurabu* (Wealth and Honor Club) intermittently published a members' newsletter and occasionally advertised for new members in one of the perverse magazines' regular cross-dressing columns.[16] These publications were important because they gave voice to a wider community of cross-dressers and enabled the development of a nonsexual discourse about cross-dressing, establishing a space for transgender practice outside of the exhibition paradigm of the sex and entertainment world.

Finding a meeting place was always a problem for amateur cross-dressers who did not seek to earn a living from their transgender interests. Unlike the luxuriantly appointed "show pubs" where newhalf entertain a clientele of heterosexual tourists (Lunsing, 2002, p. 26), amateur transgender bars are known in Japanese as *sunakku*–signifying modest hole-in-the-wall joints where drinks and simple snacks can be obtained. Some also offer the use (for a membership fee) of a backroom where customers who arrive at the bar in male attire can change their clothes and apply their makeup. The staff in these bars are sometimes referred to as "semi-professional" (*semi puro*) in that they may gain auxiliary income from serving in the bars a few nights a week while also maintaining day jobs as men. The *sunakku* also offer the chance for a wider community of "amateur" (*amachua*) cross-dressers to interact with each other and also with male customers who are interested in or admire transgenders. Most bars have a dual charge system where cross-dressed men pay substantially lower charges for tables and drinks than do the gender-normative men who come seeking companionship. However, these bars exist in established red-light districts, and not all men who like to cross-dress feel comfortable with the sexualized atmosphere that exists in these areas.

Other venues catering to amateur cross-dressers include private clubs established in rented rooms which provide opportunity to cross-dress and socialize with other cross-dressers. One of the earliest of these venues was associated with the Fuki Club which rented various rooms in Tokyo in the 1960s where men could meet, dress up and interact with one another (Mitsuhashi, 1998). However, these groups were always small and remained marginal to the wider transgender world organized around the *mizu shōbai*. It was not until larger, better publicized cross-dressing clubs such as the Elizabeth chain,[17] which opened its first club in Tokyo in 1979, developed that Japan saw a boom in amateur cross-dressing. Unlike the bars, Elizabeth and other clubs such as Studio Sapphire, do not allow non cross-dressing men to join in their activities and actively promote cross-dressing as a "hobby" (*shumi*) for men irrespective of their occupation, lifestyle or sexual orientation.

Elizabeth club was closely associated with the development of Japan's first commercial magazine dedicated to transgender issues–*Queen* (*Kuiin*), published in 1980.[18] *Queen* is distinct from other magazines that have followed, in focusing primarily on "amateur" cross-dressing as a "hobby" and consequently it does not include pornography or advertisements for bars where gender-normative men go to meet transgender partners. The development of *Queen* as a medium of communication between men with a nonsexual interest in transgender practices as well as the proliferation since the 1980s of cross-dressing social clubs which exclude "gender normative" males has provided a space for transgender practice outside of the exhibition mode of the entertainment world. Men who transgender themselves in these environments are, of course, aware of being observed by their peers but their motivation is not to perform for an audience, nor to increase their earning potential. The designation *amachua* used to describe the transgender practices undertaken in these spaces signifies not so much part-time and certainly not lack of ability, but is rather used in opposition to the term *puro* which designates an identity built around a calculated transgender performance associated with the sex and entertainment world.

While publications such as *Queen* and the development of recreational spaces such as the Elizabeth and other clubs where men can meet together and explore transgender practices and identities outside of the paradigms offered by the entertainment world have been important in widening the scope for transgender practice in Japan, the Internet has had an even greater impact on the variety of discourses surrounding transgender identities. As Miller and Slater point out, "the encounter with the expansive connections and possibilities of the Internet may enable one to envisage a quite novel vision of what one could be" (2001, p. 11). Transgender individuals in Japan were among the first to establish a Net presence, even before the birth of the World Wide Web (*Kuia sutadiizu heshu iinkai*, 1997, 33). *EON*,[19] a BBS (bulletin-board system) for "transvestites and transsexuals," was established in 1990. By 2000 there were hundreds of individual transgender Web sites as well as Web rings dedicated to providing information and contact services for transgender individuals and their admirers. In April 2000, the Web ring *Newhalf Lady*[20] was one of the first to provide an *i-mode* service enabling browsers to surf and download material from the ring's Web sites via their mobile phones thus helping close the digital divide between those with computer access and those without.

Transgender individuals from both the professional and amateur worlds make use of Internet technology: most newhalf clubs, bars and cabarets maintain Web sites promoting their services, as do individual transgender sex workers (McLelland, 2002, 2003a), and there are thousands of other transgender sites offering advice about everything from new developments in hormone therapy and female fashions to news about transgender issues in Japan and abroad. In a few short years the Internet has developed an ever expanding and practically inexhaustible databank of transgender culture and experience which has impacted upon the range of expressions available for understanding transgender in all its forms.

Lunsing comments that "the various categories of transgender that a cultural discourse provides are never adequate to fully describe actual transgender experience" (2002, p. 21). This was already apparent in the perverse magazines of the 1950s which gave space to the voices of readers whose lives did not fit into the official paradigms offered by the experts and is certainly the case with more mainstream media which primarily focus on commercial transgender identities expressed in the entertainment world. However, through the medium of the Internet, it is possible to encounter a much wider range of transgender images and practices and to contribute one's own experience to the debate. Indeed, excellent online databases of Japanese transgender culture such as *Metamorphosis*[21] have made Japan's transgender history internationally accessible and links between Japanese and Western transgender Web sites show that transgender collaboration is now worldwide.

The Internet has also been instrumental in promoting the visibility of a new kind of transgender personality–the transgender intellectual–who has entirely broken with the exhibition paradigm of the entertainment world. Mitsuhashi Junko is a university lecturer and amateur cross-dresser whose historical research into Japanese transgender practice regularly appears in *Newhalf Club* magazine as well as on her Web site. Mitsuhashi is a married biological male who teaches gender studies at Tokyo's Chuo University while dressed as a woman while also lecturing in history at another Tokyo university while dressed as a man (Josei sebun, 2000). Media response to Mitsuhashi's innovative lecture courses has been largely positive and she has been interviewed in several mainstream newspapers and magazines and appeared on numerous television and radio programs, details of which are provided on her extremely well organized and informative Web site.[22]

Another high profile transgender intellectual is also a heterosexually married father who, in his "masculine mode" (*dansei mōdo*) teaches at high school, and at the weekends, when in "feminine mode" (*josei mōdo*), becomes Miyazaki Rumiko, transgender activist, writer and lecturer who, in addition to publishing her own books and writing for mainstream print media, has run a highly successful Web site dedicated to transgender issues since 1997.[23]

Designating herself *sensei*, much as did writers for the perverse magazines half a century earlier, Miyazaki helps her readers understand the different forms that transgender expression may take and yet in her analysis, it is not transgender individuals themselves that have a "problem" but rather society as a whole which is amiss in enforcing a binary gender system on all its citizens. Miyazaki proposes a "gender free" society in which an individual's choice of dress, mode of communication, occupation and sexual orientation are not decided by their birth sex but by personal preference and disposition. However, she is well aware that in order to normalize the transgender experience she must break down its abiding association with the entertainment world. As she says in the afterword to her book *I Am Transgendered*, "Up until now the word newhalf has been well known. But so far the image of a person who works at night, singing, dancing and performing on a stage has remained strong. What I'd like the person reading this book to remember is that there are also transgendered people living beside you leading ordinary lives" (2000, p. 216). She goes on to comment that "*gender free* means living outside the narrowness of 'masculinity' and 'femininity,' it's a term, the importance of which is that you should live like yourself" (2000, pp. 217-18).

CONCLUSION

As outlined earlier, Japanese media have provided space for the discussion of a variety of transgender and sexual practices, yet the place for the enactment of these practices has overwhelmingly been the entertainment world–a situation which has worked against the development of fixed gender and sexual "identities." While transgender individuals have certainly been discussed in terms stressing their "otherness," the kind of moral and social condemnation which at times has violently erupted in English-language media has been largely absent.

In the last decade, new technologies such as the Internet have provided further opportunities for transgender people to network and challenge the sexualized images so prevalent in the mainstream press and argue for a greater range of gender expressions to be acknowledged in real life. Although the lives of many Japanese people are still very much constrained by hegemonic gender norms, there has been considerable movement in the last decade towards a more flexible society from which members of sexual minorities, in particular, have benefited (McLelland, 2003b). Indeed, there is a clear momentum toward the representation of diversity that is impacting upon the lives of all Japanese people, irrespective of their gender or sexual orientation that parallels similar trends in other postindustrial democracies (Giddens, 1991, 1992; Castells, 2000).

While there will always undoubtedly be resistance from some quarters to lifestyles and identities outside those traditionally endorsed, the proliferation of media and the power afforded minorities by new technologies such as the Internet makes the insistence upon one hegemonic mode of sex or gender identity less and less plausible. This is particularly the case in Japan which lacks a tradition of religious fundamentalism and where conservative politicians do not orchestrate moral panics about a supposed "queer menace" in order to win votes. As Giddens (1991, 1992) has argued, modernity, in Japan as elsewhere, has seen the development and proliferation of "lifestyle sectors" that challenge "traditional" lifestyle patterns and gender roles. Increasingly, individuals with transgender interests are encountering diverse transgender practices on the Internet and, through participating in activities organized by the amateur cross-dressing clubs, are critically engaging with mainstream gender narratives. Like Mitsuhashi Junko and Miyazaki Rumiko, other transgenders are pioneering nonsexualized versions of transgender identity outside the entertainment world which require a wider cultural reassessment of what we think we "know" about sex and gender, not just in Japan but around the world.

FOLLOW-UP QUESTIONS WITH DR. MARK McLELLAND

To tease out a few more intersections between bi-eroticism and trans-genderism in the work that Mark is doing on Japanese sexualities, we posed the following questions to him, and he graciously–and insightfully–responded.

Editors: You very carefully note the importance of, in Japan at least, not confusing transgender practices and "sexual identities," primarily because (if we're understanding you correctly) such practice frequently "undoes the connection between transgender practices and specific forms of 'sexual identity.'" As such, you don't apply terms such as homosexual, heterosexual, and bisexual.

Mark: I try to avoid these terms as much as possible because they don't map onto Japanese sexual subcultures in a very clear way. Historically, transgender practice was seen as a performance–it grew out of the kabuki theater and was understood more as a career choice than an expression of inner identity. This is still seen today in the all-woman Takarazuka theater where the young women who enroll in the troupe's training school have to decide early in their careers whether they will specialize in male or female roles.

The "traditional" sex and gender system which associated masculinity with activity and femininity with passivity meant that transgendered males were available as passive inserters for gender-normative men, yet also able to function as active inserters in relationships with women. However, in the first half of the twentieth century, this system began to break down and there was a stronger sense that transgender performance was tied in with a "passive" nature which was more exclusively homosexual. Yet, even in the 1950s, figures such as the *dondengaishi* or "reversibles," complicated this picture. In recent years, newhalf, many of whom pass very convincingly as women, have laid claim to a phallic agency which severely disrupts the traditional system because they are understood to be capable of penetrative sex not just with women, but more importantly, with other men. Is a gender-normative man who engages in sex with a newhalf therefore "homosexual" (because both bodies are male), "bisexual" (because he is responding to a body that has aspects of both genders) or even "heterosexual" (because many newhalf pass convincingly as women)? I don't think that this terminology is particularly illuminating here–human desire always exceeds the categories that we generate to describe it.

Editors: At the same time, your essay describes a diversity of trans identities developing in Japan over the last several years–identities that provocatively disturb set notions of masculinity and femininity, even male and female. Has there ever been a "bisexual identity" that has taken shape or form in Japan? If so, what might be its relationship with the trans identities–newhalf, blue boy, etc.–that you describe?

Mark: I don't think that the development of these trans identities in Japan is a recent development. Post-war Japanese culture saw a rapid proliferation of identities from "sister boys" to "gay boys" to "blue boys"–each a response to complex interactions between foreign influences (such as the Japan tour of Le Carrousel) and specific local conditions (such as the laissez faire attitude of the police which allowed vibrant subcultures to develop). What is new is the role that television and more recently the Internet have played in increasing the visibility of these subcultures.

One aspect of this increased visibility is that Western discourses about sexual and gender "identity" have begun to spread. Tellingly, the Japanese term most often used to express the notion of identity is *aidentiti*–an English loanword. Other loanwords such as "gay" (*gei*), "lesbian" (*rezubian*), "bi" (*bai*), "straight" (*sutoreeto*) and "transgender" (*toransugendaa*) are now commonly used throughout popular media. In the 1990s *gei* developed into an identity for some Japanese men in a manner very similar to Western gay identities but it has not displaced older indigenous understandings and is sometimes in conflict with them. Gay, lesbian and bisexual identities are not some kind of necessary future for Japanese sexual minorities; there is much else going on besides these imported understandings, as I try to show in my essay.

Editors: In terms of the "newhalf"–which you describe as an "indeterminate figure, not of mixed race but of mixed gender"–to what extent do you think that a bi-eroticism, if not a bisexual identity, accounts for "newhalf," its attractions and those who are attracted to "newhalf"?

Mark: This is a very interesting question which takes us back to an earlier understanding of "bi-sexual"–not a sexual identity which responds to the erotic potential of both male and female bodies so much as an attraction to a body which manifests both male and female attributes–known elsewhere as "she-male." What is special in the Japanese case is that the phallic potential of newhalf is publicly acknowledged. Seemingly similar categories such as the *travesti* of Brazil, although they may privately penetrate their clients, are publicly understood to be available only for "passive" intercourse. A *travesti* who was "active" in sex with a gender-normative male would contravene the Latin sex and gender system which associates activity with masculinity and passivity with femininity. Newhalf, however, through openly advertising "reverse anal fuck" as a sexual service, lay claim to a phallic potential which troubles their otherwise feminine gender performance. This does seem to be something new in Japanese society. Kabuki *onnagata* were always available for hire by women in which they would play the "active" role (as we see in the movie *Actor's Revenge*) but in Japan's pre-modern sex and gender system, it was inconceivable that an *onnagata* might be the "active" partner with another adult male.

In the 1950s "perverse magazines" that I have been studying, there is much discussion of transgender practices, including transgender prostitution but the assumption is that there is this binary relationship between the female/passive "urning" and the masculine/active "pederast." Newhalf, because of their acknowledged phallic agency, disrupt this traditional paradigm and represent a new kind of "bi-eroticism"–they are *both* male and female, *both* active and passive in the one body–and I think that this is a large part of their fascination.

Editors: You describe the plot of a fascinating movie, *An Actor's Revenge*, suggesting that "The plot is only plausible to the extent the audience understands that transgender performance is not in itself incompatible with heterosexual interests and moreover, that a transgendered man could be considered a suitable love interest for women, as is still the case today with the boys in Japan's cross-dressing 'image bands.'" To what extent are such interests bi-erotic?

Mark: This is very difficult to answer because the fieldwork which would illuminate this issue just isn't there yet. "Japanese Studies" as a discipline has yet to engage with issues of transgender performance and its reception in everyday life. There are, of course, discussions of kabuki and the Takarazuka, and a few texts that look at historical manifestations of homosexuality in the distant past but it is still hard to get grant money for fieldwork with actual transgender people or to do audience surveys to find out how people consume transgender performances in everyday life.

What work does exist looks at the relatively safe issue of women's reception of both male and female transgender performance and the explanation goes that in Japan, where gender roles are very rigid and where men are somewhat severe patriarchal figures, women feel more comfortable with men who express "feminine" characteristics—the fan base for the transgender performers I mention is almost exclusively female. This suggests that if real men were just a bit nicer and more approachable, then transgender performers would lose their appeal. This is both a sexist and heterosexist argument, assuming that what a girl really wants is a nice man! It neatly sidesteps the bi-erotic fascination that Japanese men and women both feel towards these transgender entertainers.

Editors: More broadly—you wonderfully describe the burgeoning entertainment trade that seems to focus on, perhaps even fetishize transgender identities, or performances. To what extent might such identities/performances be understood as bi-erotic? Is that a useful term for understanding part of the appeal of the trans performances?

Mark: Absolutely. The very many transgender performers in Japan all have a bi-erotic potential—not in the usual sense of the term "bisexual" which refers to sexual attraction toward both men and women, but in the sense that they integrate aspects of male and female in the same body. Japanese performers constantly draw attention to their "bi-sexual" status, particularly in their use of language. Japanese is spoken rather differently by men and women—women use a more polite register than do men and there are certain pronouns, articles and phrases used exclusively by men or by women. IZAM, a transgendered member of the boy band SHAZNA, passes very convincingly as a woman until he speaks—he uses both male speech and body language. Mikawa Ken'ichi, a transgendered singer of traditional folk songs, switches between male and female language for comic effect. Likewise, Asakawa Hikaru, a newhalf who was popular for a time on Fuji TV, became famous for the gag that her top half resembled her mother but her lower half resembled her father. Through drawing attention to the "bi-sexual" elements of her body, Asakawa is definitely encouraging us to imagine its erotic potential.

Editors: Ironically then, "bi-sexuality" is not defined *relationally*—as it is presently defined in the West (as opposed to historically in Freud's day)—but more in terms of an *individual's* expression. In other words, it doesn't matter who, i.e., what gender(s), is/are drawn to one's "erotic potential." That is not the focal point in the culture, correct?

Mark: To a degree this is true but only to the extent that these kinds of interactions take place in the fantasy space of the "entertainment world." Absent in Japan, compared with the US, is the anxiety that the gender free for all in the entertainment world will have a debilitating effect upon people's gender performances in "real life." US gender-benders such as Marilyn Manson are very popular in Japan, too, but there are no Christian or parents' organizations campaigning to have such performers banned because they are a bad influence on young people.

Editors: The construct of sexual orientation, therefore, falls by the wayside when trying to define anyone's desire of trans individuals, regardless of culture, East or West. Because, once traditional identities of gender have been mucked with, then sexual identities subsequently follow it into the murky identity waters.

Mark: I think so because desire for trans individuals is not necessarily always "sexual" in a straightforward genital sense. The Japanese term most often associated with the public's interest in transgender performance is *akogare* which is a kind of "yearning" for a state beyond gender. In Japan, daily gender performance is actually strictly codified, much more so than in the West, and so the desire to "trans" gender in the sense of "go beyond" is very evident in the entertainment sphere. Indeed, another term often used in discussion of transgender entertainers is *koeru*, a verb meaning to "exceed" or "surpass." Such individuals have a freedom lacking in ordinary life and are therefore very attractive to some.

Editors: Notice how the "exceptions" in the gender binary system confuse not just gender but sexuality as well; however, the converse is not true: bisexuals—who upset the sexual binary system (gay/straight) tend not to upset the gender binary system. Bi people are still commonly seen as "real" men or "real" women, even though some say they don't "really" have a sexual orientation.

Mark: In the 1950s magazines, bisexuality, for men, is always discussed in terms of being "acquired" through various environmental factors, such as long-term exposure to a homosocial situation like the army or on a fishing boat, past negative experiences with women or a tendency toward debauchery which leads to the search for new pleasures. Men who behave bisexually are referred to as *tachi* (from *tatsu*, "to stand"), a term best translated as "top." In focusing on the sex of the participants, as opposed to their sexual *roles*, the English term "bisexual" doesn't really map onto this kind of behavior. What would have upset the gender system is if a man were to be heterosexually "active" and homosexually "passive." I have never come across an article where this possibility was discussed, although it must have taken place.

Editors: Thus, sexual orientation rests upon the larger foundation of gender, making it–gender–the higher order structural system. Hypothetically then, one would expect greater resistance toward accepting transgender individuals than bisexuals (or homosexuals). Those transsexuals who seek to completely adopt one category for another are the "safest" ones then.

And the queer transgendered, then, are "the ones to watch out for," because their subversive goal of deconstructing/reconfiguring gender is much more of a threat (in the eyes of social or religious conservatives) than either bisexuality or homosexuality, I presume.

Mark: So far in Japan no sexual minorities have been signaled out by public or religious authorities as being particularly threatening or dangerous. Representatives from transsexual, homosexual and sex-worker organizations are in dialogue with government agencies about the particular social problems that they face. These interactions have met with mixed results but, despite some irresponsible media reporting, especially concerning AIDS, no public figures or organizations have found it expedient to demonize these groups and there is little benefit to be gained from launching anti-homosexual campaigns. So the above comment speaks more to the situation facing sexual minorities in Anglophone societies. While in Anglophone societies sexual minorities are often viewed as inherently dangerous and degenerate, in Japan, they are seen more as institutionally awkward–so long as they remain in the entertainment world, that's fine, but how does one integrate them into the school or the workforce or the heterosexual family? It is only recently that such attempts have been made by "amateur" (i.e., non-entertainer) transgenders such as Miyazaki Rumiko who take their transgender performance into the public world. Media response to Miyazaki's lectures has, on the whole, been positive–and this makes me wonder whether the anxiety and paranoia that has accompanied the gradual winning of transgender rights in the US is a necessary future for Japan. We need to wait and see.

NOTES

1. Early twentieth-century vaudeville also had a category of "female impersonators" who were considered able to give "more photographic interpretation of femininity than the average woman is able to give" but, unlike *onnagata*, "were careful to appear suitably manly offstage" (Slide, 1994: p. 172) so as not to cause suspicion of homosexuality.

2. At the beginning of the twentieth century, Vaudeville star Julian Eltinge, "the most famous female impersonator of his day," also caused women to go into "ecstasies" over him (Slide, 1994: p.158) but from around 1920 onwards, as public anxieties over homosexuality grew, female impersonation was increasingly associated with the developing homosexual subculture and went underground (Berube, 1990: pp. 72-3). Intriguingly, Eltinge's dresser was a Japanese man.

3. Many Japanese "boy bands" include members who cross-dress, often very successfully. In recent years, the most notable cross-dressing star has been IZAM of the band SHAZNA. For a discussion of IZAM, see Todd Holden's paper "I'm Your Venus/ You're a Rake," *Intersections*, issue 3: Online. Available: *http://wwwsshe.murdoch.edu.au/intersections/issue3/holden_paper4.html* (21 February 2003).

4. For a philosophical reflection of post-war decadence, see Sakaguchi (1986), originally published in the monthly magazine *Shincho* in 1946.

5. I consulted issues of these magazines while conducting archival research in Tokyo in December 2002. Titles I looked at included *Ningen tankyû* (Human research), *Fûzoku zôshi* (Sex-custom story book), *Fûzoku kagaku* (Sex-custom science), *Kitan kurabu* (Strange-talk club), and *Fûzoku kitan* (Strange tales of sex customs).

6. Prominent intellectuals who were said to frequent Tokyo's gay bars in the early 1950s included authors Mishima Yukio and Edogawa Rampo (XYZ, 1955: p. 78); the latter sometimes contributed articles to the perverse magazines–see, for example, his *"Dôseiai bungakushi ni tsuite: Iwata Jun'ichi-kun no omoide"* (On the history of homosexual literature–Iwata Jun'ichi's thoughts), *Ningen tankyû* special edition, May 1952, pp. 40-44.

7. One reader, for instance, resists the pathologizing framework of the experts when he describes how, during his honeymoon, he and his wife enjoyed swapping roles, and walked about town each dressed in the other's clothes. Y. Mishima *"Watashi no 'josô' no hanseiki,"* *Fūzoku kitan*, March 1961, pp. 180-183.

8. Nealon points out that although there was also an explosion in pulp literature in post-war America, its treatment of homosexuality was unremittingly negative since "the prevailing language for homosexuality in the 1950s was a toxic mix of psychopathological and the criminal." Homosexuality appealed to the publishers of pulp literature which focused on the "'dark side' of American life" (2001: 148-9) and it was rare to come across nonpathological descriptions of homosexual life.

9. Examples of articles discussing various homosexual and transgender types include K. Kabiya *"Danshoku kissaten,"* *Fūzoku zôshi*, July, 1953, pp. 26-30; T. Shibukawa *"Sodomia hôrôki,"* *Fūzoku zôshi* October 1953, pp. 71-77; as well as the regular advice columns *"Sodomia tsūshin"* in *Fūzoku zôshi* and *"Homo no peiji"* in *Fūzoku kagaku.*

10. This seems to be the case even today. The writer and film critic Donald Richie, who has lived by Ueno Park for over thirty years, often encounters cross-dressed male prostitutes during his evening strolls. When he enquired of one if he were married, Richie received the reply "Of course, whose clothes do you think I'm wearing?" (Personal communication).

11. February 1961, *"Geisha bōi no ryōtei wa daihanjō,"* p. 63.

12. The origin of the term "blue boy" is obscure but it has been suggested that it may derive from the famous Gainsborough portrait of that name which depicts a very feminine-appearing male youth.

13. "Black ships" or *kuro fune* refers to all the Western ships to visit Japan from the 16th century until the end of the Edo period (1867). The image of the ships, when used

as a metaphor, expresses the sense of disorientation generated by the sudden arrival of a totally new, alien culture.

14. *http://www.newhalf.net/photo* (26 November 2002).

15. *Rezu* is a broader term than the English word "lesbian" from which it derives since it can refer to sexual interactions between cross-dressed and transgendered men as well as biological women.

16. *Fūzoku kitan* (Strange talk about sex customs); see, for example, page 163 of the February issue of 1961.

17. For information on the Elizabeth chain of clubs, see their Web site: *http://www.elizabeth.co.jp/* (28 October 2002).

18. Lunsing reports that the bi-monthly circulation of *Queen* is 7,000 (2003: 22).

19. The name refers to the eighteenth-century cross-dressing diplomat Chevalier D' Eon from whence "Eonism," an early term for transvestism, is derived.

20. *http://www.newhalf.com/nhl/* (18 May 2000).

21. *http://www.geocities.co.jp/Hollywood/4349/index2.html* (19 February 2003).

22. *http://www4.wisnet.ne.jp/~junko/index2.html* (25 February 2003).

23. Miyazaki Rumiko's homepage: *http://www4.justnet.ne.jp/~r.miyazaki/* (18 February 2003).

REFERENCES

Berube, A. (1990). *Coming Out Under Fire: The History of Gay Men and Women in World War Two*. New York: The Free Press.

Castells, M. (2000). *The Power of Identity*. Malden, MA: Blackwells.

D'Emilio, J. (1992). The Homosexual Menace: The Politics of Sexuality in Cold War America. In J. D'Emilio (Ed.), *Making Trouble: Essays on Gay History, Politics and the University*. New York: Routledge. 57-73.

Dower, J. (2000). *Embracing Defeat: Japan in the Wake of World War II*. New York: W.W. Norton.

Foucault, M. (1990). *History of Sexuality Volume One: Introduction*. London: Penguin.

Fruhstuck, S. (2000). Managing the Truth of Sex in Imperial Japan. *The Journal of Asian Studies*, 55: 2, 332-358.

Furukawa, M. (1994). The Changing Nature of Sexuality: The Three Codes Framing Homosexuality in Modern Japan (transl. A. Lockyer). *U.S.-Japan Women's Journal English Supplement* 7: 98-127.

Giddens, A. (1992). *The Transformation of Intimacy: Sexuality, Love and Eroticism in Modern Societies*. Cambridge: Polity Press.

Giddens, A. (1991). *Modernity and Self-Identity: Self and Society in the Late Modern Age*. Cambridge: Polity Press.

Hirano, T. (1947). *Gunbuku no danshōtachi* (Danshō in military uniform). *Shinsō jitsuwa* (True tales). May, 114-147.

Honshi Chōsabu (Magazine Research Group). (1954). *Danshō no ijōseiai chōsa* (Research into the abnormal sexuality of *danshō*). *Fūzoku kurabu* (Sex-customs club). May, 92-98.

Ishida, H. (2002). *Yomigaeru burūbōi saiban no "seishin": Seitenkan shujutsu to sono ihōsei ni kansuru zasshi media wo mochiita monogatarironteki gensetsu bunseki* (Revived blue-boy judgments' "spirit": A discourse analysis of sex-change operations and their illegality in terms of the narrative model). *Hō to sekushuariti* (Law and Sexuality) 1:1, 85-117.

Josei sebun (Women's seven). (2000). *Junko sensei wa sei no ekkyōsha: Nippon hatsu! Wadai no chūodaigaku josō kōshi ga karada wo haritte oshieru "otoko no karada de onna no kokoro" no shakaigaku* (Japan's first! Professor Junko transgresses sex: A cross-dressing Chuo University lecturer teaches sociology from the perspective of a woman's heart in a man's body), 30 November, 55-57.

Kogure, G. (1952). *Onna demo otoko demonai otoko: [danshô] okama dekameron* (Men who are neither women nor men: An *okama* Dekameron), *Kipatsu kenkyū* (Extraordinary research). August, 22-30.

Komatsu, A. (2000). *Nyūhā fu ga kimeta "watashi" rashii ikikata* (On deciding to be a newhalf and living like "myself"). Tokyo: KK Ronguserâzu.

Kuia sutadiizu henshu iinkai (Queer studies editorial board). (1997). *Kuia sutadiizu '97* (Queer Studies '97). Tokyo: Nanatsumori shokan.

Laderriere, M. (1984). Yoshizawa Ayame (1673-1729) and the Art of Female Impersonation in Genroku Japan. In G. Daniels (Ed.), *Europe Interprets Japan*. Kent: Paul Norbury Publishing, 233-238.

Leupp, G. (1995). *Male Colors: The Construction of Homosexuality in Tokugawa Japan*. Berkeley: University of California Press.

Low, M. (2003). The Emperor's Sons Go to War: Competing Masculinities in Modern Japan. In K. Louie and M. Low (Eds.), *Asian Masculinities: The Meaning and Practice of Manhood in China and Japan*. London: RoutledgeCurzon, 81-99.

Lunsing, W. (2002). What Masculinity? Transgender Practices Among Japanese "Men." In J. Roberson and N. Suzuki (Eds.), *Men and Masculinities in Contemporary Japan*. London: RoutledgeCurzon, 20-36.

McLelland, M. (2003a). Japanese Queerscapes: Global/Local Intersections on the Internet. In C. Berry, F. Martin and A. Yue (Eds.), *Mobile Cultures: New Media in Queer Asia*. Durham: Duke University Press, 52-69.

McLelland, M. (2003b). Gay Men, Masculinity and the Media in Japan. In K. Louie and M. Low (Eds.), *Asian Masculinities: The Meaning and Practice of Manhood in China and Japan*. London: RoutedgeCurzon, 59-78.

McLelland, M. (2002). The Newhalf Net: Japan's "Intermediate Sex" On Line. *International Journal of Sexuality and Gender Studies*, 7: 2/3, 163-176.

McLelland, M. (2000). *Male Homosexuality in Modern Japan: Cultural Myths and Social Realities*. London: RoutledgeCurzon.

Miller, D. and D. Slater. (2001). *The Internet: An Ethnographic Approach*. Oxford and New York: Berg.

Mishima, Y. (1978). *Yukio Mishima on Hagakure*. Tokyo: Tuttle.

Mitsuhashi, J. (2001). *Burūbōi no shōgeki* (The blue boy impact). In *Nihon josō mukashibanashi* (Reminiscences about Japan's cross-dressers). *Nyūhā fu kurabu*, (Newhalf club) no. 31.

Mitsuhashi, J. (1998). *Saisho no amachua josō shūdan* (The first amateur cross-dressing associations). In *Nihon josō mukashi banashi* (Reminiscences about Japan's cross-dressers). *Nyūhā fu kurabu* (Newhalf club) no. 25.

Miyazaki, R. (2000). *Watashi wa toransugendā* (I am transgendered). Tokyo: Neoraifu.

Miyazono, S. (1953). *Danshoku kandan* (Gossip about male eroticism). *Fûzoku kagaku* (Sex-custom science). August 1953, 74-79.

Nealon, Christopher. (2001). *Foundlings: Lesbian and Gay Historical Emotion Before Stonewall*. Durham: Duke University Press.

Pflugfelder, G. (1999). *Cartographies of Desire: Male-Male Sexuality in Japanese Discourse*, 1600-1950. Berkeley: University of California Press.

Robertson, J. (1998). *Takarazuka: Sexual Politics and Popular Culture in Modern Japan*. Berkeley: University of California Press.

Roden, T. (1990). Taishō Culture and the Problem of Gender Ambivalence. In J.T. Rimer (Ed.), *Japanese Intellectuals During the Inter-War Years*. Princeton: Princeton University Press.

Rubin, J. (1988). The Impact of the Occupation on Literature or Lady Chatterley and Lt. Col. Verness. In T. W. Burkman (Ed.), *The Occupation of Japan: Arts and Culture*. Norfolk, Virginia: General Douglas MacArthur Foundation, 167-174.

Rubin, J. (1985). From Wholesomeness to Decadence: The Censorship of Literature Under the Allied Occupation. *Journal of Japanese Studies* 11:1, 71-103.

Sakaguchi, A. (1986). "Discourse on Decadence." *Review of Japanese Culture and Society*, 1:1, 1-5.

Shimokawa, K. (1995). *Nihon ero shashinshi* (History of Japan's pornographic photographs). Tokyo: Shōkyūsha.

Slide, A. (1994). *The Encyclopedia of Vaudeville*. Westport: Greenwood Press.

Takahashi Y. (1995). Kabuki Goes Official: The 1878 Opening of the Shintomi-za. *TDR*, 39: 3, 131-151.

Tomida E. (1958). *Gei* (Gay). Tokyo: Tōkyō shobō.

Valentine, D. and R. A. Wilchins. (1997). One-Percent of the Burn Chart: Gender, Genitals and Hermaphrodites with Attitude. *Social Text*, 15: 3/4, 215-222.

Watanabe T. and J. Iwata. (1989). *The Love of the Samurai: A Thousand Years of Japanese Homosexuality* (trans. D.R. Roberts). London: GMP.

XYZ (a pseudonym). (1955). *Danshoku kissaten/sakaba no Tōkyō chizu* (Map of Tokyo male-eroticism coffee shops and bars). *Fūzoku kagaku* (Sex-customs science) February, 72-78.

While Diving, Drink Water: Bisexual and Transgender Intersections in South Sulawesi, Indonesia

Sharyn Graham

http://www.haworthpress.com/web/JB
© 2003 by The Haworth Press, Inc. All rights reserved.
Digital Object Identifier: 10.1300/J159v03n03_15

[Haworth co-indexing entry note]: "While Diving, Drink Water: Bisexual and Transgender Intersections in South Sulawesi, Indonesia." Graham, Sharyn. Co-published simultaneously in *Journal of Bisexuality* (Harrington Park Press, an imprint of The Haworth Press, Inc.) Vol. 3, No. 3/4, 2003, pp. 231-247; and: *Bisexuality and Transgenderism: InterSEXions of the Others* (ed: Jonathan Alexander, and Karen Yescavage) Harrington Park Press, an imprint of The Haworth Press, Inc., 2003, pp. 231-247. Single or multiple copies of this article are available for a fee from The Haworth Document Delivery Service [1-800-HAWORTH, 9:00 a.m. - 5:00 p.m. (EST). E-mail address: docdelivery@haworthpress.com].

SUMMARY. This article analyzes the intersections, or to take this publication's play on words, interSEXions, between bisexuality and transgender in South Sulawesi, Indonesia.[1] While there are no equivalent indigenous terms, there are cognate identities and experiences that make such an examination valid and fruitful. The article is divided into four main sections. After a brief introduction, section one sets the scene by introducing readers to South Sulawesi. This section also examines prevailing ideas of gender and sexuality in the region. I argue that gender is a salient notion in South Sulawesi and that there are very clear models of what is expected of girls and boys when they grow up. I also posit that gender is a holistic concept, constituted by various factors, including biology, sexuality, roles, and behaviors. It is essential to develop this emic understanding of gender in order to appreciate the intersections of bisexuality and transgender. In the second section I introduce two gendered identities which fall outside normative models: *calabai'* (transgendered males) and *calalai'* (transgendered females). Through the narratives of key informants the identity and subjectivity of these individuals is revealed. In the third section I recount specific examples of bisexuality and transgender intersections. A critical analysis of these intersections reveals much about representations and understandings of desire, sexuality, and gender. The theoretical contributions which arise from this analysis are proposed in the fourth section. I argue that the conceptual categories imposed by rigid Western terminology are rendered problematic when considering the intersection between bisexuality and transgender. As such, in South Sulawesi experiences of bisexuality and transgender must be explored from a perspective which allows appreciation of their coalescence. *[Article copies available for a fee from The Haworth Document Delivery Service: 1-800-HAWORTH. E-mail address: <docdelivery@haworthpress.com> Website: <http://www.HaworthPress. com> © 2003 by The Haworth Press, Inc. All rights reserved.]*

KEYWORDS. Bisexual, transgender, sexuality, identity, Bugis (Indonesia)

INTRODUCTION

Jero', Dodid and I sit staggered on the bamboo stairs leading to Jero's house. The *muadzin* calls people to evening prayer. The sun slowly sets, silhouetted behind the large white dome that crowns Sengkang's largest mosque. Jero' and Dodid are men in their early thirties. Dodid has recently married.

Jero', however, is leaving the decision, and planning, of his wedding up to his parents. His parents are yet to find him a suitable spouse. The three of us talk about a number of things. Soon our conversation turns to ideas of gender, sexuality and identity:

Jero'	–I was once warned about *calabai'* (transgendered males). I was told, 'Don't trust *calabai'*.'
Sharyn	–Why not?
Jero'	–Well, you know *calabai'* play an important role in weddings, right. They organize the food, organize the wedding costumes, they dress the bride and groom, and do their make-up. *Calabai'* are put in positions of trust, you know. Often they are alone with the bride in the room getting her ready for the wedding. The *calabai'* is putting on her make-up and dressing her. Well, I have been told that sometimes *calabai'* rape (*memperkosa*) the bride.
Sharyn	–That doesn't really happen, does it?
Dodid	–It seldom happens, Jero'.
Jero'	–Sure, it doesn't happen often, but it does happen. Tell Serli (Sharyn) about your wedding day, and the *calabai'* who was feeling you up!
Dodid	–Well, there was a *calabai'* who was employed to organize (*mengurus*) my wedding and s/he was in my room dressing me, but s/he kept needlessly feeling my body and squeezing my arms and touching me everywhere. I was very uncomfortable.
Jero'	–Yep, while diving, drink water! (*Iye', sambil menyelam minum air,* meaning, take advantage of every opportunity).
Sharyn	–I can understand why that would happen, but why would a *calabai'*, who is attracted to men, want to rape a bride?
Dodid	–Because *calabai'* have two sides to them, mostly they're attracted to men, but sometimes to women. If their passion rises (*timbul nafsu*) then they can be attracted to women.

Jero' and Dodid's comments started me thinking about the intersections between bisexuality and transgender. Jero' alludes to *calabai'* drinking water while diving. By this he implies that *calabai'* take advantage of every sexual opportunity that comes their way. While *calabai'* are transgendered males, from Jero's perspective, *calabai'* are also bisexual. Dodid reinforces this assumption when he asserts that *calabai'* have two sides and, as such, can be sexually attracted to men and to women.

In this article I want to deconstruct and explore further the intersections between bisexuality and transgender. For simplicity, I take bisexual to mean sexually oriented toward both sexes. I take transgender to mean exhibiting appearances and behavioral characteristics not generally associated with one's sex. These definitions are certainly problematic and I will return to them in later sections. To facilitate an examination of the intersection between these concepts, the article is divided into four sections. Section one contextualizes the paper by introducing readers to South Sulawesi. This section also examines prevailing notions of gender and sexuality. I argue that gender is a salient concept in South Sulawesi and that there are very clear models of what is expected of girls and boys when they grow up. I also posit that gender be thought of in a holistic sense. Rather than sexuality being distinct from gender, for instance, sexuality actually contributes to gender identity. It is essential to develop this emic understanding of gender as it guides understanding of bisexual and transgender intersections.

In the second section I introduce two gendered identities which fall outside the normative model. These identities are introduced through the narratives of two key informants, Yulia and Ance'. Yulia is male-bodied, yet s/he does not identify as a man, nor does s/he aspire to be/come a woman. Rather, Yulia identifies, and is identified as, a *calabai'*. Ance' is female-bodied and yet s/he does not conform to the expectations of a 'good' woman. As such, Rani is not considered, nor does s/he consider herself, a woman. Rather, Ance' identifies, and is identified as, a *calalai'*. This section highlights the identity and subjectivity of individuals who do not conform to dominant norms of gender and sexuality. Having an understanding of *calabai'* and *calalai'* enables better appreciation of the intersections between bisexuality and transgender.

In the third section I reproduce a number of ethnographic narratives collected during my fieldwork period in South Sulawesi between 1998 and 2002. Dissecting these narratives reveals a fundamental intersection between bisexuality and transgender. Individuals who identify, and are identified as, transgendered are assumed to be, and often are, bisexual. Moreover, because of the cultural setting in which gendered identities are formed, transgendered individuals are often persuaded to be bisexual. This section, then, looks at ways in which transgender assumes, and persuades, bisexuality.

In the concluding section I present a critical analysis of the intersections of transgender and bisexual experiences. I argue that these intersections problematize the idea of desire. Moreover, I suggest that such experiences show how desire can be motivated and governed by cultural discourse. In effect, rather than being individual identities, transgender and bisexuality actually intersect in forming a single identity. Imposing Western terms (i.e., transgender, bisexual), which denote a separation of sexual identity from gender identity, is therefore problematic. As such, this section highlights the need to word towards developing new theoretical configurations of (trans)gender and (bi)sexual experiences.

PREVAILING NOTIONS OF GENDER
AND SEXUALITY IN SOUTH SULAWESI

Sulawesi is an orchard-shaped island located in the middle of the Indonesian archipelago. It is home to the Bugis, an ethnic group comprising around three million people. The Bugis are renowned seafarers (Ammarell, 1999; Pelras, 1996), and have undertaken extensive migrations to various parts of Asia (Acciaioli, 1989; Anderson, forthcoming). While fishing provides a livelihood for many Bugis, farming and cultivation are also important daily activities. Most Bugis identify as Muslim and Sengkang, the area where I did my field work, boasts a high percentage of people who have made the pilgrimage to Mecca. While the influence of Islam is strong, quotidian customs and practices continue to be inflected with more traditional ones. As a popular adage goes: Makassar people (the southern neighbors of the Bugis) hold tight to religion; Bugis people hold tight to *adat* (traditional customs and practices).

While gender has attracted an expanse of academic attention, in South Sulawesi it has been the focus of only a few works (Chabot, 1950 [1996]; Graham, 2003; Kennedy, 1993; Millar, 1983). These works have placed varying degrees of salience on gender. Millar, for example, argues, 'gender relations in Bugis society are almost entirely subordinate to a cultural preoccupation with hierarchical social location' (Millar, 1983, p. 477). While there is no indigenous term equivalent to 'gender'–*gender* is used in academic discourse, and increasingly in the public arena, and *jenis kelaminan* is used to describe genitalia–the concept of gender is articulated in numerous ways, and is a fundamental principle in Bugis social life. I want to go into some detail about notions of gender because an emic understanding is essential in order to grasp the intersections occurring between what in the West might be labelled 'bisexual' and 'transgender' identities.

The birth of a baby in South Sulawesi is greeted by questions concerning its sex. Genitalia thus determines whether a baby is categorized as a girl or a boy. This may seem unremarkable, and in a sense it is; throughout the world births are greeted with questions concerning the baby's anatomical sex, and babies are categorized accordingly. I make mention of this here for a particular reason. While babies are marked according to sex, a girl does not necessarily grow up to be a woman, nor a boy a man. Definitions of 'woman' and 'man' are strict is South Sulawesi, and as such, deviations from the ideal means that individuals may be excluded from these dominant categories.

Womanhood is clearly defined in Bugis society. Local and state discourses, and Islamic doctrines actively promote ideals of womanhood. A woman is considered the embodiment of her family's honor (*siri'*) (Chabot, 1950 [1996]). As such, she must be discrete and reserved in everything she does. The national government promotes the idea that a woman's greatest achievement, and indeed her natural role, is as wife and mother. It is through pursuing these functions that a girl becomes a woman, and hence a legitimate and worthy member of the Indonesian nation-state (Suryakusuma, 1991). Dove-tailing with local and national discourses are the teachings of Islam. Islamic models of womanhood shape appropriate behavior for women. Muslim women are morally required to marry. Once married, a woman can legitimately bear children, an achievement which accords her a level of status and respect (Manderson, 1980). A woman is female-bodied, heterosexual, married, a mother, and dressed modestly and appropriately (e.g., her sarong is tucked in rather than rolled down like a man's). A woman acts demurely, speaks politely, is refined and reserved, and identifies and is identified as, a woman.

What being a man means is also clearly defined in South Sulawesi. Local discourses assert that men embody and exude qualities such as self-discipline, reason, authority, physical strength, aggression, and are in control of their passions (Millar, 1983, 1989; Peletz, 1995, 1996). Men must protect their family's honor (*siri'*) (Chabot, 1950 [1996]). Making extended voyages and returning home wealthy and wise contribute to the status of a man (Acciaioli, 1989; Pelras, 1996). State ideology declares that men must be husbands and fathers, although, unlike women, men are not defined solely by these attributes. Islam compliments these models of manhood, and defines men as breadwinners who support and protect their family. A man is male-bodied, heterosexual, married, and a father. A man is assertive and aggressive and controlled.

There are thus very strict models of gender, and what being a woman and a man means is clearly defined in Bugis society. Individuals who are unable to conform to these models are often located in a separate conceptual category. There is, then, a high degree of gender variance precisely because not everyone fits the normative model. In South Sulawesi, there are five gendered identities: *makkunrai* (B, woman), *oroane* (B, man), *bissu* (B, androgynous priests), *calabai'* (transgendered males), and *calalai'* (transgendered females) (cf. Graham, 2003). Of most significance to this article are the latter two as these identities often experience intersections between transgender and bisexuality. Before I introduce *calabai'* and *calalai'*, however, I want to briefly discuss how gender is understood in South Sulawesi.

In South Sulawesi, gender is considered to be constituted by myriad factors. An individual's gender identity is not thought to be solely the result of biological sex, however, this is a fundamental consideration. As such, a girl can never become a man. In order to become a man, an individual must necessarily be male. Being male, however, does not mean that an individual automatically becomes a man. Being a man is about more than just anatomy. Sexuality, which includes who one erotically desires and the roles one performs in sexual encounters, does not define an identity, although it is an important contributor. As Murray writes for Indonesia, 'Although gender and sexuality may be distinguished analytically, they are far from being independent from each other. Indeed, outside the elite realm of academic gender discoursing, sexuality and gender generally are expected to coincide' (Murray, 1997c, p. 256; cf. Blackwood, 1999; Jackson, 1997, p. 168; 2000a, p. 417; Murray, 1994, p. 60; 1995; Wieringa, 1999). Labels such as 'bisexual' therefore lose their potency in a region where sexuality is tied in with gender–an issue which I discuss later.[2]

In addition to biological sex and sexuality, gender identity is constituted through notions of spirituality, a sense of self, roles, occupations, behavior, and dress. Because various combinations of these elements are possible for any one individual, notions of gender can move beyond binaries of masculine-male-man, and feminine-female-woman. For instance, a male-bodied individual who is employed as a wedding organizer, who ties hir sarong like a woman (i.e., tucked in rather than rolled down), is involved in a romantic relationship with a man, and who does not consider hirself a man, would identify, and be identified as, a *calabai'*. A female-bodied individual who works as a farmer alongside men, wears trousers, is involved in a romantic relationship with a woman, and who does not consider hirself a woman, would identify, and be identified, as a *calalai'*.

This section has shown that gender is an important concept in South Sulawesi, and that there are very clear models of ideal gender forms. It is precisely this strict model of legitimate gender identity, and the particular holistic understanding of gender, that produce, and provide space for, gender diversity. There are, then, more than two gender identities, and these identities experience intersections between transgender and bisexuality.

CALABAI' AND CALALAI'

In this section I introduce two of my closest informants, Yulia and Ance'. Through their story, I hope that readers get an understanding of the diversity of gender identity in South Sulawesi.

Calabai'

Yulia is one of the most respected wedding organizers in Sengkang. Hir skills as a make-up artist and dress-maker are also highly sought after. In recognition of hir expertise, s/he is often referred to as Indo' Boting (B, Wedding Mother). Yulia is economically savvy and has saved enough money to buy hir own simple, yet comfortable, house. Built in typical Bugis style, it is on stilts and is divided into three sections. The second section is where Yulia does hir dress-making.

Yulia is male-bodied and yet s/he does not conform to the expectation of being a man. Yulia does not identify as a man, and people do not consider hir a man. Neither does Yulia aspire to be a woman. S/he was born male, and in order to be a woman, s/he would have to have been born female. Yulia identifies, and is identified as, a *calabai'*. Yulia is feminine in hir behaviors and dress, although s/he does not embody the image of an ideal Bugis woman. Rather, Yulia's style of dress is influenced by Western images of fashion and s/he frequently wears short skirts and low-cut tops. Yulia is also assertive in both hir job and hir sexual relations with men, which are not feminine qualities. Yulia neither reflects the image of a Bugis man nor a Bugis woman. Rather, Yulia is *calabai'*.

Calalai'

Ance' is thirty-four years old. S/he has known for a long time that what society expected of hir as a female (to be feminine and marry heterosexually) did not fit with hir sense of self. Ance' never liked playing with girls, putting on dresses, serving guests tea and biscuits, or any of the things a girl is expected to do in order to learn to be a woman. Indeed, Ance' hated helping hir mother and older sisters so much that s/he always found an excuse to assist hir father, or to go off playing with hir brothers. While hir behavior was tolerated when s/he was young, as Ance' grew up the pressures on hir to be more feminine and marry became stronger. Ance' wanted to have children, it was just the strict model of womanhood available to hir which s/he detested.

Ance' identifies, and is identified as, a *calabai'*, a female-bodied individual who is more like a man than a woman. This does not mean that Ance' desires to be/come a man, though. S/he does not. It is just that Ance' prefers men's clothes, men's work, and men's freedom. As such, s/he is not considered a woman. But Ance' is female-bodied, so s/he can never be a man, s/he is *calalai'*.

Using the narratives of Yulia, Ance' and others, I now want to examine the intersections between bisexuality and transgender. What is revealed is that bi-

sexual and transgender experiences merge in South Sulawesi so that it is problematic to apply discrete Western-derived labels and theories. As such, there is
the potential for development of a more inclusive theoretical framework
which appreciates the intersections of bisexual and transgender experiences.

BISEXUAL AND TRANSGENDER INTERSECTIONS

I opened this article with an exchange between Dodid, Jero', and myself.
One of the themes of this passage is the perceived vacillating desire of
calabai' for men and women. Jero' revealed that, in his opinion, *calabai'* take
advantage of all situations: *calabai'* drink water while diving. Dodid noted
that *calabai'* have two sides, and if their passion rises, they can be attracted to
women as well as to men. Indeed, for many people in South Sulawesi, being
transgendered implies bisexual desire, as the following narrative suggests:

> Serli, you shouldn't go with Yulia (a *calabai'*).You shouldn't go with
> Yulia and all hir friends to (the city of) Bone. You shouldn't go because
> Yulia's man side might emerge and s/he might try to seduce you. You
> never know when their (*calabai'*) man side might emerge. (Haji Bacco')

Haji Bacco', an elderly *calabai'*, believes that even though Yulia is *calabai'*,
or precisely because s/he is *calabai'*, Yulia's man side might emerge and s/he
might try to seduce me. Yulia strongly refutes this assumption. Yulia is ada-
mant that s/he is not attracted to women, and indeed, if s/he were, s/he would
not consider herself a true *calabai'*–for Yulia, true *calabai'* are not attracted to
women, if *calabai'* are attracted to women, then they are fake *calabai'*. Never-
theless, sexual wavering is a common assumption made about *calabai'*, as the
following passage further reveals:

> So Yulia is a *simpanan* (literally, 'on the side,' a 'storage,' in this case,
> mistress) . . . she's looked after (*dipelihara*). Yeah, some guys have a
> wife and also a *calabai' simpanan* . . . they get bored with their wife, she
> always looks the same, maybe getting older and not so attractive, and she
> works around the house. Also, all they ever talk about is problems
> they're having. So men go and find *calabai'* because they have a differ-
> ent body, they're very beautiful and wear beautiful clothes, and they're
> more exciting. And most important, *bencong* (*calabai'*) can't get preg-
> nant! I too like hanging out with *bencong* sometimes. You can gossip
> and stuff and also be really frank (*terus terang*) and talk about topics that
> you can't with girlfriends. But watch out (*hati-hati*)! Don't be alone in a

room with them because you never know if their man side is going to emerge (*muncul*)! (Nabilah, a woman civil servant in her late twenties)

Nabilah states that men find *calabai'* attractive because they are not women. Such men may identify as bisexual if they were living in the West. Nabilah also reiterates the common theme that a *calabai's* man side might emerge. This passage reveals that men can be married and still form relationships with *calabai'*, revealing an intersection between bisexual men and transgendered males. *Calabai'* are also believed to be attracted to men and women. We see this again in the following quote:

> *Calabai'* are like adaptors. They're AC/DC. They 'plug in' to both women and men. (Andi Jafri, a young man)

Such perceptions underscore a significant intersection between transgender and bisexuality. Sexual desire is considered to be particularly strong among transgendered individuals because sexual desire contributes substantially to an individual's identity; for an individual to identify as transgender, their sexual motivation has to be particularly high, or else they would feasibly just conform to societal norms. Many people extend this assumption to unproblematically link transgender to bisexuality. While there is some truth in this assumption, many *calabai'*, like Yulia, vehemently refute this. Why then is this link so persistently presumed?

Calabai' have fewer restrictions applied to them than do either men or women, and they are not expected to (be able to) control their sexual passions. Moreover, *calabai'* are in a sense expected to be outlandish in their sexual desires because this in part signifies their identity. Men are required to be in control of their passions and desires (Peletz, 1996); women are assumed to have a low sex-drive. *Calabai'* differentiate themselves from men because *calabai'* are considered to have no ability to control their desires, and *calabai'* differentiate themselves from women because *calabai'* have such a high sex-drive. We find, then, that the first intersection between transgender and bisexuality is the perception that transgendered individuals are bisexual.

A second link between transgender and bisexuality stems from the cultural context in which identities are formed. As the previous section revealed, there are very strict ideas of what is expected of males and females. While there is tolerance and general acceptance of *calabai'* and *calalai'* identities, there is still pressure on individuals to marry heterosexually and have children. For this reason, and also because of personal desire, some transgendered individuals develop heterosexual relationships while maintaining homosexual relationships, as the following narrative reveals:

> There's a *calabai'* with a kid you know. Yes, there is. In the daytime s/he's *calabai'* . . . works, dresses, acts as a *calabai'* . . . but then at night s/he goes home to hid wife and kids and acts and dresses like a man and plays the role of husband and father. We call hir *amfibi* because s/he can live in the sea and on land . . . s/he can live in a woman's world and a man's world. S/he can live in two environments (*alam*). (Pak Hidya, middle-aged man).

Pak Hidya relates the case of a *calabai'* who maintains a heterosexual relationship and performs the role of husband and father. While this individual may be doing this simply to conform to societal expectations, it is an example of an intersection between bisexuality and transgender. In the following passage, Dilah notes that, although s/he is a *calalai'*, s/he wants to have children:

> Yeah, I'd like to have children, I just don't want to get married. Ugh! I could adopt a baby so I wouldn't have to sleep with a man. But if I did have to marry, you know if my parents force me, which they've tried to do before, but I always tell them their selection isn't suitable (*cocok*), then I'd just stay with him until I was pregnant and then I'd find a *linas* (a feminine woman who is attracted to *calalai'*) because you know, a *hunter* (*calalai'*) can't change hir feelings, hir make-up. You can't change your fate (*kodrat*), hey. Once a *hunter*, always a *hunter*, you know? (Dilah)

In this passage, Dilah shudders at the thought of getting married. S/he expresses a wish to have children, though, and s/he is under pressure to do this within the institution of heterosexual marriage. While there is no desire on Dilah's part to be involved in a sexual relationship with a man, marriage is the only legitimate way to have children. Understandings of bisexuality which fail to take into account the extent to which society molds sexuality, or at least prescribes legitimate avenues, are limited in their applicability to South Sulawesi.

Another *calalai'*, Ance', is also constrained in hir development of relationships. Like Dilah, Ance' wanted to have children, but s/he did not want to perform the role of wife. Ance' explains hir situation:

> We got married because two males, or two females, can't have children. At the start, [my spouse] Wawal did all the cooking and cleaning because s/he's *calabai'* and s/he knew all about that kind of stuff. I'm *calalai'* and I hate doing all that housework stuff, that's why I'm *calalai'*, because I want to live like a man. At first it was good. But then

Wawal got lazy. In the end s/he expected me to be the husband and the wife! But I have my daughter . . . (Ance')

In Ance's account, we hear of a unique solution. While Ance' wanted to be like a man, and s/he sexually desired women, s/he could neither conceive, nor legitimately raise, children in a homosexual relationship. So s/he married a *calabai'* (a transgender male). In this way, Ance could get pregnant but continue to live like a man. Identifying as transgender does not necessarily preclude marriage and children (cf. Boellstorff, 2000). Ance's gender identity meant that s/he was forced, in a sense, to be bisexual. We see again how the gender structure in South Sulawesi operates to shape sexuality. The second key intersection between transgender and bisexuality, then, stems from the way cultural norms prescribe appropriate avenues for gender and sexuality experiences.

A third intersection between bisexuality and transgender arises due to the impact of gender on sexuality. As I noted earlier, in Bugis society gender and sexuality are tightly interwoven. Who one erotically desires, and the roles one plays in sexual acts, are contributors to gender identity. As such, there is an influential relationship between transgender and bisexuality. We see this in the following account:

> You know, the most important factor [in me becoming a *calalai'*] was influence from a *linas*. You see, I was chosen and seduced by a *linas* over a long time, and this is what made me become ill (*sakit*; homosexual desire is often described in such terms). Before, I wasn't ill, I used to just act like a man (*dulu saya tidak sakit, cuma gaya seperti lelaki*). Then there was a *linas* who always approached me and wanted to be partners (*pacaran*). At first, when we became friends, I didn't think about sex. The *linas* kept paying me lots of attention but I was still scared because I still had feelings like a woman [i.e., was still sexually attracted to men]. I was still 16 then. But I was from a broken home and I really enjoyed all the attention I was getting. So finally I too became ill (*saya ikut sakit*) and became a *hunter* (*calalai'*). (Eri, a *calalai'* in hir mid-twenties)

Eri's eventual attraction to, and relationship with, a *linas* may be seen as a continuation of hir masculine behavior, which was 'like a man.' However, s/he still had feelings like a woman and so it was not necessarily a natural progression. Without the attention from a *linas*, Eri may not have developed a *calalai'* identity (i.e., s/he may have remained only sexually attracted to men). We see here how bisexuality is in some respects an extension of gender identity.

This interplay between transgender and bisexuality is evident in other accounts as well. For Dilah, a thirty-year-old *calalai'*, it was attraction to a woman which initiated hir formation of a masculine *calalai'* identity (cf. Newton, 1984). Moreover, the woman with whom Dilah developed a relationship with was married to a man:

> I met a girl who was married to a violent man who beat her all the time
> and never satisfied her [sexually] in bed. We became friends and I guess
> we started testing. At first she was scared and didn't know if it was appropriate (*cocok*), but finally we let go and 'became one body' (*bersetubuh*, a term for making love). We were both satisfied (*puas*) and we became partners (*pacaran*) because we were suitable (*cocok*). (Dilah)

This narrative adds an interesting dimension to the intersection between transgender and bisexuality. While Dilah is transgendered, hir partner is bisexual. There are, therefore, attractions between these two categories.

The passages examined in this section illustrate intersections between transgender and bisexuality. These intersections problematize the application of terms such as bisexual and transgender. Transgender and bisexual identity in South Sulawesi cannot be fully understood using Western-derived categories. Rather, the intersection of transgender and bisexuality underscores a significant way in which identity in South Sulawesi differs from Western settings: transgender and bisexual experiences may merge to form a single identity. In order to appreciate Bugis gender/sexuality categories, we need to reconfigure rigid Western approaches which dichotomize (trans)gender and (bi)sexuality. I move now to the conclusion where I highlight areas for potential theoretical development.

CONCLUSION: POTENTIAL THEORETICAL DEVELOPMENT

This article has sought to develop a nuanced understanding of the intersections between transgender and bisexuality in South Sulawesi. The first section argued that gender is an important concept in South Sulawesi, that it is clearly defined and articulated, and that gender identity is constituted through the interplay of various factors. The strict definition of ideal gender models, and the holistic understanding of gender, have both forced and fostered the development of various gendered identities. In the second section I introduced two additional gendered identities, *calabai'* and *calalai'*. Through the narratives of Yulia and Ance' the ways in which some individuals form gendered identities which do not conform to normative models were revealed. *Calabai'* and *calalai'* identities are impacted through the intersection of transgender and bisexuality. Three main intersections were thus analyzed in section three. These intersections included: transgender implying bisexuality; cultural discourses encouraging transgendered individuals to be bisexual; and gender identity initiating bisexual desire. I now want to highlight potential theoretical implications of these intersections for future gender/sexuality work.

In thinking of gender and sexuality in South Sulawesi it is problematic to apply Western-derived terms such as bisexual and transgender. There is certainly heuristic value in using these terms and as such I have used them in this article. However, they do not translate well. In Western discourse, bisexuality assumes active sexual desire for both men and women. In South Sulawesi, however, bisexuality is often molded, even prescribed, by cultural norms. In Western discourse, transgender assumes that an individual crosses from one normative gender to the 'other.' In South Sulawesi, however, *calabai'* conform neither to the model of womanhood nor of manhood. Rather, *calabai'* assert a distinct gendered identity. Trying to categorize individuals in South Sulawesi as bisexual or transgender overlooks these fundamental differences in meaning and it does not allow for appreciation of the particular environment in which identities are formed. Moreover, using discrete terms such as bisexual and transgender ignore ways in which these categories impact upon each other.

Applying Western labels to non-Western identities also poses a problem in that the meaning of concepts such as sexuality and gender differ. It is possible in the West to have an identity based on sexuality (e.g., to be homosexual, lesbian, gay, bisexual). It is also possible to have an identity based on gender (e.g., transgender). Because gender in South Sulawesi is constituted in part by sexuality, a division between a gendered identity and a sexual identity is not conceptually possible. Bisexuality is not distinguished as a sexuality, and transgender as a gender. The distinctions between Western identity labels thus become blurred because no clear break exists been gender and sexuality. As Jackson notes for Thailand, it is difficult, indeed ultimately impossible, 'to consistently sustain a difference between the notion of desire for a particular type of sexed body (whether male or female), and hence of sexual identity, and the idea of a preference for enacting a particular gender performance (whether masculine or feminine), and hence of gender identity' (Jackson, 2000a, p. 416). Western terms and theories are therefore labelled in a cultural matrix which is not applicable to South Sulawesi.

In order to appreciate gendered identities in South Sulawesi we need to develop theories which are more attune to emic understandings of gender and sexuality, and which are sensitive to the constitutive intersections between sexuality and gender in identity formation. Such theories will problematize clear conceptual categories and break down the rigidity of Western labels (e.g., bisexual, transgender). Collective understandings of the dynamic relationship between gender and sexuality will be enriched if we can take into account the different configurations of these concepts in South Sulawesi and develop theories accordingly.

NOTES

1. The ethnographic material contained in this paper is the result of sixteen months of fieldwork carried out between August 1998 and March 2002. I would like to thank the people I lived with in Sulawesi, and Rob Webb, Greg Acciaioli and Lyn Parker, for helping me develop the ideas contained in this paper. In this article, Indonesian words are rendered in Italics. Bugis words are also rendered in Italics and are signified by (B), with the exception of *calabai'* and *calalai'*. All informant's names are pseudonyms. I use *hir* and *s/he* to challenge readers to image a subjectivity beyond the dichotomous her/his, she/he. The use of *hir* further signifies the possibility of an identity not contingent on crossing from one normative gender to the other (cf. Blackwood, 1999; Wilchins, 1997) Moreover, neither the Indonesian nor Bugis languages discriminate between gender, using instead the gender non-specific pronouns *dia* and *i/na* respectively.

2. This is changing, though, in metropolitan areas such as Jakarta and Makassar (the capital city of South Sulawesi), where men are identifying as *gay* (Boellstorff, 2000).

REFERENCES

Acciaioli, G. (1989). *Searching for Good Fortune: The Making of a Bugis Shore Community at Lake Lindu, Central Sulawesi.* The Australian National University, PhD dissertation, Canberra.

Ammarell, G. (1999). *Bugis Navigation.* New Haven: Yale University Press.

Anderson, K. (forthcoming). *Like Birds in a Tree: Early Modern Wajorese Statecraft and Diaspora.* Unpublished PhD dissertation, University of Hawaii.

Blackwood, E. (1999). *Tombois* in West Sumatra: Constructing Masculinity and Erotic Desire. In E. Blackwood & S. Wieringa (Eds.), *Female Desires: Same-Sex Relations and Transgender Practices Across Cultures* (pp. 181-205). New York: Columbia University Press.

Boellstorff, T. (2000). *The Gay Archipelago: Postcolonial Sexual Subjectivities in Indonesia, PhD Thesis.* Unpublished PhD dissertation, Stanford University, Stanford.

Chabot, H. T. (1950 [1996]). *Kinship, Status, and Gender in South Celebes* (Vol. 1950). Leiden: Koninklijk Instituut voor de Taal-, Land-en Volkenkunde (KITLV) Press.

Graham, S. (2003). *Hunters, Weddings Mothers, and Gender Transcendent Priests: Conceptualizing Gender Among Bugis in South Sulawesi, Indonesia.* Unpublished PhD dissertation, University of Western Australia, Perth.

Jackson, P. A. (1997). Kathoey><Gay><Man: The Historical Emergence of Gay Male Identity in Thailand. In L. Manderson & M. Jolly (Eds.), *Sites of Desire, Economies of Pleasure: Sexualities in Asia and the Pacific* (pp. 166-190). Chicago: University of Chicago Press.

Jackson, P. A. (2000a). An Explosion of Thai Identities: Global Queering and Re-imagining Queer Theory. *Culture, Health, and Sexuality, 2*(4), 405-424.

Kennedy, M. (1993). Clothing, Gender, and Ritual Transvestism: The *Bissu* of Sulawesi. *The Journal of Men's Studies, 2*(1), 1-13.

Manderson, L. (1980). *Women, Politics, and Change: The Kaum Ibu UMNO Malaysia, 1945-1972.* Kuala Lumpur: Oxford University Press.

Millar, S. B. (1983). On Interpreting Gender in Bugis Society. *American Ethnologist, 10*(August), 477-493.

Millar, S. B. (1989). *Bugis Weddings: Rituals of Social Location in Modern Indonesia.* Berkeley: University of California at Berkeley.

Murray, S. O. (1994). Subordinating Native Cosmologies to the Empire of Gender. *Current Anthropology* (35), 59-61.

Murray, S. O. (Ed.). (1995). *Latin American Male Homosexualities.* Albuquerque: University of Mexico Press.

Murray, S. O. (1997c). Male Actresses in Islamic Parts of Indonesia and the Southern Philippines. In S. O. Murray & W. Roscoe (Eds.), *Islamic Homosexualities: Culture, History, and Literature* (pp. 256-261). New York: New York University Press.

Newton, E. (1984). The Mythic Mannish Lesbian: Radclyffe Hall and the New Woman. *Signs: Journal of Women in Culture and Society, 9*(4), 557-575.

Peletz, M. G. (1995). Neither Reasonable nor Responsible: Contrasting Representations of Masculinity in a Malay Society. In A. Ong & M. Peletz (Eds.), *Bewitching Women, Pious Men: Gender and Body Politics in Southeast Asia* (pp. 76-123). Berkeley: University of California Press.

Peletz, M. G. (1996). *Reason and Passion: Representations of Gender in a Malay Society.* Berkeley: University of California Press.

Pelras, C. (1996). *The Bugis.* Oxford: Blackwell Publishers.

Suryakusuma, J. I. (1991). State Ibuism: The Social Construction of Womanhood in the Indonesian New Order. *New Asian Visions, 6*(2, June).

Wieringa, S. (1999). Desiring Bodies or Defiant Cultures: Butch-Femme Lesbians in Jakarta and Lima. In E. Blackwood & S. Wieringa (Eds.), *Female Desires: Same-Sex Relations and the Transgender Practices Across Cultures* (pp. 206-231). New York: Columbia University Press.

Wilchins, R. A. (1997). *Read My Lips: Sexual Subversion and the End of Gender.* Ithaca: Firebrand Books.

"Outing" and "Duplicity"

Ann Tweedy

[Haworth co-indexing entry note]: "'Outing' and 'Duplicity.'" Tweedy, Ann. Co-published simultaneously in *Journal of Bisexuality* (Harrington Park Press, an imprint of The Haworth Press, Inc.) Vol. 3, No. 3/4, 2003, pp. 249-252; and: *Bisexuality and Transgenderism: InterSEXions of the Others* (ed: Jonathan Alexander, and Karen Yescavage) Harrington Park Press, an imprint of The Haworth Press, Inc., 2003, pp. 249-252. Single or multiple copies of this article are available for a fee from The Haworth Document Delivery Service [1-800-HAWORTH, 9:00 a.m. - 5:00 p.m. (EST). E-mail address: docdelivery@haworthpress.com].

OUTING

it has become almost religious: two or three times
each week, i drive an hour to see women pretend
they are men. their breasts have been wound
and flattened, their hair cut short, they are
equipped with penises of duct tape and sock.
in cowboy hats and jeans, white shirts and ties,
they lip sync in an alphabet only the body can interpret

and what of the body, who for thirty years staked
her allegiance in one nation, while admitting to break
its lesser edicts about sex and love,
who and how many? imagine that self-proclaimed outlaw
dreaming a life of prescribed normalcy

i see myself now, for six months caught between planets:
loving a man i mean to spend my days with and a woman
who dances on-stage for anyone who can afford
cover. her repertoire of male voices, from pop
to country, thrills from an underlying forgery

do you think i could write myself back into
the hewn dimensions of any single space? home is the structure
you build when nowhere else will have you

DUPLICITY

i could be the man who's lusting
after your teen-aged daughter. the man you want to tell
"get your eyes the hell off of her." you're picturing
me 40, 50 maybe, jeans that are too loose, so loose
i could pull them off without much effort.
you think i don't comb my hair and haven't washed it
in a couple of days. invariably, it's dark brown
and greasy. my gut hangs out below my t-shirt. my jobs
have been nothing to brag about, like parking
attendant, janitor, or taxi cab driver. now your guessing i'm
unemployed. you shake your head and think that's what i get
for being a high school drop out. i drink too much

cheap beer and watch trash on tv constantly, the game shows,
sports, but not the discovery channel or even jeopardy.
yes, you're sure you know who you're dealing with
and how to help your little girl avoid him (not that she'd
be interested anyway), except when you're busy hunting down
some action. this time it's a blonde-haired, green-eyed,
thirty-year-old lawyer, slight with a foal-like bone structure.
each breast would fit in a hand. you concentrate on the hips
that betray my sex no matter how skinny i get. then you survey
the hair, cropped close to the head, a little short for your taste, but maybe
you'll overlook that, just once, and ask me out for a date.

STEERING QUEER OF LGBTI IDENTITY POLITICS

Walking Through Walls:
An Immodest Proposal
for Trans-cending Sexual
Orientation

Matthew Kailey

Digital Object Identifier: 10.1300/J159v03n03_17

[Haworth co-indexing entry note]: "Walking Through Walls: An Immodest Proposal for Trans-cending Sexual Orientation." Kailey, Matthew. Co-published simultaneously in *Journal of Bisexuality* (Harrington Park Press, an imprint of The Haworth Press, Inc.) Vol. 3, No. 3/4, 2003, pp. 253-264; and: *Bisexuality and Transgenderism: InterSEXions of the Others* (ed: Jonathan Alexander, and Karen Yescavage) Harrington Park Press, an imprint of The Haworth Press, Inc., 2003, pp. 253-264. Single or multiple copies of this article are available for a fee from The Haworth Document Delivery Service [1-800-HAWORTH, 9:00 a.m. - 5:00 p.m. (EST). E-mail address: docdelivery@haworthpress.com].

SUMMARY. This article addresses the current Western cultural model of sex, gender, and sexuality, and argues that the model is confining, inaccurate, and based on false premises. Further, it addresses the need for eliminating the model and argues for a generalized concept of sexuality rather than the categories of sexuality prescribed by the current model. It also calls on transsexual, intersexed, and bisexual people to be at the forefront of eliminating the model. *[Article copies available for a fee from The Haworth Document Delivery Service: 1-800-HAWORTH. E-mail address: <docdelivery@haworthpress.com> Website: <http://www.HaworthPress.com> © 2003 by The Haworth Press, Inc. All rights reserved.]*

KEYWORDS. Transsexual, bisexual, intersexed, sexuality, male-to-female, female-to-male

Unlike sexual positions, which have been around at least since the Kamasutra, sexual orientation is a relatively new concept, seeming to take on definition in the latter part of the 19th century when the term "homosexuality" was coined by German psychologist Karolyn Maria Benkert (Pickett, 2002). Since that time, "heterosexuality," which used to refer to an abnormal obsession with the opposite sex (Katz, 1995), has become the norm, "homosexuality" has become aberrant, and "bisexuality" has emerged as a misunderstood but necessary response to the labeling of human functions and emotions. In reality, as different as these "orientations" appear to be, they all have one major similarity–they all contain "sexuality," the word and the concept, which is so universal that it is possessed in some way by every living being on earth. Sexuality is something that we all share and that we all understand to be part of us. It is also something that our modern culture has difficulty handling in its rawest form, so by dividing and labeling it, we are able to dissociate ourselves from the "lower" animals who share it, from each other, and from our own basic needs and instincts.

But regardless of the categorization of, and the connotations connected with, what was once simply a natural function of every living entity, inherent in all of the generally established terms for orientation is the concept of a binary gender system and a human sexuality that links directly to that system. It is neat and tidy and reflects all the Western cultural concepts that we hold dear: that there are two sexes, male and female, that are differentiated by invisible chromosomal structures and by visible genitalia developed in response to those structures; that there are two genders, masculine and feminine, that are cultivated as a direct result of those chromosomal structures and genitalia; and that there are three sexual orientations, the good, the bad, and the undecided, and that these orientations spring directly from the two sexes and genders. And then, in our fast-paced, catch-phrase society, we made it easy on ourselves by creating short, nonclinical labels for these three orientations–"straight," "gay and lesbian," and "bi."

It all fit together so well. We knew who was normal and who was not. We knew who was a threat and who was not. We knew which groups should be allowed civil rights and which groups should not. And we lived, and continue to live, under the belief that we can control human behavior by categorizing it and that we can eliminate that behavior that threatens to undermine our already fragile societal standards of rightness. We had categories and we could label them, a principal that served to keep the dominant social structure in place and punished those who would stray outside of it. And just when we thought we had it under control, transgendered and transsexual people came along and mucked everything up by defying the labels of sexual orientation, and the system they are based on, altogether. Instead of allowing us to move blindly along, clinging to our euphemistic categories, trans people have forced us to examine not our gayness or our straightness, not our homo-, hetero-, or bisexuality, but simply our sexuality, which can be the most frightening concept of all.

In its most clinically accepted definition, to be transgendered means to have an internal gender identity at odds with external physiology–simplistically, to be biologically female but to identify as male or vice versa. Because a major expectation in our culture is that internal identity and external genitalia will match, and that both these things will be apparent through a person's presentation of self–appearance, behaviors, and social relationships–transgendered people are often forced to deal with their incongruity in one of two ways, neither of which is wholly acceptable. The first is that they can decide on an external gender presentation that corresponds with their genitalia but not with their identity. In this case, a female-to-male identified person might choose to wear certain clothes, such as dresses, a certain feminine hairstyle, and makeup in order to conform to expected gender presentations. The other possibility is for transgendered people to present in the gender they believe themselves to be–a male-to-female in a dress, wig, and heels, perhaps–and risk ridicule at the very least and violence as an ever present reality.

But another option, one that is seen as the only option by some transgendered people, is to change the body to match the identity, thus allowing for congruity of external physiology, internal gender identity, and external gender presentation. People who undergo this physiological correction are, in our culture, generally known as transsexuals.

All the concepts discussed above are heavily rooted in Western culture and are based on the binary system described earlier. However, although the definitions are based on that structure, the reality of trans people and their sexuality completely topples it. Even those trans people who buy into the binary system, go through a gender transition, and completely assimilate into their new gender, often adopting stricter gender roles than even the mainstream culture, challenge the very assertions on which the system is based.

Consider the following examples:

A fully transitioned male-to-female transsexual, packed with estrogen and sporting female genitalia, still has an XY chromosome. For those who assign physical sex categories based on the end of the alphabet, this woman is still male. If she then has sex with a natal man, is this in fact homosexual sex? Based on her chromosomes, it would be considered such. Based on her genitalia, it would not. Her own internal identity, no doubt, is female, and she would not see this interaction as anything other than a heterosexual sex act–but she probably saw sex with men as such even prior to her transition.

A fully transitioned female-to-male who decides against genital surgery, for whatever reason, has sex with a natal man. Two men with beards, body hair, no breasts, and baritones are taking a tumble–is it a homosexual or a heterosexual sex act? Based on the transman's chromosomes and genitalia, it is heterosexual sex. Based on his physical appearance and internal identity, it is a homosexual act. If the same transman gets a phalloplasty, or surgical penis construction, what then becomes the label for the identical sex act?

In fact, based on the binary sex and gender structure that our culture has taken such pains to create, there are no good, solid answers in either of these scenarios. Thus, the structure does not hold up against the realities of gender diversity. Although we find our circumscribed sexual categories comforting, it is impossible for these limited classifications to define the range of human sexual experience.

Heterosexuality, homosexuality, and bisexuality are not sexual orientations. They are as much labels as are "straight," "gay," "lesbian," and "bi." They are limited in their scope, and the labeling process allows for no deviations. A person cannot change sexual orientations–a label is forever, leaving the recipients snugly fit in their boxes. Or maybe not.

Consider the following:

As a man-loving female for forty-two years, I was considered as straight as the Berlin Wall, until that particular facade crumbled under gender transition. Now with a mustache and goatee, a male chest, and an "M" on my driver's license and passport, I am seen by the world as a gay man, even though the world usually does not see my decidedly un-"male" genitalia. Am I a gay man? Did I, in fact, change sexual orientations?

An example I like to give college students in human sexuality classes is this: If I am walking down the street holding hands with a natal man, I am a gay man. If we are both naked and someone sees only our genitalia, I am a straight woman. If I am walking down the street holding hands with a natal female, I am a straight man. If we are both naked and someone sees only our genitalia, I am a lesbian. I can change sexual orientations and genders more rapidly than a quick-change artist, but the reality is that I haven't changed at all. Although I'm not holding hands with much of anyone these days, my hands of attraction would most likely belong to a natal male.

And although I have been accused of changing sexual orientations because, prior to transition, I was "straight" and now I'm "gay," only the culturally constructed label for my sexuality has changed. My attraction, and thus my orientation, remains as it always has.

There are people who have transitioned and discovered that, although they once found natal women the objects of their attraction, they now are drawn to natal men or vice versa. If I have not changed sexual orientations, based on the argument above, then an argument could be made here that these folks have. In fact, there are many reasons for this apparent "switch." In some cases, the attraction has always been there but has not been acted on. For example, some male-to-female transsexuals felt uncomfortable carrying out a fantasy of sexual interaction with a man prior to transition because of the stigma attached to being considered "gay." Others have found that they can only relate sexually to men in a female role. And for female-to-males, testosterone does some interesting things to sex drive, sometimes causing attractions to mix and mingle. Then there are people who transition and find that they have a heterosexual orientation regardless of their gender and others who find that they have a homosexual orientation. So those who retain the same label after transition—that of homosexual or heterosexual—have not "changed" their sexual orientation either.

It is evident that even in the case of transsexual sexual orientations that loosely follow the recognized cultural structure discussed earlier, these orientations are fraught with inconsistency. If a transsexual, whether female-to-male or male-to-female, is attracted to women prior to transition and remains attracted to women after transition, he or she has not changed orientations, only labels. He or she remains oriented to women—the object of attraction remains the same. If a male-to-female transsexual is attracted to women prior to transition and finds herself attracted to men after transition, she has not changed orientations either—she remains heterosexual, as would a female-to-male whose attractions were reversed. A transsexual who is same-sex attracted prior to transition and remains same-sex attracted after transition has not changed orientations—he or she remains homosexual. So no matter what the object of attraction is or becomes after transition, it can be logically argued, based on our current structure of sex, gender, and sexual orientation, that transsexuals do not change orientations, regardless of how it appears. But it could also be argued that they do. It simply depends on how the arguer views the concept, and the labels, of orientation.

In truth, there are very few times when I actually consider myself a "gay man." I use the term socially because it seems easier for everyone to understand. But there are boundaries to "gayness," expectations of life experience that I have not had, expectations of certain behaviors into which I have not been socialized, and expectations of certain body parts that I do not possess. The mere fact that I am expected to choose and define my sexuality with one term or another has been somewhat difficult for me when constructing a new identity after gender transition. That we, as a society, attempt to label our sexuality in the first place indicates that we need or believe we need this in order to help shape our identity, to draw specific boundaries between groups, and to allow us to belong to a particular group with distinct norms, guidelines, and social codes. But for trans people, those boundaries can be confounding, those group norms can be foreign, and those labels can help to shape identities or help to confuse them.

The sexual identities of trans people simply do not fit neatly into these established groups, which can have the positive effect of freeing them from conformity, or the negative effect of not allowing them to conform. I do not fit, and yet I am expected to choose. We are all expected to choose, trans or not, and join a particular group by default if there is no exact fit, conforming to the group's norms and guidelines even when they don't feel right–even when we have to give up a part of our identity in order to belong. To do otherwise is to drift without definition in a society that insists on it. If I decide that I am not "gay" and I am not "straight," then who am I to be homo- or heterosexual with?

The phenomenon of transsexual sexual attraction throws the whole orientation schema into a state of confusion. This occurs even before adding trans/trans attraction or bisexual attraction into the mix. If two transmen are sexually involved, is this a homosexual relationship? And, if so, is it a gay male relationship or a lesbian relationship? If one of those transmen has had genital surgery and the other has not, does it then become a heterosexual relationship? And if it does, does this mean that a transman with genital surgery who is sexually attracted to both nonsurgical transmen and natal men is bisexual? Or is he bisexual if he is attracted to both nonsurgical transmen and natal women?

And trans people are not the only ones who render useless our culture's paradigm of sexual orientation. Consider the following example:

Janet is clearly female. She has breasts, a female shape, and genitalia that appear female because she has no visible penis or testicles. She was raised as female and identifies as such. However, she has an XY chromosome and Androgen Insensitivity Syndrome, an intersex condition in which the chromosomally male fetus does not respond to androgen, the "male" sex hormone. Her testes, which were present internally at birth, have been removed to prevent complications. Although she lacks a fully developed vagina and cervix, she has chosen not to have genital surgery. She is sexually active with women. Is Janet homosexual, based on her body and her identity, or is she heterosexual, based on her chromosomal structure?

The Intersex Society of North America, citing information compiled by Dr. Anne Fausto-Sterling and colleagues of Brown University, presents the statistic that one in every one hundred people is born with a body that differs in some way from the "standard" male or female body ("Frequency," 1995-2003). In our given structure, which is based both on chromosomes and on genitalia, are intersexed people allowed to be sexual at all? And if so, with whom and what labels will the relationships be given?

Bisexual people also lay waste to our construction, even though their label is a part of it and must be inherent in the structure. When a natal male who identifies as bisexual is sexually involved with another natal male, is this a homosexual sex act, based on genitalia, or is it a bisexual sex act, based on personal identities? When that same male is sexually involved with a natal woman, is this a heterosexual act or a bisexual act? And if our theoretical bisexual male becomes involved with a transsexual female-to-male, what label is given to this act? Does it depend on the genitalia of the female-to-male? A computer, programmed to identify relationships within the established structure, would be smoking, shaking, and insisting that this "does not compute."

In reality, what does not compute is the culturally constructed paradigm of sexual orientation. It does not hold up under the litmus test of transsexual, intersexed, and bisexual people. These people move over, under, through, and around these barriers while, when necessary, slyly appearing to remain within them. We are either very good at manipulating the system or the system invites manipulation. Another possibility, probably the most feasible, is that there is no system. The emperor is naked. Human beings, in all their natural variations, do not lend themselves to sexual orientation at all. Human beings are sexual. That is all, and that is really enough. But the cultural pressure to define our behaviors is sometimes overwhelming.

Transsexual, intersexed, and bisexual people, probably more than others, are aware that they are walking through walls and ignoring structure when they are engaging in any sex act whatsoever, although there are still those who are so socialized into the dominant cultural constructs that they refuse or are unable to see their own transcendence and its importance. So ingrained is our system of labels that we who fall outside of the boundaries often feel it necessary to apply labels of sex, gender, and sexual orientation in order to allow ourselves to be sexual at all. If we cannot label or define it, then we cannot participate in it. Indeed, maybe we have no right to it at all. And often, it is not only we who suffer.

My friend is a natal female who fell in love with a male-to-female transsexual. Although there were other complications in the relationship, an overriding concern for my friend was the fact that she did not identify as a lesbian. Since she saw her lover as a female, even though no genital surgery had been performed, she was unable to sit back and enjoy the relationship without worrying over a label for her sexual orientation and for the relationship. In this case, it was not so much her concern about how she would be seen by the world, but about how her new love would assimilate into her own identity, which up until that time had carried the label "straight female."

Conversely, over the course of several years of working with female-to-male transsexuals and their partners, I have found much concern among female partners about losing their lesbian identity once their partner becomes male. This can cause serious interference in the relationship, because that label and all that goes with it, which becomes an identity in itself, is threatened by a suddenly male partner. The happy lesbian couple has now become, for all intents and purposes, a straight couple, and the life-space that was occupied by the lesbian community becomes vacant overnight.

A female bisexual friend of mine, when reporting on an upcoming date, was asked by a lesbian friend, "Which one will it be tonight–a boy or a girl?" The answer was really unimportant, but the question, which was intended to be snide, also reveals the necessity of some kind of parameter for the relationship, even if it is only a date. People on the borders of the socially accepted model are often those who most adopt its tenets, perhaps with the assumption that, by association, they will somehow be normalized. The truth lies somewhere else–what is natural, and therefore normal, is not found in a schema of human creation. What is natural, and therefore normal, is the sexuality of all living things, regardless of how that sexuality is expressed.

We are all sexual beings. What we have is sexuality. Almost all of us have the capacity, and the facilities, to relate to someone else sexually. Tacking on the prefixes of hetero, homo, or bi to that sexuality serves no purpose other than to stick that which is a natural extension of the self into a category based on gender, a category that can be changed or disrupted when a person jumps ship and changes that gender. These prefixes cause undue anxiety for sexual beings wishing to express their sexuality, because before they can express it, there is the need to label it. If it doesn't fit one of the preexisting, socially acceptable labels, then it becomes an unrecognized, and, therefore, invalid, interaction.

We are all physical beings. We have bodies and minds. Most of us have bodies and minds that respond to sexual stimuli. Categorizing our responses to that stimuli based on perceived gender and then labeling those responses serves no purpose other than to bring pride or shame to the natural reactions of the body and mind. Regardless of our particular chromosomal makeup and regardless of our particular genitalia, we react. What we react to is a product of our conditioning, our socialization, what our culture sets forth as sexually attractive, and what our individual physical and psychological makeups tell us is sexually attractive. These things can differ at different times in our lives, in our days, or in our hours. But because we are so busy trying to stick with our given definitions of who we are, we tend to ignore or filter out those things that do not jibe with our created identities.

Transsexual, intersexed, and bisexual people are sometimes better able to reject those filters and those definitions, often because we have to. For trans and intersexed individuals, the body does not always allow for conformity with the imposed structure. We are on our own to grapple with our sexuality and to try to label it if we must. But when we are able to recognize the lies of the labels, we are free to follow the natural course of our sexuality. We are liberated. Bisexual people with "standard" bodies who are living comfortably with their sexuality are also liberated, in that even as they might accept their label, they can acknowledge the freedom that it gives them. However, they can go further. They can cast off the label and realize that their sexuality simply is, and needs no definition. And all of us–trans, intersexed, and bisexual–can eventually teach others, confined in their niches, that they too can experience sexual freedom, simply by refusing to define their relationships and their sex acts.

Giving up our labels of sexuality will not result in a sexual free-for-all, as enticing as the idea might seem to some. Our attractions will not change and will not have to change. There would be no expectation that a married father of three who has admired women all his life or a swinging bachelor with an appointment book full of women's names and numbers would suddenly be forced to date men. And women or men who swoon over Brad Pitt or Vin Diesel would not be expected to hang Jennifer Lopez posters on their wall. But what they could do is forget for a moment, or a lifetime, about how their sexuality is defined and simply enjoy it, whatever it is.

There would still be gathering places for men and women who want to meet each other, for men who want to meet men, and for women who want to meet women. There would still be personal ads, church singles' groups, dating clubs,

and blind dates. There would still be marriages, although there would be no favored group who got to marry while other groups did not. What there would not
be is shame, guilt, phobias, hatred, violence, fear, mistrust, and judgment. What
there would not be is a privileged class and several nonprivileged classes based
on sexuality, which boils down to sex and gender. And what there would not be
is local or national law and policy, ranging from property rights to hospital visi-
tation rights to child custody, based on private sex acts.

Transsexual, intersexed, and bisexual people are in a position to be at the
forefront of this revolution, but only if we are able cast off our own need to label our sexuality. Even "bisexuality" is confining in that the binary gender
system is inherent in the term. Indeed, some people have begun to identify as
pansexual, omnisexual, genderqueer, or simply queer in an effort to explain a
sexuality that is not confined by either/or. But even these are labels, and although they fall outside of the system, they have been created because the system requires it. If I want you to know that I will have sex with you regardless of
your genitalia, given that we find each other sexually attractive, I also have to
let you know that I fall into one of these categories. And you had better fall into
one of these categories as well, or you're in for a big disappointment. But if
there are no categories, I am free to relate to you simply as another human being and we are free to negotiate sexual contact in whatever way we choose. We
are also free to reject each other based on any number of nonattractions. Just
because we have no label does not mean we have to have sex.

Although some say that to change the system we must work within it, there
are those of us who are so inherently outside of the system that our options are
limited to imploding rather than exploding the structure. We can apply pressure from without. And those of us who have experienced mutability in how
we relate to the structure, either through our sex, our gender, or our sexuality,
are free to carry that further. So why don't we?

Unfortunately, we have not only internalized the labeling system. We have
also internalized its main premise–that pure, unadulterated sexuality is wrong. It
is far easier to say, "I'm straight" than to say, "I'm a heterosexual." But it is easier to say, "I'm a heterosexual" than to say, "I'm sexual." It is the same with the
other categories. In our culture, proclaiming that we are sexual is tantamount to
saying that we are rampant horndogs who cannot be controlled and who will
copulate at will with anyone or anything that happens along. We live in a society
that would prefer to deny sexuality altogether, but since it cannot, it chooses to
confine it in the only way possible–by creating a multilayered, black and white,
good or bad, either/or model and fitting each of us into the given structure.

But even as we deny that the members of our society are sexual beings, we
find representations of that sexuality on every street corner, in every magazine
and video store, and on every television channel. We complain about it, we are

publicly appalled by it, and we lock our doors and turn on the television or pop in a video. Our sex industry, in all its permutations, is a multi-billion dollar operation and is a natural outgrowth of our denial. It doesn't have to be this way.

Those of us who transcend the established boundaries, because we choose to or because we have to, can make a decision to be sexual. And we can make a decision to act on that in whatever ways we decide. And we can free ourselves from the sexual roles and expectations that keep us in our places. I am sexual. How about you?

SOME DEFINITIONS

Female-to-male: A person identified as female at birth who possesses a male gender identity, lives either part or full time as a male, or has had surgery and/or uses hormones to correct the body to male.

Male-to-female: A person identified as male at birth who possesses a female gender identity, lives either part or full time as a female, or has had surgery and/or uses hormones to correct the body to female.

Natal male/female: Those people who have been given the label of male or female at birth based on physical sexual characteristics.

Transsexual: A person identified as either male or female at birth who possesses an gender identity inconsistent with the birth sex, lives full time in the role of identity and usually has had surgery and/or uses hormones to correct the body to achieve consistency with the identity. *Transman* is a term for a female-to-male transsexual, and *transwoman* is a term for a male-to-female transsexual.

REFERENCES

Frequency: How common are intersexed conditions? (1995-2003). Retrieved January 14, 2003, from Intersex Society of North America Web site: http://www.isna.org/faq/frequency.html

Katz, J. N. (New York: Dutton Books, 1995). *The Invention of Heterosexuality*. Retrieved January 14, 2003, from PBS Web site: http://www.pbs.org/wgbh/pages/frontline/shows/assault/context/katzhistory.html

Pickett, B. (2002, August 6). Homosexuality. Retrieved January 14, 2003, from the Stanford University, *Stanford Encyclopedia of Philosophy* Web site: http://plato.stanford.edu/archives/fall2002/entries/homosexuality

We Are All Others:
An Argument for Queer

Coralee Drechsler

[Haworth co-indexing entry note]: "We Are All Others: An Argument for Queer." Drechsler. Coralee. Co-published simultaneously in *Journal of Bisexuality* (Harrington Park Press. an imprint of The Haworth Press, Inc.) Vol. 3, No. 3/4, 2003, pp. 265-275; and: *Bisexuality and Transgenderism: InterSEXions of the Others* (ed: Jonathan Alexander. and Karen Yescavage) Harrington Park Press. an imprint of The Haworth Press, Inc., 2003, pp. 265-275. Single or multiple copies of this article are available for a fee from The Haworth Document Delivery Service [1-800-HAWORTH. 9:00 a.m. - 5:00 p.m. (EST). E-mail address: docdelivery@haworthpress. com].

SUMMARY. There is a certain degree of controversy about the usefulness and appropriateness of the label and identity "queer." Despite this controversy, the argument of this article is that queer is a useful and defensible label and identity that emphasizes the commonality, recognition, and respect required for an effective, inclusive social movement. This contention is supported by the challenge presented by transgender and the consequent destabilization of the concepts associated with sex and gender, as well as identities based on sex, gender, and sexuality. In addition to the transgender challenge, bisexuality also reinforces the contention, particularly in troubling the concept of sexuality. *[Article copies available for a fee from The Haworth Document Delivery Service: 1-800-HAWORTH. E-mail address: <docdelivery@haworthpress.com> Website: <http://www.HaworthPress. com> © 2003 by The Haworth Press, Inc. All rights reserved.]*

KEYWORDS. Queer, identity, transgender, transgendered, sex, gender, sexuality

As a researcher, academic, and self-identified "nonheterosexual," I have had numerous conversations in as many different contexts about the usefulness and appropriateness of the label and identity "queer." Some rejections of queer have their basis in theory, while others seem purely aesthetic–people simply do not wish to be associated with a word that has, from their perspective, such an ugly and derogatory history. While I can appreciate the various critiques, I maintain the position that queer is a useful, defensible label and identity that emphasizes commonality and the mutual recognition and respect that is required for an effective social movement. This conceptualization of queer is suggested and supported by a particular understanding and interpretation of transgender. What brought me to this particular understanding and interpretation is the research I completed concerning transgendered individuals' perspectives, and the impact of these perspectives on sex, gender, and sexuality (see Drechsler, 2002). While my research did not include anyone who identified as bisexual, bisexuality, like transgender, also challenges the linear construction of sex, gender, and sexuality.

The transgendered individuals who shared their knowledge and perspectives assisted me in my attempt to make sense of the concepts of sex, gender, and sexuality. Through this process, the definitions of associated concepts were examined, and eventually I came to the understanding that virtually everyone is oppressed by sex and gender in some way, regardless of the label with which she or he chooses to identify. With the concepts associated with sex and gender destabilized, the challenge that transgender presents to gay and lesbian identities becomes apparent. Queering sex, gender, and sexuality not only calls lesbian and gay identities, among others, into question, but it also challenges social movements based on sex, gender, and/or sexuality, including the "gay liberation movement." The importance of queer is that it offers the basis upon which to build an effective, cohesive social movement, with more inclusion and equality than has been demonstrated thus far in the mainstream gay movement.

My desire to understand the North American concepts of sex, gender, and sexuality is long-standing. There are many incidents in my personal history that remind me of the importance that these concepts have had in my life. As one example, I am still curious about my mother's objection to me wearing my sibling's hockey jersey. In her words, "It's bad enough that you have such broad shoulders. You don't have to add to it by wearing that." She does not remember this encounter and, in the interest of being true to my mother's character, she is not much of a "gender defender." Despite incidents from my childhood, my life is not characterized by strict sex/gender segregation. However, there are also obvious limits on what is considered acceptable. My mother demonstrated the bounds of sex/gender appropriateness in not wanting me to appear too masculine in the estimation of other people.

This personal interest in sex, gender, and sexuality was further developed academically as an undergraduate student. In Women's Studies class, in particular, I began to question the concepts of sex and gender, including what is meant by "man" and by "woman." While my classmates seemed comfortable with the common North American constructions of "man" and "woman," I had trouble realizing the prescription for feminism and for being a feminist. I do not mean to imply by this statement that I am a part of the contemporary backlash against, or disregard for, feminism. I acknowledge the oppression of people based on sex/gender. However, I believe that the assertion of people's rights must include all oppression based on sex/gender, not only the "mainstream," recognized oppression of "women" for the benefit of "men." These categorical assertions are too limiting and serve to create divisions between people who should be allies. Due to my personal and academic wrestling with the concepts of sex and gender, I chose to focus my research on learning and understanding the perspectives of people who defy the established categories of sex and gender in some way. This is the definition of transgender/transgendered to which I adhere and that I used in my research. Thus, transgender/transgendered covers a considerable range of experiences that challenge the concepts of sex and gender, including people who have been referred to as "cross-dressers," "drag kings/queens," "masculine women," "feminine men," "intersexed" ("hermaphrodites"), and "transsexuals." However, it is necessary to note that this definition of transgender/transgendered is neither stable nor universal. Indeed, there are individuals, I am sure, who would disagree with my definition.

Since my interest has contained the recognition of commonality for the purpose of establishing a cohesive social movement, this inclusive definition of transgender/transgendered is important. Indeed, one of the unstated goals of my research was to convey some of the ways in which individuals have been constrained by sex and gender so that the reader might relate his or her own experiences (see Drechsler, 2002). Often, when the labels transgender or transgendered are acknowledged, the usual perception is "transsexual." For many people, a transsexual is someone who definitively alters her or his body and social appearance from the sex/gender she or he was born into to the "other" prescribed sex/gender. With my use of the terms transgender and transgendered, I want to indicate that this is not always the case. In fact, while transgendered people are all in defiance of sex/gender, their actual experiences, perspectives, and decisions about how to handle this defiance vary significantly. For example, some of the individuals I learned from had only accessed support groups, others had accessed hormone therapy only, some had discontinued hormone therapy, some had opted for "top surgery" but not "bottom surgery," and others had plans for both "top" and "bottom surgery," but still had no intention of fulfilling the societal expectations associated with the physical body (see Drechsler, 2002).

The experiences, perspectives, and actions of transgendered individuals provide the basis for questioning the definitions of sex and gender, as well as the definitions of other associated concepts. Sex is often used to signify bodies according to their biological characteristics. The dominant North American conceptualization of sex is that there are only two body types, male and female. The most immediate signifier of the sex of the body is most commonly visible at birth, at which time the body of an infant is declared male according to the presence of a penis (and absence of a vagina) or female according to the presence of a vagina (and absence of a penis). Because sex is constructed as a dichotomy, any degree of confusion concerning the sex of a body, as occurs in an "intersexed" infant, must be overcome and corrected as soon as possible according to medical practitioners (Money, 1986, p. 137). The sex dichotomy is thereby further justified. As a person matures past infancy, that person is expected to display characteristics believed to be congruent with that person's sex. For the most part, these characteristics comprise the definition of gender, which is understood, contemporarily, as the social characteristics that a given culture in a given historical time attributes to the two differently sexed bodies.

However, the separation between biological characteristics (sex) and social characteristics (gender) in North American society is neither complete nor perfect. For example, the presence of facial hair in males and the absence of facial hair in females is often cited as a secondary sex characteristic and, therefore, as a biological difference between males and females. Yet some adult males do not have noticeable facial hair while some adult females do. This supposed biological difference between males and females is reinforced and perpetuated by the construction of this characteristic as a social difference. Adult females with noticeable facial hair are ridiculed, laughed at, and/or perceived as "masculine" or "male." To avoid social sanction, adult females must ensure that they are free of facial hair through methods such as shaving, waxing, tweezing, and electrolysis. Thus, a characteristic constructed as biological is also social. These biological and social elements exist simultaneously, and both reinforce and influence each other. Therefore, what is constructed as sex is also gender, and what is constructed as gender is also sex. The impossibility of separating one from the other (Butler, 1990, p. 7) is signified by my use of sex/gender or "the sex/gender system." While I do not mean to imply a belief that sex and gender are identical, I am suggesting that the reality of sex and gender should be open to question since the concepts of sex and gender, often presented as distinct in social science literature, overlap and interconnect in various ways.

Sex/gender also affects the perception of sexuality. Through the regulation and prescription of sex and gender in all their binary forms (including male/female, man/woman, masculine/feminine), the sex/gender system establishes the categories of sexuality. For instance, the definition of a heterosexual person is directly dependent upon that person's own sex/gender as well as the sex/gender of the sexual and/or intimate partner chosen by that person. A person is only considered heterosexual if she or he chooses as a partner a person of the "opposite sex." Therefore, sex/gender is essential in the establishment of heterosexuality as the accepted and expected sexuality in North American society. Indeed, when a person displays a characteristic considered appropriate to the "opposite sex," that person's sexuality is questioned. However, it is also common to question the sex/gender of a person who is known to be nonheterosexual.

Accordingly, then, North American society is organized in concert with certain beliefs about sex, gender, and sexuality, but these beliefs are not static. They change over time. One of these beliefs is that there are two sexes, male and female, and two genders, man and woman. A further aspect of these two genders is that they are each connected to certain behavioral presentations, masculinity and femininity respectively. With regard to sexuality, the dominant North American belief is that heterosexuality is the normal and preferred orientation (Butler, 1990, p. 23). The connection between sex, gender, and sexuality is presented predominantly as one of coherence and continuity (Butler, p. 17), which means that a male is a man and is mostly masculine in presentation, and a female is a woman and is mostly feminine in presentation. In addition, the ideal man and the ideal woman are also heterosexual. Clearly, both transgendered and bisexual individuals defy and challenge this linear construction of sex, gender, and sexuality. Along with the linear construction, the categories of sex, gender, and sexuality also are presented as occurring naturally when they are in fact constructed through the "effects of power" (Foucault, 1980, p. 98). Through the power of the dominant culture in North American society, "certain bodies, certain gestures, certain discourses, certain desires come to be identified and constituted as individuals" (Foucault, p. 98). Not only are the categories associated with the sex/gender system socially constructed, but they are constructed as dichotomies—an individual is a man to the extent that the individual is not a woman, and an individual is feminine to the extent that the individual is not masculine (Butler, 1990, p. 22). Sexuality may also be interpreted as binary, with heterosexuality as the norm and "nonheterosexuality" as the aberration.

Destabilizing the social constructions associated with sex, gender, and sexuality enables individuals to both challenge traditional identities and question the criteria used in defining identities. Identification is not an event, but an ongoing process (Butler, 1993, p. 105) that involves both external and internal elements, due to the dynamics of power (Foucault, 1980, p. 141). The identity of the individual is not simply the result of societal forces acting upon the individual, since the individual also has power to establish, assert, or acquiesce to an identity (Feinberg, 1998, p. 89). Not only do transgendered individuals challenge the sex/gender system by confusing the categories through physical appearance, behavior, and attitude, but they also challenge the system by refusing the identity established for them at birth. Moreover, the sex/gender system is also challenged by the insistence of some to be identified as "trans," or as another nontraditional identity. In this "resistance to categorization," transgendered individuals have some degree of freedom from the sex/gender system (Grant, 1993, p. 131).

Since transgender problematizes the concepts of sex, gender, and sexuality, lesbian and gay identities are also troubled. The transgender challenge to these identities occurs on various connected levels. First, transgender requires questioning the definitions of man and woman. Lesbian and gay identities are based on the primary recognition of a person as a woman or a man. While gay has been used as a "universal" label, gay is also used to indicate "homosexual men," while lesbian indicates "homosexual women." These labels demonstrate the significance of recognizing the sex/gender of people in terms of gay and lesbian identities. Indeed, if one is unable to tell who or what a man or woman is, then how is one to discern a person's sexuality? Just as sex/gender is vital to the definition of a heterosexual, so too is it essential to a lesbian or gay identity. In addition to this transgender challenge, bisexuality also troubles sexuality in terms of the heterosexual and gay/lesbian insistence that desire must be rigidly concentrated on only one of the two constructed sexes/genders. Moreover, both bisexual and transgender contest gay and lesbian identities by questioning who is included in what category. This is indicated by the common exclusions of transgendered and bisexual individuals from either formal or informal participation in lesbian and/or gay "communities." For example, as a member of the group responsible for the first Pride March in my hometown, I recall an offensive and lengthy discussion on whether "bisexual" and "transgender" should be officially included in any March materials. The person who was most adamantly opposed to the inclusion was a professor at the local college. While she is recognized as a lesbian scholar, she did not seem to realize that the Stonewall Rebellion involved more than lesbian and gay individuals. As I have since learned, Stonewall predominantly involved transgendered individuals, whatever their sexuality might be (see Feinberg, 1996). Had I known then what I know now, I would have argued more forcefully.

Second, transgender challenges gay and lesbian identities on the basis of the physical body. Some gays and lesbians assert that only a person born male or female is a "true" gay or lesbian person, provided that his or her sexuality involves a "same sex" partner or the desire for such a partner. However, as both feminism and the gay movement have argued, biology is not destiny. Transgendered individuals demonstrate this through the alterations they may choose to make to their bodies, including mastectomy, hormone therapy, electrolysis, and/or other surgical interventions. Considering the significant similarities and overlapping ranges of "normal" between the "two sexes" (see Hausman, 1995), it is basically impossible to discern if a person is "naturally" the sex he or she appears to be.

Third, beyond the physical body, yet still connected to it, is the transgender implication for expected social characteristics. The common perception of lesbian and gay "communities" is that they are free of heteronormativity and, therefore, free of the demands for heterosexual standards and norms in terms of appropriate social behavior and appearance (Myers, Taub, Morris, & Rothblum, 1998, p. 18). However, this is not entirely accurate. While lesbian and gay people have been freed, to some extent, from heterosexual expectations, there are lesbian and gay expectations that have taken their place (Myers et al., p. 20; Fries, 1998, p. 321; Mann, 1998, pp. 348-350). Individuals involved in lesbian and gay "communities" are often concerned with how to be recognized as a lesbian or gay person, how to be accepted, and how to be considered attractive. Moreover, failure to conform to these expectations may result in some sort of social sanction or punishment (Woolfe, 1998, p. 88). The inclusion, or even the acknowledgement, of transgender requires the further examination of the social expectations associated with lesbian and gay "communities." While these expectations are often difficult to define, they do exist and, in addition to others who may not conform in some way, transgendered individuals force the consideration of how a lesbian/gay person is supposed to present her/himself in a social context.

What is also apparent through this discussion of lesbian and gay identities and "communities" is that, despite the construction of lesbian and gay as outside the mainstream of North American society, and as centered on the ideal of equality and inclusion, these identities and "communities" have established a core and a periphery within this outside–there is a mainstream within gay and lesbian identities and "communities," and within the gay and lesbian social movement. As I have argued through the transgender challenge to lesbian and gay identities, there are members of those "communities," whether transgendered, bisexual, or with some other identity, who have been constructed as the outside. This situation also impacts upon the effectiveness of the gay and lesbian social movement. As with the contemporary women's movement, some identities and issues have been privileged over others, with a failure to recognize difference (Jagose, 1996, p. 61). The equality that the movement is supposed to achieve within North American society will not be fully realized because it has not been achieved within the movement.

My argument is that adopting queer as the identity upon which to base the movement could achieve equality within the movement. The definition of queer that I am using to make the argument includes anyone who is constrained by sex/gender in some way. As previously stated, this definition could encompass almost everyone. However, inclusion is dependent upon people's willingness to identify themselves this way. As Holmes (1998) explains, queer is the choice to be who you are without mainstream approval (p. 223). Gay and lesbian individuals are easily included in Holmes' definition of queer. With regard to sex/gender, gay and lesbian people are queer because they too have denied the linear construction of sex, gender, and sexuality. They have refused the heteronormativity of the sex/gender system. People who identify as heterosexual may also be considered queer. To be recognized and validated by others as a heterosexual man or woman requires that one fulfill the expectations associated with the respective identity. What this entails is the individual's investment in one sex/gender and the denial or suppression of characteristics connected with the other (Butler, 1993, p. 126). Thus, heterosexual people are queer because they are constrained by sex/gender. Indeed, this constraint is the basis of feminism. The ways in which men have been limited is also necessary to examine and acknowledge.

Just as with transgendered, bisexual, lesbian, gay, and heterosexual identities, a queer identity is also curiously dependent upon sex/gender, while it simultaneously rejects the mainstream prescriptions for sex/gender. Indeed, this dependence on sex/gender is apparent in my suggestion that sex/gender should be the basis for a cohesive, collective social movement. However, sex/gender oppression cannot be the only basis for this movement, since this would provide room for other oppressions to flourish. A social movement based on sex/gender must also account for other differences among its population. Racism, classism, and other forms of discrimination must be addressed for a social movement to be successful. As Feinberg (1998) argues, we must be outraged at all oppression in order to achieve unity and social justice (pp. 48, 113). If the issue of other oppressions is not addressed, some members of the movement are forced to hierarchize aspects of their identities (Phillips, 1998, p. 251; Trahan, 1998, p. 309), which undermines their identification with the movement and the solidarity that is required to affect change.

A social movement that encompasses such a significant portion of the population has the potential to affect tangible, systemic change. However, as I have acknowledged, there are serious barriers to this possibility. People must be willing to understand and accept the label and identity of queer as defined here, and recognize commonality between themselves and others who are also constrained by sex/gender, even though the experiences will vary. The research that I completed with the assistance of the participants is one small attempt to demonstrate commonality between people that I consider potential allies. A queer social movement also requires that those involved recognize their own privilege, and acknowledge and address the oppressions of others that may not directly affect them. My experience has been that people are reluctant to acknowledge their own privilege, as well as to share power and accept that they may contribute to the perpetuation of structural oppression. However, people are also capable of learning, of change, and of empathy. While this hope for a broad-based social movement based on sex/gender may seem idealistic, that is the purpose of social change–the attempt to bring about an ideal society.

REFERENCES

Butler, J. (1990). *Gender trouble: Feminism and the subversion of identity.* New York: Routledge.

Butler, J. (1993). *Bodies that matter: On the discursive limits of "sex."* New York: Routledge.

Drechsler, C. (2002). *Sex/gender and sexuality: An analysis of transgendered perspectives.* Unpublished thesis, University of Saskatchewan.

Feinberg, L. (1996). *Transgendered warriors.* Boston: Beacon Press.

Feinberg, L. (1998). *Transliberation: Beyond pink or blue.* Boston: Beacon Press.

Foucault, M. (1980). *Power/knowledge* (C. Gordon, Ed.), (C. Gordon, L. Marshall, J. Mepham, & K. Soper, Trans.). Brighton, Sussex: Harvester Press.

Fries, K. (1998). The imperfections of beauty: On being gay and disabled. In D. Atkins (Ed.), *Looking queer: Body image and identity in lesbian, bisexual, gay, and transgender communities* (pp. 315-322). New York: Harrington Park Press.

Grant, J. (1993). *Fundamental feminism: Contesting the core concepts of feminist theory.* New York: Routledge.

Hausman, B.L. (1995). *Changing sex.* Durham: Duke University Press.

Holmes, M. (1998). In(to)visibility: Intersexuality in the field of queer. In D. Atkins (Ed.), *Looking queer: Body image and identity in lesbian, bisexual, gay, and transgender communities* (pp. 221-226). New York: Harrington Park Press.

Jagose, A. (1996). *Queer theory: An introduction.* New York: New York University Press.

Mann, W.J. (1998). Laws of desire: Has our imagery become overidealized? In D. Atkins (Ed.), *Looking queer: Body image and identity in lesbian, bisexual, gay, and transgender communities* (pp. 345-353). New York: Harrington Park Press.

Money, J. (1986). *Venuses penuses: Sexology, sexosophy and exigency theory.* Buffalo: Prometheus Books.

Myers, A., Taub, J., Morris, J.F., & Rothblum, E.D. (1998). Beauty mandates and the appearance obsession: Are lesbians any better off? In D. Atkins (Ed.), *Looking queer: Body image and identity in lesbian, bisexual, gay, and transgender communities* (pp. 17-25). New York: Harrington Park Press.

Phillips, L. (1998). "I" is for intersection: At the crux of black and white and gay and straight. In D. Atkins (Ed.), *Looking queer: Body image and identity in lesbian, bisexual, gay, and transgender communities* (pp. 251-258). New York: Harrington Park Press.

Trahan, J.D. (1998). Inside/Outside. In D. Atkins (Ed.), *Looking queer: Body image and identity in lesbian, bisexual, gay, and transgender communities* (pp. 307-312). New York: Harrington Park Press.

Woolfe, K. (1998). It's not what you wear: Fashioning a queer identity. In D. Atkins (Ed.), *Looking queer: Body image and identity in lesbian, bisexual, gay, and transgender communities* (pp. 87-91). New York: Harrington Park Press.

Centering:
An Alternative Perspective

Jamison Green

http://www.haworthpress.com/web/JB
© 2003 by The Haworth Press, Inc. All rights reserved.
Digital Object Identifier: 10.1300/J159v03n03_19

[Haworth co-indexing entry note]: "Centering: An Alternate Perspective." Green. Jamison. Co-published simultaneously in *Journal of Bisexuality* (Harrington Park Press, an imprint of The Haworth Press, Inc.) Vol. 3, No. 3/4, 2003, pp. 277-285; and: *Bisexuality and Transgenderism: InterSEXions of the Others* (ed: Jonathan Alexander, and Karen Yescavage) Harrington Park Press, an imprint of The Haworth Press, Inc., 2003, pp. 277-285. Single or multiple copies of this article are available for a fee from The Haworth Document Delivery Service [1-800-HAWORTH, 9:00 a.m. - 5:00 p.m. (EST). E-mail address: docdelivery@haworthpress.com].

SUMMARY. The bipolar model of sexuality and gender expression limits us to two types of bodies: male and female; two types of sexuality: heterosexuality or homosexuality; and two types of gender expression: masculine and feminine. This view of what is central in our society marginalizes those who don't fit, inciting people to take positions of moral superiority that the author believes are damaging to the human spirit. This paper postulates that if the diversity of people living in the "in-between" zones of sex and gender were valued over monosexual exclusion, many of the "isms" that plague modern society could be alleviated. *[Article copies available for a fee from The Haworth Document Delivery Service: 1-800-HAWORTH. E-mail address: <docdelivery@haworthpress.com> Website: <http://www.HaworthPress.com> © 2003 by The Haworth Press, Inc. All rights reserved.]*

KEYWORDS. Bisexuality, diversity, moral judgment, intersex, transgender, transsexual, values

We are taught, and in fact we may have direct experience of the effects of the premise, that heterosexual people view bisexual, transgender, transsexual, and intersexed people as outside the norm. This "norm" is a presumption resulting from the logic that heterosexual people constitute a majority, and that what is experienced and interpreted by heterosexual people is therefore "right and proper." Heterosexuality and homosexuality, as relationship models, both rely on a bi-polar construct of sex and gender, a distinction between women and men that is seen as fundamental to human existence. It is almost as though those of us who are heterosexual or homosexual, both, base our ability to have intimacy on xenophobia: some of us are afraid to have–or repulsed by the thought of–relationships with people who are like ourselves, and some of us are afraid to have–or repulsed by the thought of–relationships with people who are different from ourselves–or at least like or different in particular ways related to physical sex and gender.

Gender does complicate matters. We may think gender and sex are the same thing, and what our genitals look like is enough to define our sexuality or our attractional interests, but then there are people who are comfortable with what we might call butch/femme relationships, and then there are some who are butch who only like other butches, and some who are femme who only like other femmes (notice I have not specified genital requirements–those are for each reader to apply as he or she conceptualizes this).

Bisexual people have long been arguing that the sex (genital type) of their partners does not define their relationships, or that they have the ability to love (and engage in intimacy with) people regardless of whether they are like or different from themselves. Bisexual people have been called fence-sitters and regarded as incapable of commitment. In the same way, transgendered people have been regarded as unsure of themselves, unable to figure out whether they are male or female. Likewise transsexual people, whose choices about their self-expression, or commitments to their gender, are sometimes labeled delusional. Intersexed people, in their turn, have been viewed as aberrant, incomplete; and the unfortunate conflation of all things relating to sex and gender as various moral perversions has done irreparable harm to so many innocent people through the ages. Regardless of our body type, gender presentation, or sexual interests, we are all human, and human beings are social and require validation, acceptance, identification, and belonging somehow.

Whether we are gay, lesbian, bi, trans, intersexed, queer, straight, or questioning, once we have accepted ourselves we are able to feel a sense of belonging to a group or classification of others like ourselves, even if that group is "the group of people who prefer not to be part of a group." Whether we actively participate socially in a geographically-based community or only connect with a few select others who are similarly identified, we can become part of an "in" group, even though we may be outside the mainstream.

No matter which group we belong to, our view of where the center lies is wherever we are, or wherever our values place it. We may feel that the center lies with the mainstream, the supposed majority, because we feel outside of the dominant culture; or we may feel that our own subculture is the central focus of our life. It doesn't matter, really. What matters is how we relate to and treat others with whom we share society and the responsibility for stewardship of our environment. So long as we practice viewing people who are different from us as strange, inappropriate, laughable, un-cool, undeserving, or deficient in any way, we are no different from our own ideological enemies, no matter how morally superior the group with which we have affiliated ourselves believes itself to be.

I don't know if it is possible for most people to let go of the idea that they themselves are in the center of their own world, but, just as an intellectual exercise, I would like to propose an alternate perspective of one particular type of center around which many people have organized their beliefs about themselves and others. That center is the mainstream cultural view of appropriate sexuality. This means that if you join me in this exercise, you will have to let go of your ideas about social validation relying on whether you are gay or straight, or whether your partner has genitals like or unlike your own.

I propose that the new center is somewhere in the middle of the continuum of sex and gender bi-polarity, and that this renders the majority of heterosexual and homosexual people outsiders. In this model, the majority become the periphery and must acknowledge their particular bias as a tilting of the scale toward an arbitrary edge, a limitation on their part, a fixation, perhaps an unhealthy obsession. No, I won't go so far as an obsession. Because this model offers a center that is more open than any other center, I'll resist the temptation to punish those who have unwittingly punished others by forcing them to the periphery of a cultural value. I don't mean to create a periphery that is a punishment, but rather a periphery that is an acknowledgment of a self-imposed boundary that keeps some people from approaching the center. In this model the center is the place where the greatest social validation comes from being fully self-actualized and free, a mental place where fear and judgment of others is unnecessary. And this center is one of unlimited capacity. All human beings have the potential to exist in this center, because this center does not depend on the existence of people on the outside of it to define its boundaries. Defying known laws of physics, this center doesn't depend on gravity, motion, or limitations to distinguish itself.

Now, hold that thought for a moment, the thought of a social world that does not judge people for being outside the mainstream of sexual or gender expression because the central focus of society is not one particular type of sexual orientation or behavior and the "rightness" or "wrongness" of sex or gender. Hold that thought, please, and let's consider bisexual, transgender, and intersex experience as they are generally viewed now, and as each of them might be viewed through this intellectual exercise.

Bisexual people are thought of as promiscuous and untrustworthy. Their gay partners are always worried they'll be abandoned for a straight person, and straight partners fear their own homosexual rivals. When someone declares her or his bisexual capacity or orientation, there is often a pause in their listener's response, an adjustment to the intake of unexpected information or information that causes a reevaluation: is this person so sexual that they have no discretion? Should I be nervous around them? Is he interested in me? Is she going to betray my affection? Is this person so emotionally needy that they are willing to accept anyone as a potential partner? If I become their partner, am I no longer special because I am equivalent to "just anyone"?

The ability to be physically intimate with people regardless of their sex or genital configuration is not necessarily an indicator of one's capacity for fidelity or level of self-esteem. Rather, the lack of attachment to one's partner as a definitive statement about the self could be the ultimate statement of self-confidence. If we look at bisexuality as residing between the poles of gay and straight sexuality without trying to judge it based on the polarized assumptions of those opposites, we might be able to see the in-between-ness of bisexuality as a desirable state of consciousness that has succeeded in eliminating the pressure of conformance to the relationship standards of others from the equation of social acceptability. Assuming any given bisexual person is generally psychologically healthy, he or she would ideally be able to select sexual partners based upon a variety of characteristics and the comfort of particular synergies between the personalities involved. This is no more or less than anyone expects from the search for an intimate partner, it's just that certain specific limitations around genital and/or gender type are eliminated from the equation. One may well wonder why this is regarded as such a threat to people who are incapable of such consciousness. Reflecting on the model of the center that I have proposed, I think the answer is that they cannot imagine what it would be like not to have the limitations and requirements that they have accepted for themselves. The lack of agreement about the value of whether someone can imagine doing what appeals to someone else is a component of our ability to move toward this alternative centering: if I place a higher value on my ability to concur with your personal choices than I place on our collective ability to choose at all, then I am less likely to "approve" of your choices, and less likely to accept a center that is larger than my own vision of what is "right" for me.

There are people today who are seeking an "off-center" approach to group affiliation, who are more comfortable in a group that has fewer boundaries. For them, the transgender continuum offers the "security" of an intangible label to describe a broad range of identities, behaviors, and self-concepts. Much more than the relatively simple acts of crossdressing to temporarily adopt an alternate gender identity, or of undergoing surgical sex reassignment to confirm a commitment to a particular gender identity, transgender opens up space for people to live in the in-between-ness of gender. Not that people haven't already been in-between forever, but without a language to discuss the positionality of trans-ness, those people were subject to the interpretation of others and helpless in the face of those interpretations.

But this new openness also brings with it further complications. Now transgender can mean whatever someone wants it to, and that very flexibility has thrown some people into an anxiety state. Anyone who has experimented with pronoun flexibility or "slippage" knows how easy it is to make non-transpeople feel completely confused. When non-transpeople get one definition of transgender from one person, and then hear another, completely different definition from someone else, they go on overload. They just can't process the information. They're used to having everything clear: men/women, gay/straight, with nothing in between.

Often non-transpeople can accept transsexualism so long as the transperson simply changes his or her sex and doesn't do any waffling. Crossdressing was confusing, but if given a cogent explanation for the behavior, it could be accepted, too. The trick always seemed to be to make sure the non-trans (particularly STRAIGHT, non-trans) person realized that someone else's trans behavior didn't have anything to do with them (we weren't trying to have sex with them!). Ah, I remember the days when a woman in men's clothing was generally understood to be a lesbian, end of story, whether that was true or not.

Now, a person (male or female) who identifies as trans can't simply say so without running the risk of being further misinterpreted. Many non-transpeople think that transgender means transsexual, that it means "someone who feels they were born into the wrong body," or someone who "wants a sex change." The nuances of transgender experience are very complicated. This can be hard on transsexual people, too, whose specific medical needs are often obscured or obliterated beneath transgender rhetoric. I don't think this means we have to abandon transgender language. But I do think we have to continue to emphasize the flexibility and individuality, the inherent subjectivity of the terminology. What we have to get non-transpeople to understand is that it's not such a bad thing to be uncertain about someone else's sex or gender. And it's not such a bad thing for someone to be in-between.

Many people struggle with their in-between-ness, but none more poignantly than the intersexed, particularly those born with ambiguous genitalia. The first question that is asked about us when we are born is "Is it a boy or a girl?" Parents want to know. Our images of girl and boy help us to project humanity and socialization onto the infant. Doctors want to display certitude and authority, or to at least be reassuring and authoritative in their lack of certitude. If a sex is not readily apparent, 19th and 20th century doctors believed that their responsibility lay in ascertaining one and ensuring surgically that the infant's body would conform to it as closely as possible. For over 30 years we believed that doctors knew best, but in the 1990s the people who are most dramatically affected by these medical theories and decisions began to speak out, and now we collectively rally behind the innocence of the child and the frequently damaging consequences of early surgical intervention when doctors and parents seek to assign a sex regardless of a child's gender.

Transsexual people still do not receive the same level of sympathy. Is it true that we can envision tolerating ambiguity in infants and allowing, even championing, these children to participate in their own gender/sex definition based upon their own experience and sense of self, but we cannot tolerate this in children, adolescents, or adults who have no identifiable physical anomaly? For that is the difference here: physical proof, something we can see or otherwise fit with our prevailing theories about maleness and femaleness of the body, Xs and Ys. Without this concreteness, we still can't accept the reality of a child's experience of her or his own body and gender difference.

I have frequently heard stories from people who were desperate to find the verifiably intersex component of their body that would justify their certain knowledge that they really are members of the opposite sex and, therefore, should be assisted in their transition from one physical sex to the other and not penalized socially for it–that is, we think if some physical anomaly can be found we will be vindicated and spared the humiliation of being labeled transsexual. But there are not enough tests; there is not enough research, not enough knowledge. There is not enough interest in us as a population to justify the larger society (with its 2 convenient gender boxes) spending the funds to do the testing to acquire the knowledge about us. People are more comfortable not hearing about us, not seeing us. That's why they often don't care so much if we switch boxes, so long as they don't have to see it happening, so long as we fit neatly into one box or the other. Making the kind of transition that prompts people to say, "I never would have guessed!" is held out as the ultimate reward for a transsexual person, just as it is the goal of doctors who are treating intersexed infants and children. Their objective seems to be to eliminate the center, to eliminate in-between-ness.

The most widely known and dramatic example of the folly of this line of reasoning is the John/Joan case, or the story of David Reimer, as told by John Colapinto in his book, *As Nature Made Him: The Boy Who Was Raised as a Girl* (2000). Reimer was neither intersexed nor transsexual, nor gay, lesbian, or bisexual, but he was forced into a transgendered childhood, with many of the same social consequences as those faced by intersexed children and their families, because of an accident in a hospital procedure intended to correct a problem with his penile foreskin when he was eight months old. Yet because it is so obvious that what happened to David Reimer should never have happened (because it was clearly the result of an error in the operating room), it is easy to use his case to point to the folly of trying to force a child to be someone whom he or she is incapable of being. The presumption of the innate being what is right is still with us. The "John/Joan" case, once used by the medical establishment to point to the success of genital and hormonal sex reassignment from childhood as a justification for infant sex reassignment in the case of intersex births, was shown to be a failure that was covered up for years. The Reimer case is now used, conversely, as evidence to prove that hormones and surgery cannot change a gender that is already fixed in a child's personality or mental self-image. This is all well and good for people whose gender is known to correspond with their genital sex, but still doesn't alleviate the issues faced by intersexed and transpeople who are still in-between.

In-between-ness, or living simultaneously at various points along the sex/gender spectrum isn't bad, wrong, or strange in itself, and a large part of our effort in creating protective legislation and establishing progressive policies within institutions such as employers or insurance companies or governments is the effort to educate about the ubiquity of in-between-ness. In order to become comfortable with in-between-ness, people have to learn not to be frightened when they come face to face with the unknown. That's a tall order, but it is absolutely necessary if we are to make social progress, and it relates to all issues of difference and all the "isms" we know in the Western world. It comes down to accepting people for who they are, whether we agree with their self-definition or not, whether we've ever met anyone like them before or not, whether we understand them or not. What we think doesn't matter when it comes to the existence of others, and only when we can give up on the centrality of "what I think" can we truly come to appreciate otherness. We do it on a small scale every day, usually unconsciously. Hand-in-hand with the necessity of learning to recognize and appreciate difference so that others are not diminished, we need to learn to be ourselves without being "right," without being "better than," without being the standard we judge others by.

It's a real balancing act, learning to have harmony within oneself and between oneself and others. Knowing who you are, that you are fine just the way you are, and not feeling like people who don't agree with you are somehow inferior, is not something we are taught in most cultures. But it's that ability, that quality we need to cultivate if all our recent social progress among gay, lesbian, bisexual, intersex, transgender, transsexual, queer and questioning is to mean anything and to endure. That's why a new central value–a new center–may be necessary to help us move forward.

We are approaching an historical intersection (if we are not already there) that invites us to investigate why we have decided that conformity in sexual behavior, gender identity, and genital (or other anatomic) formations are so crucial to our ability to relate to and cooperate with other human beings. A real generosity of spirit is required to open the traditional center and push any remaining boundaries to the farthest possible periphery. Can we meet in the middle? Only if we are not afraid to let go of the edge.

REFERENCE

Colapinto, John (2000). *As Nature Made Him: The Boy Who Was Raised as a Girl.* New York: HarperCollins Publishers Inc.

Index

Life or Something Like It, 196
Linas, 242,243
Love, C., 175
Love Love and Love, 173-174,175
Lunsing, W., 218

Madonna, 174,175,177
Maki, C., 213
"Male eroticism," 206
Male Homosexuality in Modern Japan, xv
Male-to-female, defined, 264
Manson, M., 225
Mardi Gras
Gay & Lesbian, 121
Sydney *Gay,* 121
Martin-Damon, K., 6,7,15
Mathy, R.M., xv, 17,94,96,98,99,104
Mattachine Society, 37,49
Maxfield Parish, 66
May I Kiss You, 178
Mays, 98
McLelland, M., xv,18,203,221-226
Meiji period, 206
Meltzer, 136
Mempperkosa, 234
Merriam-Webster's Online Dictionary, 31
Metamorphosis, 218
Metro State University, xv
Meyer, M.D.E., xv,17,151
Meyerowitz, J., 10,11,14,39-40
Miami University, Oxford, xv
Millar, S.B., 236
Miller, D., 218
Minikomi, 216
Mitsuhashi, 219
Mizu shobai, 215,217
Money, J., 81,82
Montgomery, B., 158
"Mr. Lady," 213
Muadzin, 233
Muncul, 241
Murray, S.O., 238

Mutability intersection, 12
My Gender Workbook, 5,6
Myers, L., xv
Myles, E., 66

Nabilah, 241
Nanshoku, 206
Narcissus, 59
Narrative, xiv
Natal male/female, defined, 264
"National Bisexual Liberation Group," 44
National Center for Lesbian Rights (NCLR), 50
National Comorbidity Survey, 97
National Gay and Lesbian Task Force, 90
National Institute of Mental Health (NIMH), 32
National Organization for Women (NOW), 49
NCLR. *See* National Center for Lesbian Rights (NCLR)
New Langton Art's Bay Area Award, xiv
New York City Council, 40
New York City Lesbian and Gay Community Center, 30
New York Times, 50
Newhalf, 214
Newhalf boom, 213-214
Newhalf Club, 219
Newhalf Lady, 218
Newhalf Net, 214
Newsweek, 44
Nicks, S., 175
Nikutai bungaku, 208
Nimaime, 207
NIMH. *See* National Institute of Mental Health (NIMH)
1968 Stonewall Riots, 51
1985 San Francisco Lesbian and Gay Freedom Parade, 47

Raymond, J., 41,123
RealPoetik, xiv
Reimer, D., 284
Ressner, J., 196
Rezu na kankei, 214
Rezubian, 222
Rice, A., 49
Richards, R., 42,137
Robin, L., 96
Rolling Stone, 177
Roppongi, 214
"Roppongi girl," 214
Rose, G., 213
Rosenberg, M., xvi, 18,171
Rostrow, A., 21
Roxxie, 189
Rubin, H., 41
Rubin, J., 209
Rumiko, M., 214,219,221,226

Sakit, 243
San Francisco Bisexual Center, 47
San Francisco Gay Pride Parade, 41
Sappho, 34
Saya ikut sakit, 243
Schimel, L., 75,76
Scorsese, M., 174
Scott, D.T., 21
Seabrook, L.A., xvi, 17,18,117
*Second Skins: The Body Narratives
    of Transsexuality,* 8
Semi puro, 217
Senelick, L., 175
Sensei, 209,219
Sententeki, 210
Sexing the Self, 174
Sexual orientation
    in partners of transsexuals,
        transitioning of, 140-143
    trans-cending, immodest proposal
        for, 253-264
Sexuality(ies)

prevailing notions of, in South
    Sulawesi, 236-238
transgender, in Japan, 203-230
SHAZNA, 224
Shileds, B., 137
Simpanan, 240
Sinfield, A., 14
Singer, I.B., 176
Siri', 237
Slater, D., 218
Smyth, C., 185
*Society and the Healthy
    Homosexual,* 31
Socrates, 34
"Sodomy" laws, 210
South Sulawesi, Indonesia, bisexual
    and transgender intersections
    in, 231-247
Stasia, C.L., xvi, 18,181
Stein, A., 187
Stone Butch Blues, 66
Stonewall, 90
Stonewall Rebellion, 272
Streisand, B., 175
Stryker, S., 42
Studio Sapphire, 217
Subculture, Gothic, 124
Suicide, among bisexual teens, study
    of, 96-97
Sunakku, 217
Suppotsu Nippon, 214
Sutoreeto, 222
Swingers, described, 87-92
Swinging culture, 91
Sydney Gay and Lesbian Mardi Gras,
    119,120
"Sydney *Gay* Mardi Gras," 121
Symposium, 80
Syracuse University, xvi

Tachi, 225
Taisho period, 211
Takarazuka, 223

Bisexuality and Transgenderism
InterSEXions of the Others

____ in softbound at $22.46 (regularly $29.95) (ISBN: 1-56023-287-0)
____ in hardbound at $37.46 (regularly $49.95) (ISBN: 1-56023-286-2)

COST OF BOOKS _____
Outside USA/ Canada/
Mexico: Add 20%. _____

POSTAGE & HANDLING _____
US: $4.00 for first book & $1.50
for each additional book
Outside US: $5.00 for first book
& $2.00 for each additional book.

SUBTOTAL _____
In Canada: add 7% GST. _____

STATE TAX _____
CA, IL, IN, MIN, NY, OH, & SD residents
please add appropriate local sales tax.

FINAL TOTAL _____
If paying in Canadian funds, convert
using the current exchange rate,
UNESCO coupons welcome.

❏ **BILL ME LATER:**
Bill-me option is good on US/Canada/
Mexico orders only; not good to jobbers,
wholesalers, or subscription agencies.

❏ **Signature** _____

❏ **Payment Enclosed: $** _____

❏ **PLEASE CHARGE TO MY CREDIT CARD:**
❏ Visa ❏ MasterCard ❏ AmEx ❏ Discover
❏ Diner's Club ❏ Eurocard ❏ JCB

Account #_____

Exp Date _____

Signature_____
*(Prices in US dollars and subject to
change without notice.)*

PLEASE PRINT ALL INFORMATION OR ATTACH YOUR BUSINESS CARD
Name
Address
City   State/Province   Zip/Postal Code
Country
Tel   Fax
E-Mail

May we use your e-mail address for confirmations and other types of information? ❏Yes ❏No
We appreciate receiving your e-mail address. Haworth would like to e-mail special discount
offers to you, as a preferred customer. **We will never share, rent, or exchange your e-mail
address.** We regard such actions as an invasion of your privacy.

Order From Your Local Bookstore or Directly From
The Haworth Press, Inc.
10 Alice Street, Binghamton, New York 13904-1580 • USA
Call Our toll-free number (1-800-429-6784) / Outside US/Canada: (607) 722-5857
Fax: 1-800-895-0582 / Outside US/Canada: (607) 771-0012
E-Mail your order to us: Orders@haworthpress.com

Please Photocopy this form for your personal use.
www.HaworthPress.com

BOF04